APQ LIBRARY OF
PHILOSOPHY

APQ LIBRARY OF
PHILOSOPHY

Edited by Nicholas Rescher

THE PHILOSOPHY OF CHARLES S. PEIRCE:
A Critical Introduction

ROBERT ALMEDER

ROWMAN AND LITTLEFIELD
TOTOWA, NEW JERSEY

© American Philosophical Quarterly 1980

191
P 37 z a

Library of Congress Cataloging in Publication Data

Almeder, Robert F
    The philosophy of Charles S. Peirce.
    (APQ library of philosophy)
    Bibliography: P.
    Includes indexes
    1. Peirce, Charles Santiago Sanders, 1839–1914.
    I. Title.   II. Series.
    B945.P44A7   1980   191   80–16012
ISBN 0–8476–6854–1

This book is dedicated to the memory of

An

George Almeder III,
Douglas Greenlee, and
James Cornman

TABLE OF CONTENTS

PREFACE

After reading what had been written on the philosophy of Charles Peirce, I began writing this book in an effort to comprehend the failure of able commentators to agree on the substance of Peirce's mature views on the nature of reality. Some commentators said that in the last analysis Peirce was a realist, others claimed that he was an idealist, and many even claimed that he was both. Moreover, among those who claimed that Peirce was both realist and idealist, opinions varied on the philosophical merit of such a position. Just as some felt that Peirce's position represented a unique and compelling synthesis of two doctrines traditionally considered mutually exclusive, others urged that the position was inconsistent. In short, I began writing this book to resolve a long-standing controversy.

And in the endeavor, my desire to provide a sympathetic interpretation of Peirce's thought led to a consideration of issues that could not be neglected if an adequate understanding and defense of Peirce's views was to be possible. For example, after reconstructing Peirce's arguments favoring epistemological realism, I began to wonder whether Peirce's commitment to epistemological realism was internally consistent with what he said about the nature of perception. After all, if his theory of perception was more consistent with what he said about idealism, then there would be good reason to believe that he was more an idealist than a realist. Since Peirce's theory of perception was fragmentary and open to conflicting interpretations, there was no way of dealing adequately with the force of Peirce's epistemological realism without reconstructing his theory of perception which, as it turned out, was consistent with epistemological realism and not epistemological idealism.

Also, central to both Peirce's theory of perception and his arguments for epistemological realism was his frequent claim to the effect that as long as there is no good reason to doubt a proposition, that proposition is perfectly acceptable as a premise in any line of argument. Here again, the plausibility of Peirce's epistemological realism (as well as his theory of perception) rested on an epistemological principle that would need defending. And since that principle was systematically dependent on what Peirce said about the nature of Inquiry, Meaning and Truth, an introductory chapter on Peirce's theory of knowledge would be needed. In laying out this introductory chapter, however, the task of reconstructing and defending Peirce's epistemology took on interesting proportions and turned out to be more exciting and important than the task of solving the original controversy. Still, both tasks have been discharged, I think, and in a way that serves not only the introductory needs of those unfamiliar with Peirce's philosophy but also the critical needs of philosophers in general and Peirce scholars in particular. I have tried to reconstruct and assess Peirce's views on the nature of knowledge and reality within the context of providing a generally reliable statement that meets the needs of the classroom more than any yet provided.

Further, no statement characterizing Peirce's views on the nature of reality could possibly be complete without an examination of Peirce's *logical* realism and his avowed debt to the medieval philosopher Duns Scotus. Scotus exerted a profound influence on Peirce's views, but (for reasons stated herein) the precise nature of that influence needed a careful and scholarly examination.

Although Peirce frequently changed his mind on various philosophical theses and wrote in a style that confuses many, a good deal of the adverse criticism, confusion and debate attending the study of his thought results from the failure of many to distinguish his mature views from earlier ones. In order to avoid ascribing to Peirce certain of the earlier views which he subsequently rejected or qualified in his mature years, I have weeded out those doctrines and arguments which he did not, or would not endorse after 1890, in the twilight of his tragic years. In short, this essay purports to provide an introductory statement and assessment of Peirce's *philosophically mature* views on the nature of knowledge and reality. Every section of the essay has been written with an eye to excluding anything that Peirce did not, or would not, endorse after 1890.

There are two reasons for singling out the year 1890 to mark the beginning of Peirce's mature period. First of all, in 1890, when he was fifty-one years old, Peirce 'retired' from public life and went to his farm in Milford, Pennsylvania. For the next quarter-century or so (he died in 1914), Peirce revised and refined his earlier views in an attempt to present a systematic statement of his philosophy. Hence it seems only natural to suppose that his mature philosophical views would be expressed as best they could during these last years of his philosophical activity. Secondly, I hope to show that a reasonably complete and systematic vision of the world can be reconstructed from Peirce's written works dating from 1890. Moreover, for the reasons which he offers in *The Development of Peirce's Philosophy*, I accept M. G. Murphey's thesis that Peirce's final systematic effort dates from 1890.

Although each chapter of this essay is integral to the whole, certain parts have been published as articles. Accordingly, I would like to thank the editors of the following journals for permission to reprint parts of the following essays:

Synthese, "Peirce on Meaning," vol. 41 (July 1979).

The American Philosophical Quarterly, "Fallibilism and the Ultimate Irreversible Opinion" (APQ Monograph Series, vol. 9, *Studies In Epistemology*) Jan. 1975.

Philosophy of Science, "Science and Idealism" (June 1973).

The Journal of the History of Philosophy, "The Idealism of Charles S. Peirce" (Oct. 1971).*

The Transactions of the Charles S. Peirce Society: A Quarterly Journal in American Philosophy, "Charles Peirce and the Existence of the External World" (Spring 1968); "Peirce's Theory of Perception" (Summer 1970); "Peirce's Pragmatism and Scotistic Realism" (Winter 1973) and "Peirce's Epistemological Realism" (Winter 1975).

Man and World, "Common sense and the Foundations of Knowledge" (Dec. 1974).

Finally, althouth parts of this essay are radical revisions of sections of a doctoral dissertation, considerably more than one-half (the first half of the essay) was not in any way part of that dissertation. M. G. Murphey directed that dissertation and I have benefited immensely from his critical observations on sections of this essay. For their comments and observations on various sections of the following I am likewise indebted to Milton Snoeyenbos, Paul Fitzegerald, John Smith, Max Fisch, Barton Palmer and R. L. Arrington. Naturally, too, I am grateful to Georgia State University for the released time and tangible assistance offered me for the completion of this project. My chairman, Dr. Arrington, my dean, Dr. Thomas, and my president, Dr. Langdale, have been especially helpful in more ways than I can mention.

Atlanta, Georgia.

Chapter I

Peirce's Theory of Knowledge

Charles Peirce died before he was able to provide an accurate, systematic statement of his philosophy. And of course six decades of philosophers have labored, with varying degrees of success, to reconstruct just such a statement from the rubble of his published and unpublished papers. The peculiar difficulty of the task derives from the well-known fact that Peirce presented his philosophy in a remarkably unsystematic manner, changed his mind on various crucial issues, and covered a wide range of topics in an obscure style of writing. Nevertheless, conspicuous progress has been made, and can still be made, in piecing together various parts of the puzzle.

In this first chapter I shall assemble that part of the puzzle which fits into the section reserved for Peirce's theory of knowledge. After examining Peirce's theory of inquiry, I shall discuss and evaluate his views on the nature of meaning and truth. Then his views on the status of common-sense beliefs and their role in scientific inference will be considered and defended. Finally, I hope to demonstrate that Peirce's views on knowledge constitute a theory that is distinctive, persuasive and exciting.

I. THE DOUBT–BELIEF THEORY OF INQUIRY

Peirce defined 'inquiry' as the process by which we pass from genuine doubt to stable belief. Hence the purpose of inquiry is to overcome legitimate doubts by establishing stable beliefs.[1] But we cannot understand precisely what Peirce meant by this unless we know what he meant by the psychological predicates, "belief" and "doubt". After all, given his characterization of inquiry, if Peirce meant by the statement, "x believes that p" that "x is disposed to act in some specifiable appropriate way under some specifiable conditions," then it would seem that the purpose of inquiry is to establish dispositions to appropriate behavior under specifiable conditions; whereas, if Peirce meant by the statement, "x believes that p" that "x is in a certain mental state which is characterized by his feeling sure that p," then it would seem that the purpose of inquiry is to establish certain feelings about propositions. What then does Peirce mean by the predicates "belief" and "doubt"?[2]

A. *Belief*

Peirce frequently used the term "belief" to designate a certain mental state or feeling which causes specific types of behavior. This state originates in certain habitual connections among our ideas (7.354 and 7.359), and involves definite habits of expectancy (8.270 and 8.294). In short, to say a person believes that p, is to say that he is in a certain state characterized by his having certain expectations caused by habitual connections among his ideas. Peirce claimed that this is a calm and satisfactory state that causes one to act in the way that he does. Of itself, however, this characterization of belief does not tell us whether statements ascribing particular beliefs to particular individuals are true. Indeed, although Peirce often talked about beliefs as mental states that cause us to act in particular ways, his primary concern was to provide an analysis of the concept of belief that would permit the verification of sentences ascribing particular beliefs to particular individuals and, for this purpose, he chose ultimately to identify beliefs with the behavior that is caused by habitual association among ideas (MS 682 (p. 11)). For purposes of being able to verify statements that ascribe beliefs to individuals, the term "belief" refers not to that which causes certain behavior, but rather to the very behavior itself, which is caused by habitual associations among ideas. For this reason Peirce maintained that the only way we know what a man believes is by the way he acts (5.371), and that differences in belief are distinguished by the different modes of behavior to which they give rise (5.12 and 5.398). According to Peirce, we infer what an individual's beliefs are from his behavior. But Peirce's analysis of belief in terms of behavior is not inconsistent with the existence of mental states. Indeed, it would seem that Peirce's behavioristic analysis of belief constitutes an instance of *methodological behaviorism* that is perfectly consistent with mind–body dualism.[3]

Furthermore, statements about belief, Peirce maintains, are not to be analyzed into statements about actual behavior. For example, it would be a mistake to claim that for Peirce, the statement "x believes that p" means "x behaves in an appropriate way under appropriate circumstances". He clearly professes that statements ascribing beliefs to individuals are not equivalent to statements about actual behavior; rather, they are in some sense to be equated with statements about *dispositions* to actual behavior:

> To be deliberately and thoroughly prepared to shape one's conduct in conformity with a proposition is neither more nor less than a state of mind called believing that proposition. (6.476)

> Belief does not make us act at once but puts us into such a condition that we shall behave in some certain way when the occasion arises. (5.373)

or:

> The feeling of believing is more or less a sure indication of there being established in our nature some habit which will determine our actions. (5.371)[4]

Accordingly, we infer what a person's beliefs are from his dispositions to act in particular ways under particular circumstances.

Incidentally, although it is no part of our present purpose to probe Peirce's position on the mind–body problem, it should be noted that Peirce's analysis of belief in terms of dispositional behavior cannot be dismissed as a straightforward instance of *analytical behaviorism*. As is well known, the thesis of *analytical behaviorism* maintains that sentences which ascribe beliefs to individuals are synonomous with (or strictly equivalent to) some finite set of sentences describing that individual's dispositional or actual behavior. As we shall see shortly, Peirce never endorsed, nor could he endorse, the view that sentences ascribing beliefs to an individual strictly *entail*, and are strictly *entailed by*, some finite set of statements describing that individual's dispositional or actual behavior. The most that Peirce maintained was that statements ascribing beliefs to individuals are rendered highly probable (not strictly entailed) by statements describing their dispositional behavior. This, as we shall see, followed as a natural consequence of his doctrine on the nature of meaning.[5] Given this observation, and Peirce's insistence on the existence of mental states, the well-known objections to the thesis of analytical behaviorism will not apply to Peirce's treatment.[6] This is not to say that Peirce's thesis is without problems. After all, as far as I can tell, he made no extended attempt either to clarify the concept of dispositional behavior or to explain how dispositions can be causes of behavior. But, in any event, if Peirce's analysis of the concept of "belief" is unacceptable, it cannot be for the reason that it is a straightforward instance of *analytical behaviorism*. It has been suggested that *any behavioristic* analysis of belief statements will be unacceptable primarily for the reason that no set of statements describing behavior will ever *entail* that an individual has a particular belief.[7] But if the entailment relationship is not demanded (as is the case in Peirce's behavioristic analysis of belief), then, of course, Peirce's form of behaviorism cannot be false for the suggested reason. Indeed, Quine has gone so far as to applaud Peirce's behavioristic semantics as his single and most important contribution to empiricism.

Such is Peirce's general analysis of "belief." We shall have cause to return to this topic for further consideration; but let us now turn to the notion of "doubt."

B. *Doubt*

Doubt, like belief, is a mental state; but the characteristics and effects of doubt are quite the opposite of the characteristics and effects of belief. As a mental state which generates certain effects, doubt (not disbelief) is the contradictory of belief. Just as belief is an habitual association among our ideas involving expectancy and, as such, a calm and tranquil state which causes us to act (or to be disposed to act) in a particular way under particular circumstances, doubt represents a lack of association among ideas depriving us of expectancy and, as such, is an irritating and frustrating state from which we wish to escape and in which we are deprived of the disposition to act in any particular way.[8] Further, just as Peirce analyzed statements ascribing beliefs into statements asserting certain dispositions to behave in certain ways, he also analyzed statements ascribing doubts into statements asserting a lack of dispositional behavior.[9] This suggests, of course, that the meaning of an expression like "x doubts that p" is, for the sake of verifying the statement, the same as "x is deprived of the disposition to act in a particular way with respect to p." Such an analysis has the clear advantage of allowing for the distinction between doubt and disbelief; for if a person disbelieves a proposition, he is not deprived of the disposition to act in any particular way—he acts, or is disposed to act, as if the proposition in question were false. This why doubt, and not disbelief, is the opposite of belief.

In further characterizing the concept of doubt, Peirce asserted that *real* doubt can occur only when something confidently expected fails to occur, or when something not in the least expected does occur. In other words, one cannot be in a genuine state of doubt unless he has been *surprised* either by that which he does not expect or by the absence of that which he does expect; and this implies that there can be no genuine doubt without antecedent belief. Belief and expectation came first and the power to doubt much later (5.512). Doubt, then, presupposes and is the negation of belief; it obtains only when some belief, or set of beliefs, is ruptured, that is, when one does not know how to act because some belief which one had previously endorsed surprisingly no longer allows him to facilitate his dealings with experience.

By far the most important and, unfortunately, the most frequently neglected, property of real doubt lay in what Peirce termed the 'external origin' of doubt. Because real doubt originates with surprise and because a person can no more surprise himself than he can scare himself by jumping up and shouting boo!, the surprise which engenders real doubt is caused by the recalcitrance of experience in the face of our beliefs, and is thus a psychological state forced upon us by external experience itself. Real doubt is something that happens to us and cannot be effected willy-nilly by any act of the will—for one cannot will the recalcitrance of experience. Peirce emphasized the importance of this when he said:

> It is important for the reader to satisfy himself that genuine doubt always has an external origin, usually from surprise; and that it is impossible for a man to create in himself a genuine doubt by such an act of the will as would suffice to imagine the condition of a mathematical theorem, as it would be for him to give himself a genuine surprise by a simple act of the will.[10]

Peirce's insistence on the external origin of genuine doubt allowed him to contrast his own conception of inquiry and doubt with the Cartesian position which he vociferously rejected. Recall that Descartes dreamt of establishing a system of philosophy on propositions so true that they could not conceivably be false; and so, in order to find those propositions, he began his quest for philosophical certainty by methodically calling into doubt all those propositions whose contradictories are logically possible. By his own admission Descartes also claimed that although he did not really doubt certain of his beliefs, still, they had to be considered doubtful if it were logically possible that they were false. In short, Descartes began his inquiry with the assumption that, for the sake of attaining knowledge, it is necessary and legitimate to doubt any proposition if it is logically possible that the proposition is false. As against Descartes, Peirce never tired of claiming that doubts based upon the logical possibility of error are not genuine doubts, and that legitimate inquiry cannot take place in the absence of genuine doubts. Cartesian doubt, unlike genuine doubt, lacks the felt quality of frustrating uneasiness experienced when we know not what to do (because we no longer know what to believe) and when the need for acting is present. And Cartesian doubt lacks this felt quality because it is not, in Peirce's sense of the phrase, external in origin.

But why did Peirce insist that legitimate inquiry can only occur on the occasion of doubt that is external in origin? Why, in short, did he feel that any inquiry is illegitimate if it proceeds on the assumption that a proposition is doubtful if it is logically possible that it is false? If we bypass his dubious claim that inquiry based Cartesian doubt does not provide the mind with strong enough motive to conduct meaningful inquiry (5.375), his basic reason was that where inquiry begins on the assumption that a proposition is doubtful if it is logically possible that it is false, then inquiry can be successful only if it terminates in the establishment of propositions so true that it is logically impossible that they be false (1.149). But, for Peirce, such a view of inquiry is self-defeating and effectively renders the attainment of knowledge impossible because there simply are no propositions so true that it is logically impossible that they be false. No doubt, in reaching the Cogito Descartes thought he had reached the indubitably true, that is, a proposition free from the logical possibility of error. However, for a host of reasons (which we shall see shortly) Peirce argued that all reasoning is infected with the logical possibility of error and that the Cogito is as much the product of synthetic inferences as is any other proposition (see pp. 49ff below). In short, Peirce's belief in the fallibility of all knowledge and reasoning ultimately forced him to brand the Cartesian doubt as fictive (MS 365). Since inquiry cannot begin with Cartesian doubt without ending in scepticism, inquiry must, Peirce maintained, originate with doubt external in origin and terminate in propositions we do not genuinely doubt, rather than in propositions which must preclude the logical possibility of error.

There is, I think, no way of avoiding the conclusion that Peirce's rejection of the Cartesian doctrine on doubt and inquiry is rooted in his rejection of the Cartesian conception of knowledge. Descartes' doctrine on doubt and inquiry is perfectly consistent with, and entailed by, the view that if a person knows that p, then it is not logically possible that p is false. For Peirce, however, a person's knowing that p is consistent with the logical possibility of p being false. And, as we shall also see, Peirce's explication of this thesis does *not* imply that truth is not a necessary condition for knowledge. Consequently, Peirce's repudiation of the Cartesian doubt and his subsequent rejection of the Cartesian view on inquiry are valid only if his doctrine on the fallible nature of all knowledge can be successfully defended. More on this later.

We can briefly summarize Peirce's doctrine on the nature of doubt as follows. If a person *genuinely* doubts that p, then with repect to p he is (a) deprived of the disposition to act in any particular way; (b) in an uneasy and dissatisfied state, which occurs only when some belief or beliefs previously endorsed lead to the unexpected; and (c) in this state in virtue of experience itself providing the unexpected, that is to say, he is in a state which he has not willed, nor could will, by appealing to the logical possibility of p's being false.

C. *Inquiry*

Accordingly, with genuine doubt inquiry begins and the purpose of inquiry is to overcome genuine doubt by re-establishing stable beliefs. The irritation of doubt causes a struggle to attain belief and the struggle itself is inquiry (5.374; 6.496; MS 596 (pp. 16ff); MS 753 (pp. 1ff)). Stable beliefs, which are the object of inquiry, are beliefs that lead to the expected and allow us to expedite our dealings with experience.[11] Hence the passage from genuine doubt to stable belief is the passage from a lack of disposition to act in a particular way to a disposition to act in a way that is successful:

> The irritation of doubt is the only immediate motive for the struggle to attain belief. It is certainly best for us that our beliefs should be such as may truly guide our actionsd so as to satisfy our desires; and this reflection will make us reject every belief which does not seem to have been so formed as to insure this result .... With doubt, therefore, the struggle begins, and with the cessation of doubt it ends. Hence the sole object of inquiry is the settlement of opinion. We may fancy that this is not enough for us and that we seek not merely an opinion, but a true opinion. But put this fancy to the test and it proves groundless; for as soon as a firm belief is reached we are entirely satisfied, whether the belief be true or false .... The most that can be maintained is that we shall seek for a belief which we shall think to be true.[12]

There can be little doubt that Peirce's theory of inquiry is based upon a biological model and the principle of "homeostasis." The process of inquiry begins when the organism is in a state of need and the process of inquiry is itself an adaptive response of the organism for the purpose of establishing the equilibrium necessary for survival. When inquiry terminates in modes of behavior that are adaptive, then inquiry is successful.[13]

It has been observed that in the above text (and in other texts) Peirce apparently insisted that it is not the purpose of inquiry to establish true beliefs, but rather beliefs which we shall *think* to be true. A closer examination, however, reveals that what Peirce was really attempting to say was not that the purpose of inquiry is not to establish true beliefs, but rather that the distinction between a true belief and a belief which is firmly established by inquiry is fanciful. That Peirce really meant this is evidenced in a later text (written in 1906) in which he commented on the preceding text. After insisting that inquiry seeks to establish beliefs which are satisfactory, he said:

> Is the satisfactory meant to be whatever excites a certain peculiar feeling of satisfaction? In that case the doctrine (the true is the satisfactory)[14] is simply hedonism in so far as it affects the field of cognition .... But to say that an action or the result of an action is satisfactory is simply to say that it is congruous to the aim of that action (5.559–60). ... It is, however, no doubt true that men act, especially in the action of inquiry, as if their sole purpose were to produce a certain state of feeling, in the sense that when the state of feeling is attained, there is no further effort. It was upon that proposition that I originally based pragmaticism, laying it down in the article that in Nov. 1877 prepared the ground for my argument for the pragmaticism doctrine (*Pop. Sci. Monthly* for January 1878). In the case of inquiry I called that state of feeling 'firm belief,' and said 'As soon as a firm belief is reached we are entirely satisfied, whether the belief be true or false,' and went on to show how the action of experience consequently was to create the conception of real truth. ... My paper of November 1877, setting out from the proposition that the agitation of a question ceases when satisfaction is attained with the settlement of belief, and then only, goes on to consider how the conception of truth gradually develops from that principle under the action of experience; beginning with wilful belief, or self-mendacity, the most degraded of all intellectual conditions; thence rising to the imposition of beliefs by the authority of organized society; then to the ideal of the settlement of opinion as the result of a fermentation of ideas; and finally reaching the idea of truth as over-whelmingly forced upon the mind in experience as the effect of an independent reality.[15]

Indeed, when we look to what Peirce considered the proper method for the establishment of belief in inquiry, it becomes quite clear that the use of the method of science is a necessary condition for the establishment of beliefs which satisfy the end of inquiry. For Peirce, the end of inquiry (the establishment of beliefs which allow us to expedite our dealings with experience) is not only achieved by the employment of the method of science, but also, and more importantly, there is no distinction between a firm belief established by inquiry and a true belief (4.523; 5.605).[16] Peirce is no more soft-headed for insisting that the end of inquiry is the establishment of modes of activity that facilitate our dealings with experience than is Quine for insisting that ultimately the acceptability of our conceptual schemes is a function of the degree to which they allow us to expedite our dealings with sense experience.[17]

That Peirce did insist on the method of science as the only appropriate method for the determination of belief, and why he insisted on it, is stated in an essay entitled, "The Fixation of Belief." In this essay Peirce claimed that there are only four methods of fixing belief: the method of tenacity, the method of authority, the *a priori* method, and the method of science. After characterizing and rejecting the first three, he argued that only the method of science is acceptable for the attainment of the end of inquiry. *The method of tenacity* is the method one would adopt if one were to hold to his beliefs while contemptuously refusing to consider any evidence which might disturb those beliefs. Those who fix belief in this manner are similar to the ostrich burying its head in the sand when danger approaches (5.377). Peirce rejected this method on the grounds that the social impulse is against such a method. What he apparently meant by this is that the community of intelligent men will not, and do not, accept such a method for fixing belief. *The method of authority* is the method one would adopt if one were to turn to some authoritative institution for the answer to any question he might have. Peirce's favorite example of this method of fixing belief is the Catholic church and the millions of people who turn to it as an authoritative source for the answer to any question that arises (5.739). Peirce also rejected this method as unsatisfactory because, although such a method has had wonderful results, nevertheless it constitutes a *prima facie* example of intellectual slavery and, moreover, no institution can reasonably undertake to regulate opinions upon every subject (5.380–1). Accordingly, the willful adherence to a belief and the arbitrary forcing of it upon others, must both be given up. The *a priori method* of fixing belief is the method one would employ if he were to adopt whatever opinion there seems to be a natural inclination to accept. This method is more acceptable than either of the preceding two, but its failure has been most manifest. It makes of inquiry something similar to the development of taste—but taste, unfortunately, is always more or less a matter of fashion

(5.382–3).[18] Therefore, we are driven to *the method of science* for the fixation of belief. Peirce said:

> To satisfy our doubts, therefore, it is necessary that a method should be found by which our beliefs may be caused by nothing human, but by some external permanency—by something upon which our thinking has no effect. ... Such is the method of science. Its fundamental hypothesis, restated in more familiar language, is this: there are real things, whose characters are entirely independent of our opinions about them; those realities affect our senses according to regular laws, and, though our sensations are as different as are our relations to the objects, yet, by taking advantage of the laws of perception, we can ascertain by reasoning how things really are; and any man, if he has sufficient experience and reason enough about it, will be led to the one true conclusion.[19]

Peirce's insistence, then, on the method of science as the only legitimate method for the fixation of belief was a function of his belief that only the method of science can guarantee stable belief because only the method of science can guarantee truth (3.430). The objectivity of the method of science and, because of its method, the unquestionable success of science in settling belief, clearly forced Peirce to accept it as the only reliable method for the establishment of truth (5.384).

His heralding the method of science, for the reason he so stated, indicates that, for Peirce, the purpose of inquiry is to establish true beliefs; and hence (as noted above) one cannot distinguish between a stable belief firmly established by the method of science and a true belief.[20]

These points are noteworthy because some philosophers take exception to Peirce's theory of inquiry for the alleged reason that the theory makes the establishment of a certain psychological state, rather than truth, the end of inquiry. Firmly believing a proposition, they argue, is not enough for the end of inquiry since firmly believing a proposition is consistent with the proposition's being false. So the theory must be wrong either because it makes firmly believing a proposition sufficient for the truth of the proposition (thereby reducing epistemology and logic to psychology), or because it makes the attainment of truth unnecessary for the end of inquiry. On this latter point Bertrand Russell has argued that if the end of inquiry were the establishment of firm beliefs, even when firm beliefs are understood to be biologically successful, then our inquiries would never be adequate because we need inquiries to terminate in true beliefs; and firm beliefs, no matter how biologically successful, do not guarantee truth. For thousands of years the inhabitants of Changsha, for example, firmly believed that the pactice of beating on gongs during lunar eclipses frightened the heavenly dog whose attempt to swallow the moon is the cause of the eclipse. The practice of beating on gongs never failed to be successful: every eclipse comes to an end after sufficient prolongation of the din. Thus if truth be made the end of inquiry, rather than firm and biologically successful belief, we can dispense with the practice of legitimatizing belief in propositions that may be false.[21]

But, given what we have noted above, this objection is quite unacceptable. Peirce chose the method of science for the establishment of stable belief because only the method of science pursued indefinitely could guarantee truth. His insistence on the method of science entails the view that a necessary condition for the establishment of stable (firm) belief is that the belief be true (7.77 and 3.430). In other words, the reason he gave for his choice of method makes it clear that if his theory of inquiry is wrong, it cannot be for the reason that it makes the attainment of truth unnecessary for the end of inquiry. Admittedly, inquiry shall have for its end the establishment of beliefs which are stable or biologically successful; but the method of science, wherever it can be used, is the only method likely to guarantee stable belief since it is the only method that can guarantee the truth necessary for avoiding those surprises which threaten the stability of belief.

Furthermore, the objection implies that if firmly believing a proposition were considered sufficient for the truth of the proposition, then we should be able to determine the truth or falsity of any proposition simply by ascertaining whether or not someone is in the appropriate mental state characterized by "feeling sure" that it is true or false. And this reduction of epistemology to psychology is deplorable because, they say, the truth of a proposition cannot be established by examining people's feelings about it. For this reason some have argued that Peirce could never have made the mistake of allowing that firm belief is sufficient for the truth of what is believed. Needless to say, if firmly believing a proposition were nothing more than being in a certain mental state characterized by "feeling sure," then the objection would be forceful. But, for Peirce, firmly believing a proposition as the result of inquiry is not simply a mental state characterized by "feeling sure." Although firm (stable) belief entails "feeling sure," a belief will not be said to be stable or firm if it is not established true by the method of science. Obviously, if one makes it a necessary condition for firmly (stably) believing a proposition that the proposition be true, then firmly believing a proposition will be sufficient for the truth of the proposition. Only a purely mentalistic conception of belief would forbid the inference.[22] So, although it is true that the end of inquiry is the establishment of stable beliefs, it will not do to suggest that Peirce's Theory of Inquiry is defective because it makes the attainment of stable beliefs, rather than true beliefs, the end of Inquiry.

We might, of course, be tempted to challenge Peirce's theory of inquiry for two other reasons. In the first case, it is part of the theory that if one has believed and never really doubted a proposition, then that proposition is perfectly acceptable as a premise in any line of argument. And this certainly seems to entail the questionable view that propositions never doubted and hence never subjected to inquiry are true simply because they are believed and have never been the subject of inquiry. If this is so, the truth of these propositions (i.e. those never doubted and thus never established by the method of science) turns out to be primarily a function of the biological success of the belief in them. In the second case, insisting that legitimate inquiry can begin only with real doubt suggests that no real advances can be made unless the inquiry emerges from felt need or dissatisfaction with present beliefs. But some of the more interesting advances in science have apparently resulted less from a feeling of dissatisfaction with present belief than from simple curiosity. People like Newton, for example, did not begin their speculations out of a sense of frustrating biological need occasioned by the recalcitrance of experience in the face of their present beliefs. Later we shall deal at length with the first of these objections.[23] So let us say something about the second and then proceed to other matters.

Peirce was well aware that many legitimate inquiries begin with the practice of asking questions about beliefs not really doubted. He even considered the practice a laudable and necessary art. But he refused to consider the practice of raising such questions as an instance of willfully calling into real doubt some belief not really doubted. Rather he described it as the simple and healthy process of submitting our beliefs to review to see if they are capable of honest doubt. In those cases where real advances are made as the result of such a practice, it is not because someone willfully chooses to doubt a given belief. For that cannot be done. The advances are made because the belief becomes genuinely doubtful in the course of asking such questions. Real doubt is still external in origin, but its occurence may be hastened by surprises that arise with the asking of pointed questions which present beliefs unexpectedly fail to answer. Peirce had this view in mind when he said:

> It will be wholesome enough for us to make a general review of the causes of our beliefs; and the result will be that most of them have been taken upon trust and have been held since we were too young to discriminate the credible from the incredible. Such reflections may awaken real doubts about some of our positions. But in cases where no real doubt exists in our minds inquiry will be an idle farce, a mere whitewashing commission, which were better let alone.[24]

Newton and others, for example, may have begun their inquiries by asking questions about beliefs they did not really doubt, or even questions that apparently had nothing to do with the adequacy of their present beliefs. But their inquiries were legitimate because the practice of asking those questions sooner or later pointed to the explanatory inadequacy (readily felt) of beliefs not previously questioned. At that point real doubt emerged and was properly laid to rest by the use of scientific method. Accordingly, it would be a mistake to characterize the result of such inquiries as proceeding from mere curiosity and in the absence of real doubt.

II. MEANING

A. The Pragmatic Maxim

Peirce claimed that before we can employ the method of science to determine the truth of any given proposition, we must first know what that proposition means; and to that end he provided a criterion of meaning, the pragmatic maxim, as early as 1878:

> Consider what effects, that might conceivably have practical bearings, we conceive the object of our conception to have. Then our conception of these effects is the whole of our conception of the object.[25]

Peirce understood this maxim to imply that the meaning of any proposition is itself given in another proposition which is simply a general description of all the conceivable experimental phenomena which the assertion of the original proposition virtually predicts (5.427; 5.412; MS 618 (p. 1); MS 619 (p. 2); MS 289 (pp. 8ff); MS 292 (p. 11); MS 290 (pp. 33ff)). In short, the meaning of any 'intellectual concept' or proposition is to be conveyed by another expression or proposition which mentions only the observable properties or effects that one would expect under certain circumstances if the original proposition were true. This latter expression Peirce dubbed the 'logical interpretant' (5.480ff). Thus, for example, the meaning of the term 'hard', or the proposition 'This is hard', is expressed by 'Not scratchable by many other substances' or 'This will not be scratched by many other substances' respectively (5.403; 5.483; 8.176; 8.195).

More specifically, however, the meaning of any given expression is obtained by translating that expression into a set of conditional statements, the antecedents of which prescribe certain operations to be performed, while the consequents of which specify certain observable phenomena which should and would occur as the result of performing those operations if the proposition were true.[26] For example, consider again the expression 'hard'. As just noted, the expression means 'not scratchable by many other substances'; but, given that the *logical interpretant* is also equivalent to a set of conditionals, the expression 'not scratchable by many other substances' means more properly '*If* you *were* to take some object which is said to be hard, and if you *were* to scratch it with many substances, *then* it would not be scratched.[27] In an example of what is meant by saying that the meaning of a concept or proposition lies in a corresponding conditional, Peirce tells us that the term 'lithium' or the expression 'This is lithium', means:

> ... If you search among minerals that are vitreous, translucent, grey or white, very hard, brittle and insoluble, for one which imparts a crimson tinge to an unluminous flame, this mineral being titurated with lime or witherite rats-bone, and then fused, can be partly dissolved in muriatic acid; *and* if this solution be evaporated, and the residue be extracted with sulfuric acid, and duly purified, it can be converted by ordinary methods into a chloride, which being obtained in a solid state, fused and electrolyzed with half a dozen powerful cells, will yield a globule of pinkish silvery metal that will float on gasoline: *then* the material of that is a specimen of lithium.[28]

In short, for Peirce, the meaning of what he calls an 'intellectual concept' or proposition is simply the conditions of its verification (5.412; MS 327).

Moreover, in spite of the unfortunate phraseology, the pragmatic maxim, as stated, is not so much a criterion for the meaning of concepts or words as it is a criterion for the meaning of certain propositions or sentences. Even though Peirce frequently slips into talking about the meaning of a concept or word, generally he talks about the meaning of a concept in terms of the meaning of a sentence such as 'this is lithium', 'This diamond is hard' or 'The sun is blue' (8.183ff). And apart from the fact that Peirce frequently claimed that it is not words or concepts, but rather *sentences* that are meaningful (MS 316 (p. 44); 8.184; 8.178; 8.195; 2.296), the fact that the meaning of a concept or term is construed by Peirce in terms of the conditions of its verification, suggests that, for Peirce, talking about the meaning of a concept or a word is in fact talking about the meaning of a sentence or proposition; for only sentences and propositions (and not concepts or words) can be verified.[29] So, while Peirce's infelicitous phrasing of the pragmatic maxim would appear to suggest the opposite, it would be a mistake to urge that Peirce's theory of meaning takes concepts or words as the primary source of semantic focus or significance. More on this shortly.

Also, in further reflecting on the import of the pragmatic maxim, we can note that the conditional statements which express the meaning of any concept or proposition state, in effect, the law governing the object of the proposition or conception. For example, the above cited conditionals which express the meaning of the proposition 'This is lithium' imply the law-like generalization 'All lithium is translucent, vitreous, insoluble, etc.' And this is what Peirce meant when he claimed that the meaning of any concept or proposition is a general description of all the experimental phenomena which the assertion of the proposition virtually predicts (5.427; 8.195 MS 327). And it is also what he meant when he said:

> To say that a body is hard, or red, or heavy, or of a given weight, or has any other property, is to say that it is subject to law and therefore is a statement referring to the future. (5.450)

The law (or habit)[30] which is tacitly expressed in the meaning of a concept or proposition and which accounts for the meaning of our propositions, is what Peirce called *Thirdness*, or the element of generality, continuity, or mediation in our experience. Thirdness enters into the meaning of all our propositions since all our propositions express some law in virtue of which the meaning of statements about those objects is expressed. Hence it is the lawlike character of our experience which accounts for the meaning of our concepts and propositions; for it is the lawlike character of our experience which accounts for the properties, a descriptions of which constitutes meaning. Indeed, Peirce claimed that, in the end, it is the law itself which is expressed in the conditionals, which constitutes the ultimate meaning of a proposition (5.491). His reason for saying as much is that the *logical interpretant* is itself meaningful in virtue of another *logical interpretant*. And if we are to avoid an infinite regress of *logical interpretants*, we must maintain in the last analysis that the ultimate meaning (*ultimate logical interpretant*) is the very law which the logical interpretants (conditionals) express.[31]

In addition to all this, Peirce effectively argued for the view that the conditional statements which express, or give, the meaning of a proposition are non-terminating or open-ended, as it were. No set of conditional statements can ever logically exhaust the meaning of the original statement. And this is because the generalization of the conditionals is, as a general description, incapable of fully identifying an object. The meaning of any sentence is exhausted by its sensory implications, but the sensory implications are unlimited. In other words, the meaning of any given proposition can only be partially specified in terms of a previously understood empirical vocabulary. This aspect of Peirce's theory of meaning, an aspect generally overlooked although essential for understanding his fallibilism, derives in part from his claim that, strictly speaking, all utterances are in some significant respect indeterminate in meaning, and hence to a certain degree vague or imprecise. Of course, for the purposes of ordinary discourse, this is not much of a problem since we can generally render our utterances sufficiently precise to avoid being misunderstood. Explaining what he meant by claiming all propositions are vague, Peirce said:

Accurate writers have apparently made a distinction between the *definite* and the *determinate*. A subject is *determinate* in respect to any character which inheres in it or is (universally and affirmatively) predicated of it, as well as in respect to the negative of such character, these being the very same respect. In all other respects it is *indeterminate*. The *definite* shall be defined presently. A sign (under which designation I place every kind of thought, and not alone external signs), that is in any respect objectively indeterminate (i.e. whose object is undetermined by the sign itself) is objectively *general* in so far as it extends to the interpreter the privilege of carrying its determination further. *Example:* 'Man is mortal.' To the question, 'What man?' the reply is that the propositions explicitly leaves it to you to apply its assertion to whatever man or men you will. A sign that is objectively indeterminate in any respect, is objectively *vague* in so far as it reserves further determination to be made in some other conceivable sign, or at least does not appoint the interpreter as its deputy in this office. *Example:* 'A man whom I would mention seems to be a little conceited.' The *suggestion* here is that the man in view is the person addressed; but the utterer does not authorize such an interpretation of any other application of what she says. She can still say, if she likes, that she does *not* mean the person addressed. Every utterances naturally leaves the right of further exposition in the utterer; and therefore, in so far as a sign is undeterminate, it is vague, unless it is expressly or by a well-understood convention rendered general. Usually, an affirmative predication covers *generally* every essential character of the predicate, while a negative predication *vaguely* denies some essential character. In another sense, honest people, when not joking, intend to make the meaning of their words determinate, so that there will be no latitude of interpretation at all. That is to say, the character of their meaning consists in the implications and non-implications of their words; and they intend to fix what is implied and what is not implied. They believe that they succeed in doing so, and if their chat is about the theory of numbers, perhaps they may. But the further their topics are from such precise, or 'abstract' subjects, the less possibility is there of such precision of speech. In so far as the implication is not determinate, it is usually left vague; but there are cases where an unwillingness to dwell on disagreeable subjects causes the utterer to leave the determination of the implication to the interpreter; as if one says, 'That creature is filthy, in every sense of the term' (5.447). ... In those respects in which a sign is not *vague*, it is said to be *definite*, and also with a slightly different mode of application, to be precise, a meaning probably due to praecisus having been applied to curt denials and refusals. (5.447)

And in further explicating the above text, Peirce stated in a footnote:

These remarks require supplementation. Determination, in general, is not defined at all; and the attempt at defining the determination of a subject with respect to a character only covers (or seems only to cover) explicit propositional determination. The incidental remark (5.447) to the effect that words whose meaning should be determinate would leave 'no latitude of interpretation' is more satisfactory, since the context makes it plain that there must be no such latitude either for the interpreter or for the utterer. The explicitness of the words would leave the utterer no room for explanations of his meaning. ... At the same time, it is tolerably evident that the definition, as it stands, is not sufficiently explicit, and further, that at the present stage of our inquiry cannot be made altogether satisfactory. For what is the interpretation alluded to? To answer that convincingly would be either to establish or to refute the doctrine of pragmaticism. Still some explanations may be made. Every sign has a single object, though this single object may be a single set or a single continuum of objects. *No general description can identify an object.* But the common sense of the interpreter of the sign will assure him that the object must be one of a limited collection of objects. Suppose, for example, two englishmen are to meet in a continental railway carriage. The total number of subjects of which there is any appreciable probability that one will speak to the other perhaps does not exceed a million; and each will have perhaps half that million not far below the surface of consciousness, so that each unit of it is ready to suggest itself. If one mentions Charles the Second, the other need not consider what possible Charles the Second is meant. It is no doubt the English Charles Second. Charles the second of England was quite a different man in different days; and it might be said that without further specification the subject is not identified. But the two Englishmen have no purpose of splitting hairs in their talk; and the latitude of interpretation which constitutes the indeterminacy of a sign must be understood as a latitude which might affect the achievement of a purpose. ... The October remarks (i.e. those in the above paper) made the proper distinction between the two kinds of indeterminacy, viz.: indefiniteness and generality, of which the former consists in the sign's not sufficiently expressing itself to allow of an undubitable determinate interpretation, while the (latter) turns over to the interpreter the right to complete the determination as he pleases. (emphasis mine)[32]

From these long texts and others, it seems clear that the meaning of any given proposition can never be fully specified because the generalization of the conditionals that express the meaning is a general sign that, in being general, cannot completely identfy the object of which it is a sign. Sometimes Peirce claimed that the reason for this natural indeterminacy of propositional meaning, or the reason why no general description (or sign) can identify an object, reflects the fact that all propositions are hypothetical assertions about the nature of our perceptual experiences which are always imprecise owing to the action of the universe upon the perceiver (5.540 n.; 3.93). More frequently than not, however, he professed that the indeterminacy of all propositions is rooted in the natural indeterminacy of the objects of perception or the objects the sign is supposed to represent. Indeed, when talking about the indetermancy of meaning, Peirce invariably located the source of that belief in his contention that there is no object that is absolutely determinate with respect to its having or not having every known property:

The absolute individual can not only not be realized in sense or thought, but can not exist, properly speaking. For whatever lasts for any time, however short, is capable of logical division, because in that time it will undergo some change in its relations. But what does not exist for any time, however short, does not exist at all. All, therefore, that we perceive or think, or that exists, is general. So far there is truth in the doctrine of scholastic realism. But all that exists is infinitely determinate, and the infinitely determinate is the absolutely individual. This seems paradoxical, but the contradiction is easily resolved. That which exists is the object of a true conception. This conception may be made more determinate than any assignable conception; and therefore it is never so determinate that it is capable of no further determination. (3.93 n. 1)

Thus Peirce's denial of the existence of absolute individuals provided the logical foundation for his doctrine on the indeterminacy of meaning. Since no object in the universe can ever be fully determinate with respect to its having or not having every known property, it follows that any proposition about the universe is vague in the sense that it can not hope to fully specify a determinate set of properties. I believe that it is for this reason also that, for Peirce, the meaning of any proposition is always open to further specification by the utterer, although an exhaustive specification cannot be given.[33]

If only for the sake of future discussion, it should be pointed out that Peirce came to designate his denial of the existence of absolute individuals as the doctrine of *synechism* (all that is, is general) and he insisted that the doctrine could be established in at least two ways. First of all, the doctrine recommends itself as the only one consistent with an evolutionary cosmology. Secondly (as is hinted at in the last of the preceding texts), the doctrine can be independently established in virtue of the infinite divisibility of the continuum as soon as it is shown that all things exist in the continuum of time and space.[34] It is because all things swim in the continuum of space and time that it is theoretically impossible for us to specify all their properties and hence render our propositions fully determinate with respect to meaning. This second argument convinced Peirce that the mathematics of the continuum would provide a logic for the universe and, in effect, the key that would open the door of his cosmology; but it also furnished the logical foundation for a most distinctive characteristic of his theory of meaning.

Before turning to other aspects of Peirce's theory of meaning in the context of assessing Quine's evaluation of it, we can reflect on the scope and ontological implications of the pragmatic maxim.

Peirce said that his primary motivation in enunciating the pragmatic maxim was to day away with, as cognitively meaningless, all those propositions that could not be verified in accordance with the method of the physical sciences (5.6; 5.423). But this should not be taken to imply that the adoption of the pragmatic maxim entails the view that all and only those sentences are meaningful which are empirically verifiable. Indeed, for Peirce, there are a host of propositions that are meaningful but not empirically verifiable. Imperatives, explicatives, and interrogatives, for example, are meaningful; they have what Peirce calls 'emotive' or 'energetic' interpretants (and not 'logical' interpretants) and this is to say that they are meaningful, but not 'cognitively' meaningful because they cannot be either true or false (5.480ff). Accordingly, it seems safer to say that Peirce enunciated the pragmatic maxim

not to brand as meaningless all propositions in principle univeri-
fiable, but rather to specify a criterion of meaning suitable for
purportedly factual assertions (assertions about what there is), a
criterion that he believed necessary for the purpose of theoretical
inquiry. Recall that, for Peirce, philosophy is a branch of
theoretical science. It is concerned with the conditions for the
ascertainment of what is fact and hence, has nothing to do (qua
philosophy) with propositions which are not in principle verifiable
(3.560; 1.659; 5.432; 5.107; 5.14 n. 1; 5.61).

But even when we grant that the pragmatic maxim, as thus far
explicated, was intended as a criterion of meaning for factual
propositions, it should not be thought that its adoption proscribes
as meaningless any statements trafficking in assertions about
abstract entities—as though it could not be a fact that there are
abstract entities. Because Peirce once claimed that pragmaticism is
a species of prope-positivism, and because of his insistence upon
the method of the natural sciences as the only method for the
ascertainment of truth, there has been, I think, a strong tendency
to believe that the pragmatic maxim is a forerunner of that rather
narrow form of verificationism generally identified with the Vienna
Positivists who subsequently were to argue that factual assertions
about abstract entities are meaningless because in principle not
verifiable. Verificationism, as so construed, renders empirically
meaningless all sentences which are not reducible by way of
suitable paraphrase to sentences about physical objects either
directly or indirectly observable. And, from a logical point of view,
it is difficult to see how this form of verificationism could attain
any measure of plausibility independently of a justification rooted
ultimately in a Humean reduction of ideas to impressions of sense
and the consequent insistence that the truth (and hence the
meaning) of empirical sentences is a function of whether they
originate from, and are reducible to, sensory impressions. I submit,
however, that Peirce did not think that the concept of verification
(or verifiability) should be so narrowly construed as to render
belief in abstract entities meaningless. Nowhere does he say that a
belief in abstract entities is a meaningless belief. And there is
nothing in his empirical criterion of meaning that implies it. What
the pragmatic maxim asserts is that the meaning of any proposition
is nothing more than the conceivable practical effects which the
assertion of the proposition would imply—if the proposition were
true. Our conception of these effects, which might conceivably have
practical bearing, just is our conception of the object. The word

'practical' of course, is ambiguous and has been variously construed by different philosophers. But, given what has been argued above, I think it should be construed to refer to those conceivable effects which, in terms of scientific practice, would count for verifying the proposition if it were asserted. This does not imply that one cannot verify belief in the existence of abstract entities. Unless one holds that belief in the existence of abstract entities has no observational results that could count for verifying the belief, there is nothing in the pragmatic maxim which implies that statements about abstract entities are meaningless.

Moreover, the plausibility of this line of reasoning is further enhanced when we consider that Peirce argued for the existence of certain abstract entities and never even considered whether it was inconsistent with his commitment to naturalism. After all, he argued for what he called his "Neglected Argument for the Existence of God" (MS 841 (p. 1); 6.49ff). And he spent a good deal of ink commenting on the existence and nature of the Absolute Mind. Indeed, when he argued that matter is effete mind because the phenomena of consciousness cannot be accounted for under mechanistic laws (1.162) he was, whether we agree with the argument or not, arguing for the existence of an abstract entity on the ground that such a belief leads to certain observable effects which cannot be explained by appealing to any purely materialistic alternative. And when he took a dim view of Telepathy it was not because belief in such a phenomenon was a matter of believing in an abstract entity, but rather because belief in the thesis did not, at the time, allow for observable, predictable and controllable effects that would count for verifying the phenomenon (MS 881; 1.115). For similar reasons he also argued for the existence of real modalities, possibilities (4.547).[35] So, even though Peirce's pragmatic maxim sustains a verificationist interpretation, its adoption does not render meaningless statements about abstract entities. Peirce's naturalism implies a concept of verification which extends beyond the view that only sentences about physical objects, defined in sensory terms, can be verified. And in every case where Peirce committed himself to belief in the existence of an abstract entity, it was simply because he felt that the purposes of an adequate explanation required it, that proceeding on purely physicalistic assumptions did not in fact succeed, and, moreover, that what exists is what is asserted to exist in an adequate explanation. Naturally, all this raises the question as to what, for Peirce, is an adequate explanation; but it seems clear that, however he construed it, an adequate explanation need not require appeal to only physical objects. And all this is further evidenced by not only in Peirce's criticism of Comte for construing verification in such a way that only those hypotheses are verifiable which contain reference to only directly observable facts (7.91; 2.511 n.; MS 475 (p. 58); MS 318 (Prag. 21)) but also by his explicit claim that "science is approaching a critical point; its old and purely materialistic conceptions will no longer suffice" (7.158 n. 5).

Finally, it is difficult to see how the narrow form of verificationism can be defended independently of the view that the truth of empirical sentences is a function of whether they originate from, and are reducible to, sentences descriptive of sensory impressions. It is well known, however, that, for Peirce, the truth of a sentence or belief is not a matter of how it originates, but rather a matter of whether what the sentence predicts will continue to be confirmed by the scientific community. And this seems to be another reason for disparaging the narrow verificationist's interpretation of the Pragmatic Maxim, since such an interpretation would require of Peirce a certain view on the nature of truth which he clearly did not endorse.

All the above considerations reflect rudimentary characteristics of Peirce's theory of meaning; and, in evaluating it, which I shall do after examining his semiotic justification for the theory, certain other aspects of the theory will come to light, aspects which are crucial but which can best be fleshed out in the course of some critical reflection.

B. *Meaning and Signs*

Peirce claimed that the problem of what the 'meaning' of a proposition is can only be solved by the study of the *interpretants*, or proper significant effects, of signs (5.475). And because he frequently claimed that his theory of meaning derives from, and is justified by, his theory of signs (8.118ff and 8.191), something certainly should be said about the extent to which Peirce's theory of signs in fact justifies, derives from or otherwise illuminates his pragmaticism. To be sure, Peirce's theory of signs is sufficiently complex and controversial to warrant a considerably more detailed and cautious examination than is here possible. Still, by examining the basics of his theory we can gain some insight into the role the semiotic serves to justify and illuminate pragmaticism.

For Peirce, then, the study of logic divides into three branches of which the first is *Speculative Grammar*, or the general theory of the nature and meaning of signs whether they be icons, indices or symbols. So, the study of signs (semiotic) is the first branch of logic, *Speculative Grammar*.[36] And Peirce called it both a descriptive and a formal science.

In explicating its nature as a descriptive study, he noted that Speculative Grammar is

> an analysis of the nature of assertion, which rests upon observations, indeed, but upon observations of the rudest kind, open to the eye of every attentive person who is familiar with the use of language and which, we may be sure no rational being able to converse at all with his fellows, and so to express a doubt of anything, will ever have any doubt. (3.432)

And in characterizing semiotic as a quasi-necessary, or formal, science he said

> By describing the doctrine as 'quasi-necessary,' or formal, I mean that we observe the characters of such signs as we know, and from such an observation, by a process which I will not object to naming *Abstraction*, we are led to statements, eminently fallible, and therefore in one sense by no means necessary, as to what must be the characters of all signs used by a 'scientific' intelligence, that is to say, by an intelligence capable of learning by experience. (2.227)

So, it would appear that the study of semiotic consists in phenomenologically analyzing, or describing, the signs we know until we are led through a process of abstraction, or inductive generalization, to what *must* be the characters of all signs.

As for the nature of the sign itself, and how the definition of the sign leads to a classification of signs, Peirce offered the following in 1908:

> I define a *sign* as anything which on the one hand is so determined by an object and on the other hand so determines an idea in a person's mind, that this latter determination, which I term the *Interpretant* of the sign, is thereby mediately determined by that object. A sign, therefore, has a triadic relation to its Object and to its *Interpretant*. But it is necessary to distinguish the *Immediate Object*, or the Object as the Sign represents it, from the *Dynamical Object*, or really efficient but not immediately present Object. It is likewise requisite to distinguish the *Immediate Interpretant*, i.e. the interpretant represented or signified in the Sign, from the *Dynamic Interpretant*, or effect actually produced on the mind by the sign; and both of these from the *Normal Interpretant*, or effect that would be produced on the mind by the Sign after sufficient development of thought. On these considerations I base a recognition of ten respects in which signs may be divided. I do not say that these divisions are enough. But since every one of them turns out to be a trichotomy, it follows that in order to decide what classes of signs result from them, I have 3^{10}, or 59049, difficult questions to carefully consider;

and therefore I will not undertake to carry my systematic division of signs any further, but will leave that to future explorers. (8.343)[37]

Notice that for every sign there must be an object, or that for which the sign stands; and there must also be an effect in an interpreter, which effect is called an *Interpretant.* On the basis of the relationship between a sign and its object, signs can be divided most basically into icon, index and symbol. We can reflect briefly on this latter division of signs and then turn our attention directly to Peirce's notion of an *interpretant.* Thereafter we should be able to see how Peirce intended the semiotic to justify pragmaticism.

For Peirce, any sign which stands for something merely because it resembles it, is an *Icon* (3.362). Icons are similar to their objects and the similarity between them is not established by the fact that the similarity is noted by an interpreter. The basis of the similarity between the Icon and its Object is present in the sign vehicle whether or not there is any corresponding object. We call something an *Icon,* then, when it is related to its object by similarity. And Peirce offers the following fuller definition:

> An *Icon* is a sign which refers to the Object that it denotes merely by virtue of characters of its own, and which it possesses, just the same, whether any such Object actually exists or not. It is true that unless there is such an Object, the Icon does not act as a sign; but this has nothing to do with its character as a sign. Anything whatever, be it a quality, existent individual, or law, is an icon of anything, in so far as it is like that thing and is used as a sign of it. (2.247)

By way of its function, the value of an icon consists in exhibiting the features of a state of things regarded as if it were purely imaginary (4.448). When the interpreter considers the sign as similar to something else, then the sign is useful for learning about the characteristics of the object. But, as Peirce would have it, the icon does not provide us with knowledge about how things stand in fact:

> A pure icon can convey no positive or factual information; for it affords no assurance that there is any such thing in nature. But it is of the utmost value for enabling its interpreter to study what would be the character of such an object should it exist. (4.447)

As examples of the icon, Peirce offers diagrams (4.418), paintings (2.92) and statues all of which are similar to, or resemble, their objects even if their objects do not actually exist.

In turning to the second way in which signs can be divided in terms of their relationship to their objects, Peirce defines the index as follows:

> An *Index* is a representamen which fulfills the function of a representamen by virtue of a character which it could not have if its object did not exist, but which it will continue to have just the same whether it be interpreted as a representamen or not. (5.73; 4.447; 2.92)

The reason why the index is fit to lead its interpreter to the object is because of some real existential connection between it and the object. As examples of the index, Peirce claims that a weathercock is an index of the wind's direction just as a low barometer with moist air is an index of rain (2.286). And elsewhere he observes that:

> Of the ... relatively genuine form of Index, the hygrometer is an example. Its connection with the weather is dualistic, so that by an involved icon, it actually conveys information. On the other hand a mere landmark by which a particular thing may be recognized because it is as a matter of fact associated with that thing, a proper name without signification, a pointing finger, is a degenerate index. (5.75)

So, an index is a sign which directs the attention of the interpreter to the object of the sign, and since there is an existential connection between the index and its object (which, unlike the object of the icon, actually exists) the index provides information about its object without describing it (1.369).[38] Whereas icons do not denote existing objects, indices do; and that is why indices provide factual information whereas icons do not.

> ... the third (or symbol) is the general name of description which signifies its object by means of an association of ideas or habitual connection between the name and the character signified. (1.369)[39]

This definition implies that, unlike the icon or the index, there is no natural fitness in the material quality of the symbol for its being a sign of the object it represents. The symbol acquires its *fitness* to represent its object by the mind. For example, the sentence "All cats are flea-ridden" is a sign. But unlike a symphony, photograph, painting or diagram, there is no natural likeness, or existential connection between the material quality of this sign and what it represents. The sentence is a symbol which represents its object because it is invested with that function by the mind's habit of associating that sentence with what the mind imagines as the object of that sentence or what the sentence stands for. Every symbol, then, is an *ens rationis* (4.464) and it functions to represent its object because of the mental habit of associating that symbol with its object.[40]

Moreover, since the symbol is a general name or description, what it represents must be general or indeterminate. It is only through the symbol that generality, thirdness or habit enter into our thinking because the symbol, being general description, can only represent what is general. The fact that the symbol is general or indeterminate indicates that its function is to represent a generality, habit or law in the universe; and it achieves this function not because the material quality of the symbol is like the object signified, but rather because the mind, by convention, associates the symbol with generality or law by letting it stand for such generality or law as we directly perceive in the world.[41] As Peirce said:

> Any ordinary word as 'give,' 'bird,' 'marriage,' is an example of a symbol. It is applicable to whatever may be found to realize the idea connected with the word: it does not, in itself, identify these things. It does not show us a bird, nor enact before our eyes a giving in marriage, but supposes that we are able to imagine those things and have associated the word with them. (2.298)

Although ideas in the mind of the interpreter are essential for the representing function of the symbol, the symbol is still determined to represent what it does by the object that it represents. What the symbol represents is the object of the thought which the symbol calls forth in the mind of the interpreter. The symbol, then, achieves representing function by calling forth in the mind of the interpreter another sign whose object is the object of the symbol. In an interesting passage in which Peirce reviews the nature of the symbol, he also tells us why symbols are important and what is achieved by the division of signs into icon, index and symbol:

> First, an analysis of the essence of a sign (stretching that word to its widest limits, as *anything which, being determined by an object, determines an interpretation to determination through it, by the same object*), leads to a proof that every sign is determined by its object, either first, by partaking in the characters of the object, when I call the sign an *Icon*; secondly, by being really and in its individual existence connected with the individual object, when I call the sign an *Index*; thirdly, by more or less approximate certainty that it will be interpreted as denoting the object, in consequence of habit (which term I use as including a natural disposition), when I call the sign a *Symbol*. ... Symbols afford the means of thinking about thoughts in ways in which we could not otherwise think of them. They enable us, for example, to create abstractions, without which we should lack a great engine of

discovery. These enable us to count; they teach us that collections are individuals (individual = individual object), and in many respects they are the warp of reason. But since symbols rest exclusively on habits already definitely formed but not furnishing any observation even of themselves, and since knowledge is habit, they do not enable us to add to our knowledge even so much as a necessary consequent, unless by means of a definite preformed habit. Indices, on the other hand, furnish positive assurance of the reality and the nearness of their Objects. But with the assurance there goes no insight into the nature of those Objects. The same Perceptible may, however, function doubly as a Sign. That footprint that Robinson Crusoe found in the sand, and which has been stamped in the granite of fame, was an Index to him that some creature was on his island, and at the same time, as a Symbol, called up the idea of a man. ... This division of Signs is only one of ten different divisions of Signs which I have found it necessary more especially to study. I do not say that they are all satisfactorily definite in my mind. They seem to be all trichotomies, which form an attribute to the essentially triadic nature of a Sign. I mean because three things are concerned in the functioning of a Sign; the Sign itself, its Object, and its Interpretant. I cannot discuss all these divisions in this article; and it can well be believed that the whole nature of reasoning cannot be fully exposed from the consideration of one point of view among ten. That which we can learn from this division is of what sort a sign must be to represent the sort of Object that reasoning is concerned with. (4.531)

Peirce had a good deal more to say about symbols; and, indeed, a good deal more can be said. But, for our present purposes, the important point to keep in mind is that every general description is a symbol which, in being general, functions to represent real law, habit or generality in the world. This is important because, as already noted, the pragmatic maxim is a criterion for the meaning of intellectual concepts or, in other words, descriptive propositions. Given that descriptive propositions are symbols, we cannot avoid the conclusion that descriptive propositions function principally to represent real habit, law or generality. Moreover, given the way in which symbols achieve their representative function, it will also follow that descriptive propositions achieve their representative function by creating in the mind of the interpreter another like sign whose object is the same object as that of the symbol itself. And all this provides a good deal by way of justifying the pragmatic maxim as we have outlined it above. But, we are getting a bit ahead of ourselves. Let us turn to considering the interpretants of signs. Thereafter we can summarize the way in which Peirce's prag- maticism is an outgrowth of his division of signs in terms of their objects and interpretants.

As noted earlier, the effect any sign has on an interpreter Peirce called the *interpretant*. More specifically, he says that "that determination of which the immediate cause, or determinant, is the sign, of which the mediate cause is the object may be termed the Interpretant" (6.347).[42] Thus the effect the sign has on those for whom it is a sign is the interpretant, and interpretants can be basically classified into immediate, dynamical and final.

The *Immediate Interpretant* is not the immediate effect a sign actually has on the interpreter; rather it is "the quality of the impression that the sign is *fit* to produce and does not consist in any actual reaction" (8.315). The immediate interpretant, then, does not consist in any effect on the interpreter. It consists in the natural interpretability that the sign has before it actually gets interpreted. As Peirce noted in a letter to Lady Welby (dated 1909) "My immediate interpretant is implied in the fact that each sign must have its own peculiar Interpretability before it gets any interpreter" (letters; p. 36). Hence Peirce's concept of an immediate interpretant is a bit of a misnomer since it consists not in any actual effect it produces in an interpreter but rather in the effect that the sign is naturally fitted to produce. Just what effect the sign is naturally fitted to produce is revealed, as Peirce says, "in the right understanding of the sign itself " (4.536).

The *Dynamical Interpretant* is "the actual effect which the sign determines" (4.536) or, alternatively, "it is the direct effect actually produced by a sign upon the interpreter of it" (4.536). And the dynamical interpretant itself divides nicely into the emotional, the energetic and the logical interpretant. What the emotional, energetic and logical interpretant consists in we shall discuss shortly.

Finally, there is the *Final Interpretant* which Peirce defines as "that which would finally be decided to be the true interpretation if consideration of the matter were carried so far that an ultimate opinion were reached" (8.184). Although he frequently defined the final interpretant in this way, it's a bit difficult to say precisely what Peirce had in mind; for he sometimes defines the final interpretant differently, and in the end confessed to being somewhat 'misty' in his conception of this third interpretant (4.536). But, as defined above, the final interpretant would appear to be the effect the sign finally has, or would have, on the fully developed mind of the scientific community. It is that effect which the sign would finally produce, or have, on the mind of the scientific community were it allowed an indefinite amount of time to investigate. At this juncture we need not enter into a prolonged discussion of the difficulties involved in understanding Peirce's concept of the final interpretant; for our principle concern is with the dynamical interpretant. And this because it is only the dynamical interpretant which has an actual effect on the interpreter. The immediate interpretant refers more to the interpretability of the sign and the final interpretant refers to the effect the sign would have on the mind of the scientific community allowed to investigate successfully and indefinitely (8.343). Thus, if, as Peirce claims, the meaning of a proposition can only be solved by the study of interpretants or proper significant effects of signs (5.475), then since it is only the dynamical interpretant that bespeaks an *actual* effect of the sign of the interpreter, it is only the analysis of the dynamical interpretant that will give us an analysis of meaning. So let us turn to it.

As noted above, the dynamical interpretant divides into three kinds, namely, the emotional, the energetic and the logical interpretant. On the nature of these three kinds of dynamical interpretants, Peirce said:

> The first proper significant effect of a sign is a feeling produced by it. There is almost always a feeling which we come to interpret as evidence that we comprehend the proper effect of the sign, although the foundation of truth in this is frequently very slight. This 'emotional interpretant' as I call it, may amount to much more than that feeling of recognition; and, in some cases, is the only proper significant effect that a sign produces. Thus the performance of a piece of concerted music is a sign. It conveys and is intended to convey, the composer's musical ideas; but these usually consist merely in a series of feelings. If a sign produces any further proper significant effect, it will do so through the mediation of the emotional interpretant, and such further effect will always involve an effort. I call it the energetic interpretant. The effort may be a muscular one, as it is in the case of the command to ground arms; but it is much more usually an exertion upon the Inner World, a mental effort. It can never be the meaning of an intellectual concept, since it is a single act (while) such a concept is a general nature. But what further kind of effect can there be? ... In advance of ascertaining the nature of this effect, it will be convenient to adopt a designation for it, and I will call it the *logical interpretant* without as yet determining whether this term shall extend to anything beside the meaning of a general concept. ... (5.476)

Hence the *emotional interpretant* is principally the feeling of recognition produced in the interpreter by the signs, whereas the *energetic interpretant* causes an effort (internal or external) on the part of the interpreter. If a sign has only an emotional interpretant, then it has only an emotional meaning; whereas if a sign has an energetic interpretant (mediated by the emotional interpretant), then it has, what for want of a better term, we can only call an energetic meaning. Some signs (for example, a concerted symphony) may have only an emotional interpretant; and other signs (for example, the command to ground arms) have both an emotional and an energetic interpretant. But no sign can have any significant effect beyond the emotional unless mediated by an emotional interpretant. After all, we must feel that we recognize the sign if it is to have any further effects on us.

Notice, too, Peirce's elusive claim that the energetic interpretant can never be the meaning of an intellectual concept because, as he says, it is a single act while such a concept is of a general nature. This reflects Peirce's claim that the interpretant of a sign must be of the same general nature as the sign itself.[43] And since intellectual concepts (propositions) are general, the dynamic interpretant of them cannot reduce to either the emotional or the energetic interpretant.

To explicate the proper interpretant of those signs called intellectual concepts, Peirce introduced the concept of the logical interpretant, which, since it must be as general as the concept itself, can only be another sign of the same general nature. The logical interpretant is itself another sign which expresses the generality of the first sign. Intellectual concepts, then, produce in the mind of the interpreter another sign of the same general nature as the original. This effect (the logical interpretant) can only be another proposition which expresses or signifies precisely what is expressed or signified by the original sign.[44]

But the logical interpretant is not the meaning of the original sign. Rather it expresses, or gives, the same meaning that the original sign expresses. The meaning of the original sign itself, and which is expressed in the logical interpretant, is not itself a sign but rather the habit or Thirdness which the sign itself expresses and which is subsequently expressed in the logical interpretant. This 'habit' which is expressed by the sign is the meaning of the sign and Peirce frequently calls it the *ultimate logical interpretant.*[45] With this brief, and admittedly rough, survey of the essentials of the semiotic, I think we are now in position to appreciate Peirce's claim that Pragmaticism is the logical upshot of the study of signs and that the semiotic provides a justification for pragmaticism. So let us turn to it without any further delay.

To begin with, recall that in explicating the essentials of what Peirce meant by the pragmatic maxim we urged that, for Peirce,

(a) the meaning of a proposition (or intellectual concept) is given in, or by, another proposition (the logical interpretant) which is the proper effect produced by the original proposition on the mind of the interpreter; (b) the logical interpretant is not itself the meaning of the original proposition, but rather expresses the same meaning that the original proposition expresses; (c) what is ultimately expressed or represented by the original proposition, and which is re-expressed in the logical interpretant is simply the properties of the object of the proposition. These properties the object manifests because the object is governed by law or habit. So, the ultimate logical interpretant, what the proposition and its logical interpretant express or represent, is not another proposition, but rather the properties of the object of the proposition. And our conception of these properties (captured in the description provided by the logical interpretant) is the whole of our conception of the object; and finally (d) the meaning of any proposition or intellectual concept is general, that is, can never be fully specified.

Observe that (a) follows naturally from Peirce's claim that every descriptive proposition (or intellectual concept) is a sign (symbol) whose meaning is conveyed by its logical interpretant which, because it must be like the original sign and is not reducible to either the emotive or energetic interpretant, can only be another proposition. In other words, Peirce's thesis that the meaning of any descriptive proposition is given or expressed by another proposition (and that this latter proposition is equivalent to a generalized description of the properties of the object of the original proposition) follows from his semiotic conclusion that the meaning of any given sign is provided by its dynamical interpretant and that the dynamical interpretant of some signs (namely, descriptive propositions) does not reduce solely to either the emotional or energetic interpretant because the interpretant must be like the original sign which, since it is general, can only have its proper interpretant in another proposition.

Secondly, notice that (b) also follows naturally from Peirce's earlier noted argument to the effect that, if we are to avoid an infinite series of logical interpretants, the logical interpretant of the sign cannot be the meaning of the sign, but instead expresses or conveys the meaning of the sign. The meaning of the original sign itself (which meaning is expressed in the logical interpretant) is not itself a sign but rather the habit or thirdness which general signs (symbols) express.

Thirdly, (c) follows from Peirce's contention that since the meaning of the proposition is ultimately what is expressed by the proposition, and since what is expressed or represented by the proposition is not another proposition or sign (although it is conveyed by another proposition which is the logical interpretant), what the proposition ultimately expresses can only be the properties of the object of the proposition. Hence our conception of the properties or effects of the object of the proposition is our conception of the object; and the meaning of the proposition can only consist in its representing the properties or effects of the object of the proposition. The fact that a generalized description of these properties or effects is a generalization indicates that the object of the proposition is basically a matter of habit or generality which is to be expected because such propositions are symbols.

Finally, (d) follows from Peirce's argument that no sign can profess to completely express or represent all the properties of the object of the sign. As far as I can see, however, (d) follows less from a disinterested (or phenomenological) analysis of the sign relation than it does from his argument that all descriptive signs or propositions are to some degree indeterminate in meaning because the objects of these signs are part of an ongoing synechistic universe whose continuous nature will always allow some further determination of the properties of these objects. Accordingly, Peirce's semiotic defense or derivation of (d) would seem to presuppose the truth of synechism since the reason given for the natural indeterminacy or generality of all signs (leading to the view that the meaning of any given proposition can never be exhaustively specified) lay in the synechistic, or non-determinate, nature of the objects of the signs. If this is not so, then I do not know how Peirce could ultimately defend his claim that no sign ever adequately represents its object. And if this *is* supposed to follow from a phenomenological analysis of signs, it is not at all clear how it does.

At any rate, we can now see why Peirce thought that his pragmaticism was merely the end product of a fully developed theory of signs and the study of their significant effects. Hence he was by no means underestimating the importance of the semiotic as a justification for pragmaticism.

Whether Peirce actually succeeded in providing a neutral, or presuppositionless defense of pragmaticism would appear to involve a careful discussion of the nature of meaning and what it is that could possibly justify any proposed theory of meaning. While it is not likely that we could do justice to such a discussion here, still, the following minimal observations seem to be in order.

Certainly every sentence is a sign. And if it makes sense to say, as there seems every reason to suppose, that some sentences are meaningful, then their meaningfulness would certainly be a property of the sign relation. Hence a complete analysis of signs should, as Peirce argued, provide us with an account of what it is that makes sentences meaningful. But it is a bit difficult to show in any clear and compelling way that Peirce actually succeeded in providing a semiotic justification for his pragmaticism. This is because so much of what Peirce said about signs is 'indirect' and admits of different interpretations—as is evidenced by the various scholarly disputes over Peirce's concept of the sign, the ultimate logical interpretant and the nature of habit.[46] As a result, given the somewhat intractible difficulties involved in clearing up these disputes, and given that this is principally an introduction to Peirce's thought, it might be wise at this point to forge ahead on the assumption that it is by no means obvious that Peirce failed to provide a semiotic justification for the import of his famous pragmatic maxim. Elsewhere I shall argue that he did so succeed, but for now let us proceed to an assessment of Peirce's theory of meaning in the light of some contemporary considerations. Thereafter we shall consider his views on the nature of truth and knowledge.

C. *Assessment of Peirce's Theory of Meaning*

In reflecting on the merits of Peirce's theory of meaning as thus far stated, we can underscore its attractiveness by reflecting on Quine's recent assessment of Pragmatism in general and on Peirce's pragmaticism in particular.[47]

Quine argues that although all classical pragmatists belong to the empiricist's tradition, pragmatism followed, rather than led, empiricism in its five most interesting turns for the better (p. 1). He describes these five turning points and then examines the professing (classical) pragmatists with respect to them in an attempt to determine the extent to which these pragmatists either fostered or favored the most important developments in empiricism. Roughly, Quine concludes that the classical pragmatists, including Peirce, were not very impressive empiricists since the five distinctively important advances in the history of post-Humean empiricism were not either fostered or abetted by the classical pragmatists in any clear way. They were in fact followers at best and not leaders in the empiricist tradition.

As Quine lists them, the first of the five turning points in the advancement of post-Humean empiricism was the shift of semantic focus from ideas to words, a shift Quine credits to John Horne Tooke. The second turning point was the shift of semantic focus from terms to sentences, and this, Quine says, is to be credited to Bentham. The third is the shift of semantic focus from sentences to systems of sentences; and on this point Duhem made the contribution. The fourth is methodological monism which is simply the abandonment of the synthetic–analytic dualism. Quine is characteristically modest in not ascribing this development to his own efforts. And finally, the fifth major advance in the empiricist's tradition is the commitment to Naturalism which bespeaks abandonment of first philosophy prior to science (pp. 2–9).

In confronting Peirce's empiricism in the light of these turns for the better, Quine urges that, perversity of expression aside, Peirce's pragmatic maxim is implicitly a criterion of meaning for sentences and is, in short, the verification theory of meaning echoed in the Vienna Circle (p. 11). But Quine hastens to add that it is difficult to regard the verification theory of meaning as distinctive of pragmatism. The verification theory of meaning is, he says, what any empiricist could be expected to come out with when asked the meaning of sentences (p. 11).

According to Quine, however, acceptance by both Peirce and the Vienna Circle of the verification theory of sentence meaning does not go far enough. For Quine, an adequate empiricist theory of meaning must hold out for a holistic or system-centered semantics, which is the third important turning point for the better in post-Humean empiricism. As Quine construes it, holism is the view that the meaning of any empirically significant statement is not always to be specified in terms of any unique set of sensory experiences whose occurrence would uniquely confirm the sentence. Any theoretical sentence can be held as true if we are willing to make drastic enough adjustments in the theory. The truth of the theoretic sentence (as opposed to the observational sentence) is a function of the truth of the theory as a whole; and since the meaning of the sentence is the conditions of its verification, it is the theory as a whole which provides the meaning of the theoretical sentence. On this score, Quine agrees that there are many passages in Peirce which could be cited to show that Peirce was aware that scientific theory confronts its evidence holistically. But, Quine adds, Peirce's awareness here is "hard to reconcile with his facile account of pragmatic meaning, or of one's conception of an object" (p. 12). Besides, on Quine's view we cannot derive semantic holism from Peirce's limit theory of truth because that theory of truth is unacceptable.[48] So, for these reasons Quine claims that, unfortunately, Peirce was by no means clearly committed to a holistic or system–centered semantics.

On Quine's reckoning, semantic holism carries with it a repudiation of the analytic–synthetic distinction; and repudiating that distinction makes Fallibilism come easy if we also repudiate first philosophy as an ideal. Repudiating the analytic–synthetic distinction is the fourth turning point which bettered empiricism after Hume. Curiously enough, however, Quine does not make any attempt to determine whether Peirce also repudiated the distinction and if so, for what reasons. In short, as Quine sees it, Peirce's theory of meaning did not clearly embrace either semantic holism or the repudiation of the analytic–synthetic distinction.

Quine does grant, however, that Peirce scored a major point for Naturalism, the fifth step in the evolution of empiricism, in envisaging behavioristic semantics, a semantics which defines belief in terms of dispositions to act. But even here it is a matter of damning with faint praise; for, on Quine's view, Peirce's behavioural account of belief is not one to rest with (p. 19). And this is because there is no hope of carrying it out sentence by sentence. Dispositions to behave are bad criteria for determining beliefs. What is laudable, then, about Peirce's contribution here is simply that it is behavioristic in spirit (p. 19). In spite of its apparent limitations in the hands of Peirce, behaviorist semantics, Quine says, might well be considered the sixth great step in post-Humean empiricism; and Quine grants that it is a distinctively pragmatic (and Peircean) contribution to empiricism.

In summarizing his analysis of the pragmatist's place in empiricism Quine says:

> The professing pragmatists do not relate significantly to what I took to be the five turning points in post-Humean empiricism. Tooke's shift from ideas to words, and Bentham's from words to sentences, were not detectible in Peirce's pragmatic maxim, but we found that Peirce's further semantic discussions to be sentence oriented in implicit ways. Peirce seemed at odds with Duhem's system centered view, until we got to Peirce's theory of truth; but this we found unacceptable. Other pragmatists were sentence oriented in an implicit way, but still at odds with the system centered view, until we made hypothetical deductive

sense of Schiller's humanism. On the analytic–synthetic distinction and on naturalism, the pragmatists blew hot and cold.

Thayer tried to formulate the distinctive tenets of pragmatism, but the result was complex, and to make it come out right he had to pad his roster with some honorary pragmatists. In limiting my attention to the card carriers, I have found little in the way of shared and distinctive tenets. The two best guesses seemed to be behavioristic semantics, which I so heartily approve, and the doctrine of man as truth-maker, which I share in large measure. (p. 20)

So much for Quine's assessment of Peirce's theory of meaning. The question now is whether this assessment is right, and I shall argue that it is not.

Given our earlier reflections on the pragmatic maxim, and Peirce's explication of its meaning and intent, we can agree with Quine that, infelicitous phrasing aside, the pragmatic maxim was offered as a criterion for the meaning of sentences. For the reasons mentioned earlier, however, Peirce's provision of the pragmatic maxim as a criterion for the meaning of sentences is quite explicit in the various ways he explicated the import of the maxim. Secondly, and for reasons also noted above, it is wrong to suggest without qualification that the pragmatic maxim is simply the expression of the verificationist theory of meaning "echoed in the Vienna Circle". To do so is misleading and represents a fundamental misconstrual of pragmaticism because it tends to suggest (given the fairly common reading of Vienna positivism in terms of narrow verificationism) that, for Peirce, sentences asserting the existence of abstract entities are meaningless because not verifiable. This may well have been part and parcel of the early positivist's theory of meaning but, as we have seen, the adoption of the pragmatic maxim does not carry in its train a repudiation of abstract entities, just as it does not carry with it the view that only those sentences are meaningful which are either analytic or empirically verifiable. The most that can be said here is that Peirce, like the positivists, held that the meaning of a descriptive proposition is the conditions of its verification; but that does not imply repudiating abstract entities and it does not require that only those sentences are meaningful which have truth conditions.[49]

Quine applauds the shift of semantic focus from terms to sentences but sees nothing very distinctive in the pragmatist's endorsement of the view (p. 11). This predictable criticism derives from his mistaken belief that the pragmatic maxim amounts to nothing more than an early statement of the verification theory of meaning, echoed in the Vienna Circle, and his identification of the shift with the adoption of the verificationist's theory of sentence meaning. At any rate, and for the reasons noted above, it is distinctive of Peirce's pragmaticism that, in providing for the shift, it did not thereby imply a commitment to narrow verificationism. On Quine's view, however, the shift of semantic focus from terms to sentences was especially welcome because it allowed for paraphrase and the elimination of reference to abstract entities (p. 4). It is important, I think, to note that this virtue, which Quine now attributes to the shift, can obtain only if verificationism is understood to imply a complete repudiation of abstract entities. After all, the shift of semantic focus from terms to sentences could hardly have had the effect of supporting the nominalist's reservations unless the nominalist had assumed (as the early Quine certainly did) that *any* meaningful sentence utilizing abstract terms can, without loss of meaning, be paraphrased into a sentence committing us to the existence of physical objects only. Certainly, verificationism, as Quine here construes it, could not have been (and cannot be) the view that *some*, but not *all*, empirically meaningful statements utilizing abstract terms admit of physicalistic paraphrase; for, if that were the case, distinguishing between those meaningful statements that *do*, and those that *do not*, admit of physicalist paraphrase would be arbitrary. How could we distinguish between sentences which are meaningful but not capable of physicalist paraphrase, and sentences which are meaningless because not capable of physicalistic paraphrase? In short, there is a contradiction involved in saying that verificationism had (or has) the virtue of purging some but not all abstract entities; for if it succeeds in purging *any* at all, it could only do so under the assumption that *any* sentence not capable of physicalistic paraphrase is meaningless. In other words, if verificationism has any virtue at all by way of purging reference to abstract entities, it can only succeed in doing that on the condition that any sentence not so paraphrasable is meaningless. Quine, of course, says that although we cannot purge all reference to abstract entities in science, still, the virtue of the shift of semantic focus from terms to sentences was that it allowed the nominalist to pursue his reservations more fully than was previously possible (p. 4). And, for the reasons mentioned I am arguing that it could not have had that virtue and still allow for belief in some abstract entities. In sum, Quine urges that, from an empiricist's viewpoint, what was distinctive and important about the shift was that it abetted the nominalist's program; and this, I submit, it could not have done unless we assume that the shift carried with it a commitment to narrow verificationism. Peirce's verificationism, however, does not principally seek to sustain nominalism. And how Quine can consistently urge that abstract entities in science cannot be wholly eliminated and yet, at the same time, claim that the virtue of verificationism is that it allowed us to pursue our nominalistic reservations more fully is, I have argued, quite questionable.[50] Peirce's verificationism, and hence his naturalism, is distinctive in that, unlike Quine's, it *consistently* allows for belief in abstract entities and its importance is underscored by the fact that such a form of verificationism would appear to be a necessity, given that science cannot dispense with reference to abstract entities.

Secondly, and more interestingly, Quine claims that although we can doubtlessly find texts which show that Peirce was unquestionably aware that scientific theory confronts its evidence holistically; still, such awareness is hard to reconcile with Peirce's facile account of pragmatic meaning, or of one's conception of an object (p. 12). And if we are tempted to think that holism is implied by Peirce's theory of truth, then Quine argues that Peirce's theory of truth is all wrong. So, for these reasons Quine asserts that Peirce cannot be thought to have successfully endorsed semantic holism, the third important turning point in post-Humean empiricism. Moreover, Quine does not stand alone on this point. Føllesdal, for example, has argued that Quine's thesis on the indeterminacy of translation is nothing more than the combination of Duhem's holism and Peirce's verificationism.[51] Bypassing momentarily the discussion of whether Peirce's verificationism is the same as the verificationism Quine has in mind in the thesis on the indeterminacy of translation, Føllesdal's equation implies, or at least strongly suggests, that semantic holism is not a thesis we can attribute to Peirce. And there are probably a good many others who might agree.

In reply to this line of reasoning, the first thing to note is that there a number of texts which indicate that Peirce was unquestionably aware that scientific theory confronts its evidence holistically.[52] On Peirce's view, for example, we will always find discrepancies between theory and observation (1.132); and when we seek to verify a law, the discrepancies between theory and observation can either be written off to errors in observation (1.332) or can be used to modify the theory to fit the observations

(1.74; 2.771). And this reflects what he elsewhere argued, namely, that any sentence can be held in the face of disconfirming evidence by adjusting other sentences in the theory (MS 290 (pp. 2–3)). He even suggests that we keep our theories as flexible as possible to accommodate wayward data (5.376 #2 note #1). Moreover, for Peirce, verification is ultimately a matter of finding out how much like the truth our hypothesis is, that is, what proportion of its anticipations or predictions will be verified (2.775). So, predictions need not *always* come out for the law to be true; for, what we are seeking is a matter of statistical corroboration (8.194).

To suggest that these texts are not to be taken seriously because they are hard to reconcile with Peirce's "facile account of pragmatic meaning or of one's conception of an object" seems too enigmatic as a reason for disparaging the holistic dimensions of Peirce's semantics. Moreover, were we to urge that Peirce's holism is readily implied by his frequent endorsement of the view that the truth of any descriptive proposition is a function of whether or not it would be endorsed by the scientific community in the idealized long-run, then Quine would remind us that such a theory of truth is unacceptable. Although considerations of space do not here permit it, I would argue that Quine's criticism of Peirce's theory of truth is itself unacceptable because Quine's criticism is predicated on the false but generally accepted contention that Peirce has a limit theory of truth.[53] And if this is so, it would appear that Quine's strongest reason for rejecting the view that Peirce favored holism is deficient. For the moment, however, I think we can conclude that there is ample textual evidence favoring the position that Peirce was committed to holism.

The last two turning points in post-Humean empiricism are (a) the shift to methodological monism (which implies and is implied by, the repudiation of the analytic–synthetic distinction) and (b) the move to Naturalism. With respect to (b), Peirce was an undaunted naturalist simply because he never tired of insisting upon the exclusive use of the method of the natural sciences for the ascertainment of truth (1.128; 5.6). Moreover, it is interesting to note that with regard to (a), Peirce's reasons for rejecting the analytic–synthetic distinction do not feed on nominalistic scruples; and since this is a pointed consideration in his naturalism, we can reflect briefly on it now.

Traditionally understood, analytic propositions are propositions that are so true that it is inconceivable that they should ever be false in any universe of discourse. But, for Peirce, what we cannot conceive today, we may be able to conceive tommorow (8.191), and so 'inconceivability of the opposite' is by no means an index of absolute certainty in the sense of 'true in all possible universes of discourse' (2.29). Moreover, apart from the liability of error in all forms of reasoning, and apart from the history of science which teaches us that even our most exact theories are only rough approximations subject to continual revision, Peirce claimed that all reasoning is fundamentally synthetic (based ultimately upon observation and inductive inference) and hence a matter of probability and not certainty (3.528; 2.693; 2.685; 8.83; 2.778). Just as Peirce's espousal of *synechism* provided him with the logical foundation for this thesis on the inherent indeterminacy (vagueness) of all propositions, the inherent indeterminacy of all our propositions accounts for their being not exactly true.[54] And he clearly extended this view to include the propositions of mathematics and logic. His reasoned acceptance of a thoroughgoing synechism especially convinced him of the fallible nature of mathematics.[55] And on this latter score, he argued that the apparently necessary character of mathematical and logical reasoning is obtained by means of observation and 'experimentation' upon the objects of our own creation, diagrams. In short, the apparently necessary character of mathematical and logical reasoning is due simply to the circumstance that the subject of the observation is a diagram of our own creation, a hypothetical state of affairs the conditions of whose being we know all about since we create it (3.560; 2.778).[56] Because the propositions of mathematics and logic are about hypothetical states, the reasoning can be necessary, that is, not subject to empirical falsification; but since the same propositions are dependent upon diagrammatic observation, they are as fallible as any conclusion based upon observation.[57] These are dark sayings, of course, but the fact that Peirce construes the subject matter of math and logic in terms of hypothetical entities created by us and whose properties are inferred by us from diagrammatic observations of them, speaks in favor of the view that, for Peirce, while mathematics and logic may make use of abstractions, mathematical entities are not real platonic abstract entities since they don't exist independently of minds. Mathematical and logical truths are truths about hypothetical entities, entities which exist only conceptually; but even then, the truths about such entities are only *apparently* necessary because the truths proceed by way of inference from diagrammatic observation which is subject to error. Or so it would seem.

Whether Peirce is right in all this is a long story which we cannot enter into here. But even if he were wrong in claiming that the propositions of mathematics and logic are dependent, to some relevantly important degree, upon observation and experiment, still, it would certainly seem that fallible nature of *all* propositions follows from a thoroughgoing synechism, a synechism which he quite clearly extended, by way of its fallibilistic implications, into a domain of mathematical and logical reasoning. However rough and ready these reasons may appear, it is significant that Peirce did not eschew analyticity, either directly or by way of implication, for the reason that failure to do so would have committed him to belief in the existence of abstract entities.[58] More on this shortly.

In the light of the above considerations, we can conclude that, Quine's assessment notwithstanding, Peirce espoused the five turning points which have doctrinally advanced empiricism since Hume. But the resulting empiricism is radically non-Humean owing to the broad verificationism implied by the adoption of the pragmatic maxim. More importantly, however, Peirce's theory of meaning would appear to advance the empiricist enterprise in at least two ways heretofore not noted.

In the first place, because the pragmatic maxim does not rule against belief in abstract entities, it provides a solid intuitive base for an empiricism which cannot quite swallow the view that science can effectively dispense with all reference to abstract entities. It is because Quine does not see this as part of Peirce's theory of meaning that he fails to see this as something distinctive and important by way of providing comfort for a naturalism which, like Quine's, cannot effectively jettison belief in abstract entities. In this regard Peirce's theory of meaning is not so much an extension of post-Humean empiricism as it is a repudiation in favor of an idealized empiricism.

Quine, of course, has most recently come out in favor of an ontology of real platonic abstract entities, numbers.[59] It is, however, difficult to see how this ontological turn is consistent with the narrow verificationism Quine endorses. After all, if, as Quine claims, the virtue of verificationism is that it allows us to pursue our nominalistic aims (a virtue which I have argued above is inconsistent with belief in the existence of *any* abstract entities and which Quine wrongly supposes to be implied by Peirce's endorsement of the shift of semantic focus from terms to sentences), then holding on to the verificationist theory of meaning, as so construed, would seem to be inconsistent with, because rendering

meaningless, an ontology of abstract entities. Peirce's verificationism, however, is not at odds with such an ontology and
hence furthers the ends of an idealized empiricism; whereas
Quine's verificationism undermines his idealized empiricism by
rendering its ontology meaningless. It is only by returning to a
Peircean verificationism that Quine could justify his ontology of
abstract entities.

In the second place, methodological monism, identified with the
rejection of the analytic-synthetic distinction, seems more plausible
in Peirce's hands than it does in Quine's. This is because Quine's
rejection of analyticity ultimately rests on nominalistic scruples
and is thus inconsistent with his ontological turn to abstract
entities, whereas Peirce's rejection of that distinction does not feed
on such scruples and hence is not at all inconsistent with such an
idealized empiricism. Let me explain.

Schuldenfrei has argued, convincingly I believe, that Quine is a
radical positivist whose attack on analyticity in "Two Dogmas of
Empiricism" is best viewed as an attempt to purify positivism by
moving against an aspect of positivism which he sees as inconsistent with a purified naturalism, that is, a naturalism that can
have no truck with modalities necessary for explaining analyticity.[60] And Quine himself has said that in "Two Dogmas of
Empiricism" he was not arguing for pragmatism but rather seeking
to repair empiricism.[61] We now know, of course that the repair job
consisted in scotching the analytic–synthetic distinction and urging
the doctrine of holism. On Quine's view, if we take verificationism
seriously, something which even the positivists themselves did not
do,[62] then we must rule against analyticity since analyticity
involves a commitment to belief in modalities the existence of
which, since they are abstract entities, cannot be verified.
Accordingly, it seems reasonable to view Quine's attack on
analyticity as motivated by the belief that a purified naturalism
requires a verificationism that is inconsistent with belief in abstract
entities. And if this is so, how can Quine's abandonment of
analyticity be consistent with his liberalized ontology? Boorse has
argued that Quine's liberalized epistemology is inconsistent with
his semantic positivism, that sustaining the former implies abandoning the latter, and that with the abandonment go all the
arguments for indeterminacy of translation.[63] I am further suggesting that Quine's rejection of the analytic–synthetic distinction
is inconsistent with his liberalized ontology since that rejection is
also based upon radical semantic positivism, or, as I have called it

above, a narrow verificationism. Keeping the ontology implies abandoning the semantic positivism, and, with that, Quine's attack on the analytic–synthetic distinction falls to the ground carrying with it his defense of methodological monism. Peirce's defense of methodological monism does not suffer such criticism because his rejection of the analytic–synthetic distinction is not rooted in semantic positivism or a narrow verificationism. These considerations also seem to suggest that an idealized or liberal empiricism can undermine the analytic–synthetic distinction only if it repudiates nominalism; and in the case, the rejection of the distinction (which rejection is essential for methodological monism) would require a theory of meaning consistent with a commitment to abstract entities. For this reason Peirce's assault on the analytic–synthetic distinction provides a more coherent empiricist foundation for methodological monism than does Quine's assault on the same distinction. And all this should lend force to the view that there is something distinctively important to be learned from Peirce's theory of meaning if an adequate empiricism is to sustain methodological monism.

In sum, I have been arguing that Quine has misconstrued Peirce's verificationism, overlooked Peirce's rejection of the analytic–synthetic distinction and has unjustifiably slighted Peirce's espousal of holism. Moreover, for all the reasons mentioned above, Peirce's theory of meaning represents a naturalism consistent with an idealized empiricism, an empiricism which Quine adopts but which, owing to his narrow verificationism, he cannot justify.

Finally, something should be said briefly about Peirce's empiricism as it relates to Quine's doctrine on the indeterminacy of translation. As noted above, Føllesdal has urged that the doctrine on the indeterminacy of translation is nothing more than the combination of Peircean verificationism and Duhemian holism. Since I have argued that Peirce was clearly committed to the doctrine of holism, it might be tempting to suggest that, in the end, Peirce too would adopt the doctrine on the indeterminacy of translation. But nothing could be further from the truth because Peirce's verificationism is not at all the same form of verificationism that Quine adopts; and Hintikka has been quick to note that Føllesdal's equation is guilty of conflating the two without careful examination.[64] Hintikka claims that Føllesdal's equation hides the extraordinarily narrow interpretation Quine puts on notions like observability and possible observation, notions which are presupposed in any concept of verificationism. For Quine, possible observations do not include observations that would have been made had another possible course of events been realized (p. 8). Hintikka, I think, is right; but I would add that the reason why Quine does not do as much is because it would entail a commitment to modalities which his narrow verificationism does not allow. Peirce is not at all committed to such a narrow interpretation of possible observations because he does not espouse such a narrow verificationism. Not only is Quine not close to the pragmaticism of Peirce, he is, unfortunately for his liberalized ontology, at odds with it. From an ontological viewpoint, Peirce is just not in the Humean traditional and Quine is trapped there with an ontology that won't fit it.

Moreover, ignoring Boorse's argument that the indeterminacy of translation falls to the ground with a theory of meaning that would be consistent with Quine's liberalized ontology, the ontological upshot of the indeterminacy thesis is something that Peirce would not endorse. Without caring to argue the details just now, I think we can grant that Peirce was well aware that physical theory is underdetermined by observational data (7.117). But that there could be *unto eternity* mutually incompatible, but empirically equivalent, translation manuals for current theory is something he could not endorse because it would be inconsistent with his view that science, unto eternity, is progressive and that, given time, we shall find out the way things substantially are. Defending this latter claim, however, involves defending Peirce's theory of truth, a theory which I now hope to show is sorely misunderstood but capable of strenuous defense.

III. *TRUTH AND FALLIBILISM*

We have noted that, as Peirce would have it, the meaning of any descriptive proposition is expressed by a set of conditional statements predicting what sensory experiences should occur as a result of our performing certain operations. More specifically, every empirically meaningful proposition is a prediction to the effect that if we do such and such under such and such conditions, then a certain specifiable and sensible result should occur if the proposition is true. Thus to determine the truth of any descriptive proposition we need only determine whether or not its corresponding conditional is true; and that is a matter of seeing whether or not what is predicted in the consequent of the conditional obtains, or would obtain, with the satisfaction of the antecedent. For example, the sentence "The object is hard" means (in part) that "*If* we were to take this object and scratch it with many other substances under 'normal' conditions, *then* this object would not be scratched by many other substances." So, to ascertain whether or not the sentence is true, we need only scratch the object in question with many other substances to see if the object is in fact scratched by many other substances. If it *is*, then the sentence "This object is hard" is false; for to say that an object is hard *means* that it wouldn't be scratched by many other substances if one were to scratch it with many other substances.[65] If, however, it is *not* scratched by many other substances, then the proposition is positively supported as true. But this is not quite to say that a proposition supported as true is in fact true; for Peirce defines a true proposition as a proposition belief in which would *never* lead to a negative instance (5.565; 5.569; 5.168ff; 6.526; MS 1147(s) (p. 5)). The fact that a proposition is positively supported does not show that it will continue to be supported or that it will never lead to a negative instance. We can never be certain that a fact of a certain sort will not occur and falsify our most cherished of beliefs. For this reason Peirce held that a proposition cannot be rendered true by one positive instance of it. Rather, each confirming instance of the proposition increases the likelihood or probability that the proposition is true (5.168; 5.569; 5.2; 6.526; 7.206; 5.2). Since the number of potentially confirming instances of a proposition is infinite (owing to the fact that the meaning of any given proposition is indeterminate) we can never rule out the *theoretical* possibility that the proposition will be falsified. For the same reason, we can never be logically certain that the proposition is in fact true. The most we can say is that the probability of the proposition's being true approximates the probability value of 1 with each confirming instance of the proposition as well as with each failure to falsify the proposition (2.729; 1.120; 2.730 n. 1).[66] Naturally, if a probability value of 1 is needed for any proposition to be true, then no proposition can ever be more than approximately true since the class of possible confirming instances can never be exhausted.

And all this would seem to suggest what many have indeed claimed, namely, that Peirce has a limit theory of truth; a theory of truth under which no proposition is quite true, but the probability of its being true asymptotically approaches the value of 1 as a mathematical limit with each confirming instance. On this common view of Peirce's theory, truth is an ideal concept, that is, it is a property our beliefs aim at though never quite reach.

But I will argue below that this common interpretation of Peirce's theory of truth is not correct. For one thing, I shall urge that, on Peirce's view, the community of scientific inquirers *will* come to a final irreversible opinion on any answerable question and that this final irreversible opinion is true. On this view, with each confirming instance of a proposition or hypothesis what is approached as a mathematical limit is not truth but a probability value of 1 that the proposition is true. And this will mean that attaining to a probability value of 1 that a proposition is true is not necessary for the truth of the proposition. Rather it is only necessary (and sufficient) for the truth of the proposition that the probability value of its being true gets sufficiently close to 1 as to render it *practically* (as opposed to *theoretically*) certain that the truth value assigned to the proposition will not be revised. In other words, when the probability value of a proposition's being true gets sufficiently close to 1 as to render the margin of error negligibly small, then the truth is reached, although reaching the truth in this way should not be thought to reflect a relationship of complete correspondence between language and the world. Complete correspondence between language and the world could only be reached with the attainment of certainty; and Peirce hastens to add that even if we were to reach a probability of 1 that some proposition is true, still, that is not certainty (5.158; 7.214). But all this is getting us ahead of ourselves. These and other aspects of Peirce's theory of truth will be discussed more fully below.

What is non-controversial, however, is Peirce's commitment to the view that, owing to the theoretical possibility that any proposition can be falsified, the truth value assigned to any proposition can never be taken as an index of absolute certainty in the sense of "true in all possible universes". This sentiment, which is part of what Peirce means by Fallibilism, extends, as we have seen, to the even more radical claim that there are no strictly necessary truths or analytic propositions as traditionally under-stood.[67] And he does not hesitate to provide a full defense of this view.

Apart from the liability of error in all forms of human reasoning, and apart from the history of science which teaches us that even our most exact theories are only rough approximations subject to continual revision, Peirce, we have seen, claimed that all reasoning is fundamentally synthetic (based upon observation and inductive inference) and hence, is a matter of probability (3.528; 2.693; 2.685; and 8.3). And, as also noted above, even if it were to establish the truth of a proposition on the basis of a probability of 1, still, we would not have certainty. Most fundamentally, however, Peirce's Fallibilism is a logical extension of his commitment to synechism. Just as Peirce's espousal of *synechism* provided him with the logical foundation for his thesis on the inherent indeterminacy (vagueness) of all propositions, the inherent indeterminacy of all our propositions accounts for their being not exactly true:

> The second order of induction only infers that a theory is very much like the truth, because we are so far from ever being authorized to conclude that a theory is the *very truth* itself, that we can never so much as understand what that means. Light is electro-magnetic vibrations, that is to say, it (is) something very like that. In order to say that it is precisely that, we should have to know precisely what we mean by electro-magnetic vibrations. Now we can never know precisely what we mean by any description whatever.[68]

By 'the *very truth* itself' Peirce here means, I submit, the property which our theory (or proposition) would have if the truth value assigned to it were not in principle subject to revision. And if the truth value assigned to a proposition is not in principle subject to revision, then that proposition is analytic or necessarily true. So, since no proposition can express the very truth itself, no proposition can be analytic or necessarily true.

Because the inherent indeterminacy of meaning is rooted in, and implied by, the doctrine of *synechism,* Peirce's Fallibilism finds its justification in the doctrine of *synechism.* Even as late as 1897 Peirce held that *synechism,* or the doctrine that all that exists is continuous, entails Fallibilism at least in so far as Fallibilism implies that the truth value assigned to any proposition is in principle subject to revision and hence not necessarily true, certain or strictly analytic;

> If I were to attempt to describe to you in full all the scientific beauty and truth that I find in the principle of continuity, I might say in the simple language of Matilda the Engaged, 'The tomb would close over me e'er the entrancing topic were exhausted'—but not before my audience was exhausted. So I will drop it here. Only, in doing so, let me call your attention to the natural affinity of this principle to the doctrine of fallibilism. The principle of continuity is the idea of fallibilism objectified. For fallibilism is the doctrine that our knowledge is never absolute, but always swims, as it were, in a continuum of uncertainty and of indeterminacy. Now the doctrine of continuity is that all things so swim in continua. ... The ordinary scientific infallibilist—of which sect

Buchner in his *Kraft und Stoff* affords a fine example—can not accept *synechism*, or the doctrine that all that exists is continuous—because he is committed to discontinuity in regard to all those things which he fancies he has exactly ascertained, and he has exactly ascertained to be *certain*. For where there is continuity, the exact ascertainment of real quantities is too obviously impossible.[69]

Moreover, that Fallibilism is logically entailed by synechism is clearly supported by a host of other texts in which Peirce claimed that it is ultimately *synechism* which led him to the belief that all human knowledge is fallible.[70]

In claiming that *all* human knowledge is fallible, Peirce, we saw, included the propositions of mathematics and logic which are traditionally considered necessarily true or analytic. Here again, Peirce reasoned that the principle of continuity covers the whole domain of experience in every element of it. Hence *every* proposition is to be taken with an indefinite qualification (7.566). Peirce's reasoned commitment to a thoroughgoing *synechism* even prohibited him from assuming that the propositions of mathematics are absolutely certain:

> Thoroughgoing synechism will not permit us to say that the sum of the angles of a triangle exactly equals two right angles, but only that it equals that quantity plus or minus some quantity which is excessively small for all the triangles we can measure. We must not accept the proposition that space has three dimensions as certainly strictly accurate; but can only say that any movements of bodies out of the three dimensions are at most exceedingly minute. We must not say that phenomena are perfectly regular, but only that the degree of their regularity is very high. ... Now, as no experimental question can be answered with absolute certainty, so we never can have reason to think that any given idea will either become unshakably established *or be forever exploded.* But to say that neither of these two events will come to pass definitively is to say that the object has an imperfect and qualified existence. Surely, no reader will suppose that this principle is intended to apply only to some phenomena and not to others,—only, for instance, to the little province of matter and not to the rest of the great empire of ideas. (7.568–9)

In conjunction with his appeal to complete synechism as the foundation for the fallible nature of mathematics and logic, Peirce argued that the apparently necessary character of mathematical reasoning is obtained by means of observation and experiment upon the objects of our own creation, diagrams. Hence the apparently necessary character of mathematical and logical reasoning is due simply to the circumstance that the subject of the observation and experiment is a diagram of our own creation, the conditions of whose being we know all about (3.560).[71] But since the propositions of mathematics and logic are fundamentally dependent upon observation and experiment they are as fallible as any conclusion based upon observation and experiment (2.447).[72] Whether Peirce is right in this latter regard is, once again, a long story. However, even if Peirce were wrong in claiming that the propositions of mathematics and logic are dependent in some sense upon observation and experiment (and it is not at all clear that he is), it would certainly seem that the fallible nature of *all* propositions follows from a thoroughgoing *synechism*. It might further be pointed out that Peirce's denial of strict analyticity could be supported by other considerations of the sort which Lewis has suggested and which seem to be clearly implied in Peirce's theory thus far stated.[73] Indeed, given Peirce's thesis that the acceptability of any proposition or theory is ultimately a function of the degree to which its adoption allows us to predict, control, and expedite our dealings with experience, it would be only a short step to the thesis that the propositions of mathematics and logic are contingently analytic pending our pragmatic concerns.

IV. *FALLIBILISM AND THE ULTIMATE IRREVERSIBLE OPINION*

It would be a serious mistake to characterize Peirce's Fallibilism as a doctrine embracing *no more* than the view that knowledge is always of propositions in some sense contingent. More fully characterized, the doctrine also asserts the apparently more dubious radical claim that because one cannot attain to absolute certainty on any matter, *knowledge* itself must always admit of some possibility of error (see MS 663 AR 4). The difference between the two characterizations is the difference between saying 'I know that p and p is a statement whose denial is non-contradictory' and 'I know that p but I may be mistaken.' In claiming that all knowledge is based upon synthetic inference which always admits of some possibility of error (1.145; 2.141; 7.82; 6.523; 7.55), Peirce was also committed to the latter characterization; and the question is whether the latter can make any sense at all. It's one thing to be told that there is a world of difference between fallible knowledge and no knowledge at all (MS 971 (p. 1)), and quite another thing to make sense of the notion of fallible knowledge.

Many philosophers argue that the concept of 'fallible knowledge' is a contradiction in terms. In any non-jocular sense of 'knows,' the expression 'I know that p' cannot be coupled consistently with 'but I may be mistaken;' and this is because saying 'I know that p' offers a guarantee which saying 'but I may be mistaken' withdraws. Even more fundamentally, in saying 'I know that p' I am asserting that *p* is true, that what *p* describes is the case; the addition of 'but I may be mistaken' withdraws what is asserted by 'I know that p' and amounts to asserting simultaneously that *p* is true but possibly it isn't and possibly it is; and what's wrong with this is that the statement *p* is either true or false; it cannot be both true and possibly false since the state of affairs described by *p* either is or is not the case—it cannot be both the case and possibly not the case.[74] If this line of reasoning is correct, then, given what we usually mean by 'knows,' a fallibilist like Peirce is committed to something contradictory. Further, if he is to avoid the apparent contradiction involved in saying 'I know that p but I may be mistaken,' he must redefine knowledge in such a way that the truth of *p* is not a necessary condition for knowing that p; and this will be utterly unacceptable because if there is anything that philosophers generally agree upon it is that knowledge cannot be false. Knowledge without truth, they say, makes knowing an act that cannot tell us how things really are. Can Peirce's Fallibilism survive such an objection?

First of all, Peirce claimed that the task of defining a concept is not a matter of accurately reporting the sense people usually assign to a term but rather a matter of specifying what meaning *should* be assigned to a term. In other words, in explicating the concept of knowledge in such a way that all knowledge turns out to be fallible, we can assume that Peirce was defining the concept stipulatively as a bit of technical terminology.[75] Apart from the fact that Peirce generally advocated the employment of technical definitions because, as he said, they are more precise and thus lend themselves more fruitfully to systematic discussion, we can also assume that his basic reason for insisting upon a technical definition of 'knows' was that the concept of knowledge is usually understood to imply the absolute impossibility of mistake. And this concept of knowledge, however well it *may* reflect the sense of 'knows' embedded in ordinary discourse, does not and cannot reflect the sort of knowledge we actually possess.[76] Thus the fact that the concept of 'fallible knowledge' may not reflect the meaning of 'knows' as it is ordinarily understood in non-technical discourse, does not show that fallibilism is false or incoherent. It only raises the question whether the concept of knowledge as it is usually understood in ordinary discourse, is philosophically adequate as a characterization of the knowledge we actually do and can possess. That it is not is the thrust of Peirce's arguments in favor of Fallibilism and the fundamentally synthetic nature of all inference.

Secondly, and more importantly, it is simply not true that the fallibilist must drop truth as a necessary condition for knowing if he is to redefine knowledge and avoid the apparent contradiction involved in saying 'I know that p but I may be mistaken.' To see that this is so, let us begin by making a few assumptions which will demonstrate the point. Thereafter we shall argue that, given what the assumptions imply and given what Peirce actually argued, we have excellent reasons for believing that Peirce endorsed the assumptions. In addition to showing Peirce's Fallibilism coherent, the overall effect of proceeding to this fashion will be to provide a panoramic view of what might otherwise appear a hodgepodge of fundamentally inconsistent assertions on truth and knowledge. Later we shall make the effort to determine whether or not the assumptions are acceptable.

Assuming that truth is a necessary condition for knowing, let us just suppose that (A) the predicate 'is true' as it applies to assertions, designates a word–word relationship of semantic authorization relative to our current conceptual framework. In other words, saying that a statement p is true means that the rules of confirmation embedded in the conventions of our current conceptual framework fully authorize our asserting p or writing it down for acceptance.[77] Further, let us also assume that (B) conceptual frameworks evolve progressively through ever more adequate systematizations of the universe and will (assuming indefinite progress) terminate in some final conceptual framework wherein what is semantically authorized as true also designates a word–world relationship of adequate, although not complete, correspondence. And finally, let us suppose that (C) we cannot ever be absolutely certain that we have attained to the final conceptual framework; and so we must assume that whatever is authorized as true in our current conceptual framework is subject to overthrow in possible future and more adequate conceptual frameworks.

Given this set of assumptions, the expression 'I know that p but I may be mistaken' need not *inconsistently* imply that p is true and possibly it isn't. Rather it would simply mean that, given the semantic rules of our current conceptual framework, the assertion (or inscription) of *p* is authorized although it is *logically possible* that the conceptual framework in which p is presently authorized may be replaced by a future and more adequate conceptual framework in which the assertion (or inscription) of *p* may not be authorized. And there is nothing at all contradictory about this.[78]

Notice further that the adoption of assumptions (A), (B) and (C) would imply the following propositions:

(i) What is established as true amounts to no more than that we are authorized in asserting (or writing down) relative to our present body of information; and so what is true today may not be true tomorrow (2.64; 2.775; 4.517; 7/671; 5.589; 5.451; 5.419; 5.416; 5.498; 5.603; 2.140ff; 1.120; 1.138; 1.234; 2.74ff; 2.775; 7.187; 7.671; 8.191; 6.498; 6.527; 5.589; 5.568ff; 5.414–420; 6.498; 2.75; MS 426 (Logic II, p. 51); MS 473 (p. 26); MS 425 (Logic 78);

(ii) The opinion reached in the final opinion unlike opinions reached earlier, shall never be overthrown although the degree to which the final opinion corresponds to fact admits of indefinite (but not substantial) refinement. So what is true in the final opinion will be true forever even though it is characteristically possible that the opinion will be falsified (4.62; 2.32; 2.75; 7.77ff; 8.226; 5.565; 1.151; 3.43ff; MS 678 (p. 28);

(iii) Because the opinion reached in the final opinion admits of indefinite refinement, absolute certainty cannot be a property of the final opinion. Moreover, since even if we had reached the final opinion we could not be asolutely sure that we had, we must assume that all our beliefs and established truths admit of overthrow (4.63; 7.78; 5.258; 1.141; 5.565; 2.75; 2.141; 7.78; 8.226; 7.108; 5.565; 1.55; 1.151; 7.108; MS 603 N 24);

(iv) The final opinion destined to be reached is *per se* fallible because it will admit of further refinement although it will be *practically infallible* because it will not be subject to overthrow. Furthermore, even if we had reached the final opinion on any given matter we would be obliged to consider it, like any other established belief, subject to overthrow and indefinite refinement (2.79; 4.62ff; 7.78; 7.108; 2.75; 7.78; MS 473 (pp. 26 and 40));

(v) Although we cannot be absolutely certain of having attained to the final opinion on any given matter (since we cannot assume that we have attained to the final conceptual framework) it by no means follows that what is authorized as true in our current conceptual framework is not the opinion which will be authorized in the final conceptual framework. It may very well be that what is authorized as true in the present conceptual framework is the opinion which will be authorized in the final opinion wherein what is authorized designates a word–world relationship of correspondence, although the correspondence can never be complete and although we can never be absolutely certain that the opinion reached at any given moment is the final opinion. (4.62ff; 8.43; 7.78; 5.172; MS 1369 (p. 26); MS 603 N. 24)

And finally,

(vi) Knowledge and truth admit of at least three different characterizations: (1) Relative to the body of presently available information (relative to our current conceptual framework) knowledge is the opinion we are fully authorized in asserting—the opinion we do not really doubt and cannot really doubt on the available evidence; (2) Relative to a complete body of information (relative to the final conceptual framework) knowledge is the final and irreversible compulsory belief destined to be agreed upon by the community of scientific inquirers; and (3) Knowledge is the opinion which is absolutely certain. Where knowledge is understood in the first sense, then the truth of what one knows would not consist in anything more than what one is fully authorized in asserting or writing down. Where knowledge is understood in the second sense, then the truth of what one knows, without ceasing to be a matter of what one is fully authorized in asserting, would designate a word–world relationship of adequate although not complete correspondence. And where knowledge is understood in the third sense, then the truth of what one knows would designate a word–world relationship of complete correspondence.

Given that we cannot assume to have attained to the final opinion on any given matter, we cannot profess to possess knowledge in the second sense, although we know (in the first sense of 'knows') that such knowledge and truth must obtain sooner or later. Given that the final opinion (when reached) admits of indefinite refinement, knowledge and truth in the third sense can never be had but at best only approached indefinitely as one would a mathematical limit. Finally, since we can never profess to know with certainty that we have attained to the final opinion on any given matter, we must assume that the only knowledge and truth we possess is knowledge and truth in the first sense.

Although Peirce did not explicitly argue for (vi), we can legitimately infer that he was committed to (vi) as a generalization of what is implied in (i)–(v).

Apart from the fact that assumptions A, B and C render fallibilism non-contradictory, it is difficult to see how anyone could consistently argue for propositions (i)–(vi) without being logically committed to assumptions A, B, and C. Admittedly, Peirce does not explicitly assert A, B and C; but the question is whether or not A, B and C represent the most plausible and consistent inter-pretation of what he actually said. Assumptions A, B and C are internally consistent and are consistent with what Peirce actually argued, namely, propositions (i)–(vi). Moreover, the fact that propositions (i)–(vi) are implied by the assumptions A, B and C provide us with excellent reason for believing that the inter-pretation implied in A, B and C is not only suggested by what Peirce said but also is required by what he said if we are to provide a maximally consistent and plausible reading. After all, in the absence of A, B and C, how could we, for example, make sense of the claim that what is true today may not be true tomorrow but what is true in the final opinion is true forever—and fallible?

The point worth repeating is that the final opinion is fallible in two senses. Although it is the opinion which shall not be overthrown (and in that sense practically infallible), it admits of indefinite refinement (like the value of π) and cannot for that reason profess to be absolutely certain or necessarily true. Moreover, since *we* cannot be absolutely certain that we have attained to the final opinion on any given matter, we must assume that whatever we are authorized in asserting is subject to future possible impeachment. Alternatively put, given the synthetic nature of all reasoning 'I know that p but I may be mistaken' represents an attitude that we must take even if it happens to be the case that *p* is in fact the opinion that will be endorsed in the final irreversible opinion. Without dropping the truth condition for knowledge, the locution 'I know that *p* but I may be mistaken' is, as we noted above, coherent only if we must assume the possibility of future conceptual frameworks wherein what is presently authorized may not be authorized; and this possibility is something we must assume even if it be false. Thus because every opinion admits of some indefinite refinement and because *we* cannot ever be absolutely certain of having attained to a final belief that shall not ever be overthrown, we must consider all our beliefs fallible although we have already reached the final opinion on many matters. And this means (among other things) that from our point of view the predicate 'is true' as it applies to assertions must be considered to designate a word–word relationship of semantic authorization.

Peirce defined truth (with a capital T) in terms of correspondence and reckoned such correspondence the property of the final opinion destined to be agreed upon by the community of scientific inquirers;[79] and he defined knowledge in terms of this final irreversible opinion.[80] This, I think, will be generally granted.[81] But I submit that there is good reason to think that Peirce was also committed to the view that truth is a property of propositions warrantedly assertible under the canons of acceptance relative to one's current conceptual framework[82] and that knowledge is to be understood in terms of propositions that are so warrantedly assertible. After all, he frequently urged that we must consider as true those propositions which are inductively established by the method of science even though the truth value assigned to the propositions may be subsequently revised in the light of future evidence (MS 426 (Logic II, pp. 52 and 53); MS 600 (L1); 1.634; 2.775; 6.527; MS 473 (p. 40); 2.86; 1.120; 1.116; 1.232; 2.75; 7.49; 5.142; MS 673 (p. 46)). And this seems to suggest that truth is a property of those propositions that we would be fully warranted in asserting relative to the canons of acceptance embedded in our current conceptual framework. Moreover, Peirce generally argued that science, as we know it, is a body of *knowledge* (MS 673 (p. 46); MS 600 (L2); MS 603 N12; MS 744 p. 12; MS 427 (Logic II, p. 16), that *knowledge* is the result of correct inference and that as long as we have no real doubt about a proposition, it is perfectly acceptable to write it down as a premise in any line of reasoning that we call a demonstration (5.376; 5.365; MS 1 (p. 9); MS 309 (p. 37)) even though what we do not doubt today we may doubt tomorrow (5.421; MS 473 (pp. 26 and 40); 8.191; 1.234; 6.134; 5.568; 5.589; 6.498; 1.138; 5.603). And this seems to suggest that knowledge is what one has when one is fully warranted in asserting a proposition under one's current conceptual framework even though the proposition's assertibility may lose its warrant under future conceptual frameworks.

Of course, we might be tempted to say that these sorts of texts merely suggest that truth in terms of correspondence and knowledge as the final compulsory belief is what scientific inquiry aims at and *will, ceteris paribus,* achieve; but since we can never be certain of having attained to that end we must *call* truth and knowledge what we are fully warranted in asserting at any given moment although it may not in fact represent what will be warrantedly assertible under the final opinion wherein what is warrantedly assertible implies a relationship of correspondence between language and the world. Something like this is certainly plausible especially since Peirce did, on at least a few occasions, characterize science as opinion in search of truth.[83] But what makes this view less plausible than the view that Peirce was committed to two distinct conceptions of truth and knowledge (in addition to the third mentioned above) is that (a) Peirce was generally insistent that truth is a necessary condition for knowledge (5.605; MS 600 (L2); 4.239; 7.49; 1.497) and (b) in nearly all his tirades against Cartesian epistemology, he inveighs against the view that knowing requires the preclusion of the logical possibility of error and insists that the requirement of knowing the premises of a demonstration (one must know the premises if he is to know what the premises demonstrate, and he cannot know the premises unless they are true) is adequately satisfied when one writes down as premises of the argument propositions free of all actual doubt although they, and the conclusions demonstrated by them, may be doubted and revised tomorrow (6.498; 5.265; 5.416ff; 5.43f; 5.376 #2 and 1; 5.589; 1.120). Thus the truth of what is demonstrably known is ultimately and only a matter of what we are authorized in writing down relative to a present body of information. And all this simply won't fit with Peirce's definition of truth as correspondence and knowledge as the final compulsory belief unless we suppose that he has at least two distinct conceptions of truth and knowledge.[84] Moreover, on the supposition that Peirce held to only the one conception of truth and knowledge, he would have been obliged to characterize the body of scientific knowledge as a body of warranted opinion in search of truth (as correspondence) and knowledge (as the final opinion). But if this is so, how could he then justify his claim that science has already reached the final opinion on some matters (which ones we do not know and cannot profess to know)? Saying that it is quite certain that we have reached the final opinion on some matters (MS 1369 (p. 26); 8.43) seems inconsistent with the view that science is a body of opinion in search of truth, if truth be understood solely in terms of correspondence and knowledge as the final irreversible opinion. The air of inconsistency dissolves, however, if there are two concepts of truth and knowledge related to one another as noted above under assumptions A, B and C. For these reasons, then, it appears that Peirce, in addition to defining truth in terms of complete correspondence and knowledge as absolute certainty (neither of which is attainable), also espoused these two other concepts of truth and knowledge.

In the end, Peirce's theory of knowledge, so characterized, represents a rather interesting and unprecedented blend of both conceptual idealism and epistemological realism. Given that his definition of truth and knowledge in terms of what we are authorized in writing down relative to our current conceptual framework implies something like a coherence theory of truth and knowledge relative to evolutionary conceptual frameworks, there can be no grounds for inferring correspondence between what is known and what is the case in a world of extra-linguistic fact; and thus there can be no entailment between what is known and what is the case in a world whose existence and properties are logically and causally independent of finite minds. Further, where the predicate 'is true' designates a word–word relationship of semantic authorization relative to our current conceptual framework, then we could not even be sure that there is an external independent world that knowledge informs us about. But when one adds (as Peirce did) that inquiry pursued indefinitely *will* terminate in knowledge as a final compulsory belief the truth of which is a matter of word–world correspondence, we end up with a system which is both fundamentally realistic in countenancing a world of knowable physical objects and at the same time conceptually idealistic in being committed to the view that we can never profess to know in the sense of capturing an independent world in the way that it is. In other words, because we cannot at any given time transcend our conceptual framework and because we cannot rule against future and more adequate conceptual frameworks, we must consider truth and knowledge a matter of what we are fully authorized in writing down relative to our present conceptual framework (8.191ff); and logically this cannot entail that there is any correspondence between what we now know and a world existing independently of mind. But the conceptual idealism thus implied is eclipsed or conditioned with the addition of the thesis that inquiry pursued indefinitely will terminate in a final irreversible opinion the truth of which shall tell us how things substantially are.

Assuming that Peirce's thought is systematized under assumptions A, B, and C, the question is whether or not we should accept the assumptions as adequate proposals. Obviously we cannot ask whether these proposals are true.

If we acknowledge, as I think we must, the evolutionary character of conceptual frameworks and the fundamentally synthetic nature of all reasoning, then we cannot be certain that we have ever attained to any final conceptual framework; and this would constrain us to the view that the truth value assigned to any statement is in principle subject to revision in light of future experience. And if this is so, then the predicate 'is true', as it applies to specific assertions, needn't be thought to designate a word–world relationship of correspondence rather than a word–word relationship of semantic authorization realtive to our current conceptual framework. In other words, where truth–value revision is in order, we cannot infer from a proposition's being assigned 'is true' that *that* proposition describes the way the world is, or 'corresponds' to the facts. Hence where truth–value revision is in order the predicate 'is true' can only designate a word–word relationship of semantic authorization (or warranted assertibility) under the rules of acceptance in our current conceptual framework.[85] In short, the acceptability of assumption C entails the acceptability of assumption A; and C is acceptable because, given the evolutionary character of conceptual frameworks (which we shall consider more fully below) there is simply no way of knowing for sure that we have attained to some final conceptual framework systematizing the world better than all conceivable others. So, we need only determine whether or not assumption B is acceptable.

Granting the evolutionary nature of conceptual frameworks, the problem with assumption B is that if the predicate 'is true' designates a word–world relationship of correspondence which obtains as the product of the ultimate and destined opinion (or conceptual framework) of the community of scientific inquirers, then there will be no truth so designated nor knowledge as the final compulsory belief unless we have good reason for believing that inquiry pursued indefinitely will terminate in some final compulsory belief that shall tell us how things substantially really are. And even if this were shown, we should still need to show that scientific inquiry *will* continue indefinitely if such truth and knowledge is to obtain. But how could Peirce prove either of these propositions? If either proposition cannot be shown, then, however strenuously Peirce tried to avoid conceptual idealism he would have failed in the end. Before considering some contemporary objections to Peirce's definition of truth as the product of the final opinion, we must consider the arguments he gave for the view that destiny decrees an ultimate settlement of opinion and further examine the extent to which he qualified the thesis. In the end, we shall see that although contemporary objections to Peirce's definition are unacceptable, the thesis needs further argumentation which we shall provide; and if our arguments are acceptable, then the theory of knowledge implied by assumptions A, B and C is in the main correct, if not, then we may well be forced to conclude that Peirce failed to successfully synthesize realism and idealism.

In general, Peirce provided two arguments in defense of his claim that science pursued indefinitely will terminate in a final and irreversible answer to any answerable question that may be asked. These arguments presuppose what we shall discuss later, namely, that scientific inquiry will continue indefinitely. His first argument can be reconstructed as follows:

Premise 1 It is inconceivable that induction should fail as a legitimate source of knowledge in any universe (5.345ff).

Premise 2 All inductive knowledge is probable inference (2.783; 2.693; 2.685; 8.3 and 3.528).

Premise 3 With respect to inductive knowledge, probable inference is to be understood in terms of the frequency theory of probability. Hence, probable inference is a matter of statistical generalization (7.177; 2.673; 2.650 and 2.268).

Premise 4 The frequency theory of probability assumes that the probability value assigned to a proposition will converge to a definite limit as the members of the class of phenomena (in which the frequency of the predesignated characteristic is to be found) approaches infinity (7.22; 7.13; 7.23; 2.776; 7.208 and 2.769).

Therefore: It is a necessary condition for the validity of inductive knowledge (which is everywhere valid) that we assume that probable inference will converge towards a definite limit.

Stated in this way, the argument implies that truth, understood as designating a relationship of *complete* correspondence between language and the world, is indefinitely approximated as one would a mathematical limit. So understood, such truth (and knowledge as freedom from all margin of error) can only be approached, and thus functions as nothing more than a regulative ideal. I suspect that when some people urge that Peirce has a limit theory of truth, it is this argument which they have in mind. But Peirce elsewhere tells us quite implicitly that the final irreversible opinion is not approached as a limit (MS 473 (p. 36 and 39ff); MS 333 (p. 14); MS 289 (p. 16); 5.494; 5.608; 5.416, MS 374 (pp. 9 and 13)). So, if we take the above argument and supplement it with Peirce's reasons (to be noted below) for thinking that the final opinion cannot be approached as a limit, we should conclude that for Peirce, what is approached as a limit is not truth as the product of the final irreversible opinion, for the final irreversible opinion will be reached; rather what is approached as a limit is the probability value of 1 that the proposition is true. And this seems to suggest that the final opinion is reached when the probability of its being true gets sufficiently close to 1 as to render it *practically* certain that the truth value assigned to the proposition will not be revised although there will always be some probability, however small, that the truth value will be revised. And this, as we noted above, provides a clear sense in which the final opinion can be true and yet fallible. In another sense, too, the final opinion is fallible because it does not profess to be certain, which is more than a probability of 1. So, when Peirce talks about the *very truth itself* being approximated by successive confirmation (7.119), he seems to be referring to the fact that the probability that a proposition is true approaches 1 as a limit although this is perfectly consistent with attaining the final truth which occurs in the process of confirmation when the probability of the proposition's being true gets sufficiently close to 1 as to render the margin of error very very small. Somewhere in the process of confirmation, the margin of error implied by the probability assignment becomes substantially negligible and thus the truth value assigned becomes set although the correspondence implied admits of further indefinite refinement. When this occurs, the final opinion—the opinion which is substantially irreversible—is reached.

Peirce sometimes likened the process to the process of computing the value of π. Sooner or later we shall compute the value to 3.14 and that is to say that the probability value assigned to π's being 3.14 admits of a margin of error negligibly small. Should the need present itself, we could compute the value of π indefinitely further to the 7th decimal place. The precise value of π admits of indefinite refinement and what π is exactly can only be approached as a limit (5.565; 8.226; 7.78). But further computation won't reveal that π is substantially anything more or less than 3.14. As the computations increase it won't happen, for example, that π will turn out to be 3.12 or 3.17. Prior to reaching the value of 3.14, had we computed π at 3.04, the probability that π was 3.04 admitted of a substantial margin of error—certainly enough to be consistent with reassigning the truth value to the statement 'The value of π is 3.04'.

In substance then, the thrust of this first argument is that the very method which science employs for the determination of truth, implies that the truth value assigned to a proposition tends toward fixity as inquiry progresses and as the margin of error with respect to our probability assignments tends toward zero—which it will as the proportion of unexamined cases to examined cases decreases (2.650 and 7.210). Given that we have no good reason to call into question the validity of inductive inference as a source of knowledge, we must accept the presupposition upon which it is based. If we add to this the legitimacy of Peirce's reasons for thinking that the final opinion is not approached as a limit, then we can conclude that, in virtue of the scientific method, inquiry tends to, and will reach the final opinion.

The first three premises of the above stated argument are relatively unproblematic and the fourth is entailed by 'the law of large numbers.'[86] Shortly, I shall argue that Peirce's reasons for urging that the final opinion is not approached as a limit can be made quite persuasive. And if that is so, we can conclude with Peirce that the inductive method is essentially self-corrective and it could not be such if we were not to assume that in the long run inquiry will converge to a definite answer on any answerable question.[87] This latter point brings us to Peirce's second argument.

The second argument for his view that inquiry pursued indefinitely will terminate in a final irreversible answer to any answerable question is based upon the history of science and can be stated rather simply: Unless we assume that inquiry on any given topic will, in general, converge in a final definite opinion on the part of the scientific community, we can have no way of accounting for the apparent success of science in the way of settling controversies and providing more and more answers in the course of time. In short, we cannot acknowledge the triumphs and progress of science without thereby noting the general tendency of inquiry to converge in a definite opinion (4.547ff; 8.43; 5.494; and 2.150).

By 1885 Peirce began to admit that for any given question it is logically possible for inquiry to continue forever without coming to a final opinion (8.43; 8.225; and 8.237). For example, it is conceivable that we might never be able to answer a question such as "How frequently did Pollonius cut his hair?" But of course we do not know that any specific question of this sort will *not* be answered in some final definite opinion (so we must treat them all as answerable); and the fact that it is logically possible for inquiry to continue indefinitely without producing a final answer to some specific question only shows that some questions may not be answerable (MS 4096 (p. 82)). It does not show that for any question *which admits of an answer* there will not be any final answer—assuming indefinite inquiry. In other words, the two arguments cited above should be viewed as supporting the thesis that for any given question which admits of a final answer, inquiry pursued indefinitely will reach the final irreversible answer.

Further, Peirce claimed that the sense in which the final opinion is destined to come (on questions that admit of answer) is not the sense in which it is logically necessary that the final opinion will obtain, but rather the sense in which a pair of dice, thrown often enough, will be sure to turn up sixes some time, although there is no logical necessity that they should. He said:

> I take it that anything may fairly be said to be *destined* which is sure to come about although there is no necessitating reason for it. Thus, a pair of dice, thrown often enough, will be sure to turn up sixes some time, although there is no necessity that they should. The probability that they will is 1: that is all. *Fate* is that special kind of *destiny* by which events are supposed to be brought about under *definite circumstances* which involve no necessitating cause for those occurrences. (4.547 n. 1. See 7.335)

Before attempting to determine in detail whether the above two arguments establish what Peirce needed to show, let us pause for a moment to consider some contemporary objections to Peirce's definition of truth as the object of the final opinion.

In commenting on Peirce's definition of truth as the product of the final irreversible opinion, Israel Scheffler has urged that (a) Peirce's reference to truth as a "fore-ordained goal" which no man can escape cannot be taken literally since Peirce can have no way of knowing that fate decrees an ultimate settlement of opinion;[88]

(b) Peirce has no way of knowing that the ultimate settlement of opinion fixes upon truth (it is surely not logically contradictory that perfect agreement is reached in a falsehood and is never reversed); and (c) it is difficult to imagine how such a notion of truth is consistent with a commitment to Fallibilism. Moreover, Professor Quine, unlike Scheffler, thinks that Peirce has a limit theory of truth; and he has offered the following observations:

> Peirce was tempted to define truth outright in terms of scientific method, as the ideal theory which is approached as a limit when the (supposed) canons of scientific method are used unceasingly on continuing experience (5.407). But there is a lot wrong with Peirce's notion; besides its assumption of a final organon of scientific method and its appeal to an infinite process, there is a faulty use of numerical analogy in speaking of a limit of theories, since the notion of limit depends on that of 'nearer than' which is defined for numbers and not for theories. And even if we bypass such troubles by identifying truth somewhat fancifully with the ideal result of applying the scientific method outright to the whole future totality of surface irritations, still there is trouble in the imputation of uniqueness ('the ideal result'). For, as urged a few pages back, we have no reason to suppose that man's surface irritations even unto eternity admit of any one systematization that is scientifically better or simpler than all possible others. It seems likelier, if only on account of symmetries or dualities, that countless alternative theories would be tied for first place. Scientific method is the way to truth, but it affords even in principle no unique definition of truth. Any so-called pragmatic definition of truth is doomed to failure equally.[89]

Finally, Bertrand Russell is also of the opinion that Peirce has a limit theory of truth, and he offers the following criticism:

> The main question is: Why does Peirce think that there is an "ideal limit toward which endless investigation would tend to bring scientific belief"? Is this an empirical generalization from the history of research? Or is it an optimistic belief in the perfectability of man? Does it contain any element of prophecy, or is it a merely hypothetical statement of what would happen if men of science grew continually cleverer? Whatever interpretation we adopt, we seem committed to some very rash assertion. I do not see how we can guess either what will be believed, or what would be believed by men much cleverer than we are. Whether the theory of relativity will be believed twenty years hence depends mainly upon whether Germany wins the next war. Whether it would be believed by people cleverer than we are we cannot tell without being cleverer than we are. Moreover, the definition is inapplicable to all the things that are most certain. During breakfast, I may have a well-grounded conviction that I am eating eggs and bacon. I doubt whether scientists two thousands years hence will investigate whether this was the case, and if they did their opinions would be worth less than mine.

"Truth," therefore, as Peirce defines the term, is a vague concept involving much disputable sociology.[90]

All the above objections deserve comment.

First of all, with respect to Scheffler's objections, all three are unacceptable. The first objection (that Peirce has no way of knowing that fate decrees an ultimate settlement of opinion) comes without any consideration of the two arguments (cited above) which Peirce gave in defense of his view that if inquiry were to continue indefinitely on any answerable question fate decrees an ultimate settlement of opinion. Moreover, the objection makes no attempt to ascertain whether Peirce argued for the view that inquiry will continue indefinitely. This we shall do shortly. Further, if the substance of the first objection is that it is logically possible for inquiry to continue forever without convergence of opinion on any answerable question, Peirce would fully agree without thereby feeling compelled to abandon his thesis. Peirce did not believe that a strict demonstration guaranteeing the preclusion of the logical possibility of error was possible for any thesis; and hence his thesis was put forth as a matter of inductive necessity on the grounds that the thesis is presupposed by the validity of inductive inference and is inductively necessary if we are to account for the observed success of science in the way of settling controversies in the course of time (8.43). Also, as previously noted, Peirce argued that simply because it is logically possible that a proposition is false, by no means indicates that the proposition is doubtful. Scheffler's second objection (it is logically possible for agreement to be reached on falsity) implies that the thesis is defensible only if the logical possibility of agreement being reached on falsity is precluded. Once again, Peirce would agree that it is logically possible that agreement be reached on falsity just as it is logically possible that dice thrown forever will not turn up sixes; but since the thesis is put forth as a matter of inductive necessity (probability 1) the exclusion of such a logical possibility is not required. The third objection (such a conception of truth seems inconsistent with a commitment to fallibilism) does not carry much weight in the light of our previous discussion on the sense in which the final *opinion can be final* and fallible. We need not repeat those considerations.

Secondly, it is apparent from the passage cited above that Quine is opposed to Peirce's definition of truth primarily because (a) there is a faulty use of numerical analogy in speaking of truth as a limit of theories, since the notion of limit depends upon 'nearer than' which is defined for numbers and not for theories; and (b) we have no reason to suppose that man's surface irritations will ever admit of any one systematization better or simpler than all possible ones. With respect to (a), Peirce did not argue that our theories or beliefs approach truth as a mathematical limit. Rather he argued that what is approached as a limit is the probability value 1 that the theory (proposition or hypothesis) is true. Otherwise, the final truth is reached when the likelihood of truth is sufficiently close to 1 as to render it extremely unlikely that truth value revision will occur.

With respect to (b) Quine, like Scheffler, has failed to notice the two arguments Peirce gave for the thesis that scientific inquiry pursued forever will beget a final answer to any question which admits of an answer. Further, he also fails to consider what, if any, arguments Peirce may have given for the belief that science will, as a matter of fact, continue indefinitely. Moreover, Quine does not provide us with a clear reason for believing that man's surface irritations will not admit of any one systematization better or simpler than all contending ones. His claim that it seems likelier, "*if only on account of symmetries of dualities,* that countless alternative theories would be tied for first place," is certainly worthy of explication. Finally, at the end of the passage cited above Quine asserts that scientific method is the way to truth, but affords no unique definition of truth. On this score it should be pointed out that Peirce uniquely defined truth (his second conception of truth) in terms of correspondence (1.578; 2.652; 2.135; 7.659; 8.104; 8.144; 5.549; 8.126) and reckoned it the product of the final opinion destined to obtain if inquiry progresses indefinitely.[91]

Thirdly, Russell's objection is wrong for a number of reasons. In the first place, he, like so many others, would have it that for Peirce the ultimate answer to any answerable question is an ideal limit towards which endless investigation would tend to bring scientific belief, when in fact Peirce claimed that this limit is not approached as a mathematical limit. I believe that Russell (like Quine and others)[92] sees a limit theory of truth in Peirce because Peirce so frequently defined truth as the property of the final opinion which the scientific community *would* agree upon if it *were* to continue inquiry indefinitely. But it should be noted that later in life, when Peirce was searching for reasons to defend the view that science *will* progress indefinitely (see pp. 75ff below) he asserted that he had made a mistake in defining truth in terms of what *would be* rather than in terms of what *will be* (MS 289 (p. 16)).

The question Russell should have asked is: Why does Peirce believe that endless investigation will terminate ultimately in a final irreversible opinion on any answerable question? And the answer lies in the two previously considered (but not yet assessed) arguments on pp. 59–62 above. So, it is certainly wrong to suggest, as Russell does, that Peirce's belief that endless inquiry will approach some final answer involves nothing more than a bit of sociological prophesying. Moreover, Peirce's thesis makes no profession to predict *what* people much cleverer than ourselves will believe in the future; and so it should not be faulted for intending as much. The thesis only implies that, given infinity, whatever will be ultimately agreed upon by the community will be the final answer to the answerable question.

Finally, Russell's claiming that Russell ate eggs and bacon on that morning does not make the proposition any truer or more certain than if he had claimed to be Napoleon on the same occasion. Of course, if Russell ate eggs and bacon on that morning, then he *might* have known it; but whether he did or did not eat eggs and bacon, whether his claim is true or false, is not established simply by Russell's asserting it (he could have been mistaken although he felt certain); rather it is established by whether or not the belief that he did is one that will be impeached by future research. Columbus, it will be remembered, claimed to have discovered America, and we can be sure that Columbus felt as certain of having done so as Russell was certain of having eaten eggs and bacon on that particular morning. But, for all that, it is not at all certain that Columbus discovered America. Whether Columbus discovered America will be something determined by future research, and if research goes on forever then we shall ultimately get the answer—if the question can be answered. This, at any rate, is how I think Peirce would reply to Russell's claim that the definition does not apply to things of which we are most certain (5.565).

Independently of these considerations, one might be inclined to suggest that the nature of the scientific enterprise affords in itself ample reason for believing that no ultimate and irreversible opinion will be reached on any matter. After all, if, as the history of science clearly shows, we can not assume that any theory represents an ultimate and irreversible systematization of our surface irritations, then it would seem likely, given the nature of the scientific enterprise itself, that no theory will ever constitute the ultimate and irreversible systematization of experience. To this line of reasoning Peirce replied that no argument based upon the history of science can ever prove that an ultimate convergence of opinion will not obtain.[93] The *most* such an argument shows is that we cannot assume that the ultimate convergence of opinion has obtained on any answerable question. But the argument cannot show that convergence will not obtain. As a matter of fact, given Peirce's second argument in defense of the thesis that inquiry will converge in an ultimate and irreversible opinion, the history of science should be taken to indicate just the opposite conclusion.[94]

The only objections that should be raised to Peirce's definition of truth as the product of the destined ultimate opinion are (a) How does Peirce know that endless investigation will terminate in a final irreversible opinion on any answerable question? and (b) How can Peirce show what he needs to show, namely, that inquiry will continue indefinitely? Answering the first question involves assessing Peirce's two previously mentioned arguments (pp. 59–62), and answering the second involves considerations we have not yet mentioned. All of which we shall now do.

As against Peirce's first argument supporting the view that inquiry pursued indefinitely will terminate in a final irreversible answer on any answerable question, certain objections should not be taken seriously. For example, it won't do to claim that there is no inductive necessity that a final answer be reached since we can conceive of the final answer as an ideal limit successively approximated by our inquiries but never actually reached. Peirce ruled against this sort of reply by asserting (as we noted above) that the final answer is not approximated as a mathematical limit, although the probability that the final answer is true approaches 1 as a limit (5.565; 8.226). And one good reason for believing that Peirce was right in refusing to consider the final answer approachable as an ideal limit is that it would imply that a theory can be true and acceptable only if the theory precludes all possible margin of error. This is a requirement which is unrealistic and for which we have no inductive justification in the history of science. We do not, and should not, demand of our theories even to the end freedom from a margin of error infinitely small. If freedom from a margin of error infinitely small is required for the establishment of a final theory, then there could be no real final theory and the idea of approximating such a theory becomes unintelligible. At best, this would make progress in science ideal rather than real and if scientific progress consists in approximating an ideal and in principle unspecifiable theory, it's hard to see how science can be progressive in any real sense at all.

Peirce's second argument, namely, that we have no way of accounting for the general tendency of scientific inquiry to provide progressively more adequate solutions unless we acknowledge a general drift of inquiry towards a final satisfactory answer which endless inquiry would reach, admits of rejoinder. After all, we can certainly *conceive* of science as a body of funded knowledge such that given an endless process the body of funded knowledge expands *ad infinitum* without ever reaching a final theory. Under such a conception science would still be progressive without it implying that endless progressive research will terminate in some final theory better than all conceivable others. Although this is certainly conceivable, the problem with this objection is that there is no reason to think it likely that science actually does progress in this way. In order for science to progress *ad infinitum* without coming to a final theory one would need to show that (a) the universe is infinitely complex and that an infinitely complex universe cannot in principle be systematized in a single theoretical framework, or (b) there is some other evidence sustaining the view that science is committed to an infinite number of explanatory models or levels of explanation. With respect to (a) William Kneale has argued that the main trouble with (a) is that there seems to be no sense in which nature can be said to be so complex as to require perpetual revolution. He says:

> For if by 'the infinite complexity of nature' is meant only the infinite multiplicity of the particulars it contains, that is no bar to final success in theory making, since theories are not concerned with particulars as such. So, too, if what is meant is only the infinite variety of natural phenomena, since that may be comprehended in a unitary theory just as infinitely many mechanical phenomena are covered by Newton's law of gravitation. If, however, what is meant is precisely what Bohm and Vigier state as a consequence of the principle, namely that there cannot be a final satisfactory theory, there is no point in trying to approach such a theory, either by scientific reforms or revolutions. For if there is no truth there cannot be any approximation to truth, and the whole enterprise of theory making is futile.[95]

We should expect of course that proponents of perpetual revolution might reply by simply refusing to describe the scientific enterprise as one which approximates truth in the sense of approximating a final goal. In which case it could be replied that the proponent of perpetual revolution begs the question against final success since he certainly has not established by appealing to the infinite complexity of the universe that science progresses in the way that it would need to in order to sustain his view.

Similarly, with respect to (b) Kneale has also observed:

> What Bohm and Vigier say about the present state of theoretical physics is attractive, and may be true, for all I know. But extrapolation *ad infinitum* from two revolutions, one of which has not yet got beyond the manifesto stage, does not carry conviction to an inductivist like myself, and I doubt whether it makes sense to one who works with ordinary logic as opposed to dialectics. For although the special form of their infinite regress of explanations has the apparent merit of making it seem possible for scientific research to have a direction without having a goal, it does not remove the fundamental difficulty of the principle of infinite complexity, namely that, if the principle excludes all hope of final theory, it does so by excluding all determinate structure such as scientists might wish to present in a final theory. On the contrary, it puts the difficulty in the bright light of paradox, since it implies that nature is indeterminate even with respect to the contradictory opposition of determinism and indeterminism. (pp. 37 and 38)

Thus, if Kneale's observations are sound, the program of perpetual revolution in science cannot be justified by appealing to the infinite complexity of the universe without either begging the question against final success or extrapolating explanatory models *ad infinitum* on insufficient inductive grounds. Hence, although it is conceivable that endless research does not terminate in any final answer to the answerable question, what would be required to make the view likely cannot, according to Kneale, be provided. On the other hand, Peirce's first argument (cited on pp. 59ff above), *suitably supplemented with the reasoned assertion that the final answer cannot be approached as an ideal limit,* does provide us with a good reason for believing that endless research will reach a final irreversible answer on any question in principle answerable by the use of the scientific method.

A rejoinder to Kneale's argument, however, can be supplied by appealing to Nicholas Rescher's recent and forceful argument that although scientific progress must enter into a stage of progressive deceleration, still, scientific progress will never stop.[96] Interestingly enough, Rescher also argues that the position he defends is distinctively Peircean since it is clearly suggested as a consequence of Peirce's basic and much neglected views on the economy of research—plus a few other considerations which Peirce failed to consider.[97] Rescher's argument for his position is as follows.

Given Planck's principle that every advance in science makes the next advance more difficult and requires a corresponding increase in effort, ever larger demands are made of the researchers in science as it progresses. If we combine this conclusion with the thesis that real qualitative progress in science is parasitic upon advances in technology and that these advances in technology are in turn ever more costly, then we shall need to conclude that scientific progress will get slower and slower because experiments will be harder to make, they will be increasingly more expensive in a world of diminishing resources, and there will be fewer people to do them. In short, if we factor into our understanding of scientific progress the cold hard economic fact of increasing costs for technology and decreasing resources, then a logarithmic retardation in scientific progress is inevitable. On this view, while major discoveries will never come to a stop, the time between significant discoveries grows larger with the passage of time. By way of analogy, Rescher asks us to consider such progress similar to a person's entering a Borgesian infinite library but with a card that entitles the bearer to take out one book the first week, one for the second two weeks and so on with increasingly long periods of delay. On this model, our ever-expanding knowledge grows at an ever-decreasing rate. Scientific revolutions will go on forever, but the time gap between them moves toward infinity and carries with it a substantial slowdown in science as an activity.

Moreover, that there could not be a finite number of empirically answerable questions follows, Rescher argues (pp. 245ff), from what he terms the ' Kant-Proliferation Effect'. This is to say, along with Kant, that unending progressiveness follows from the very real phenomenon that in the course of answering old questions we constantly come to pose new ones. For this reason, no matter how far science progresses, there will still be questions that we will never be able to answer. Moreover, even in the infinite long run, these questions will remain unanswered because their being answered depends on a greater concurrent committment of resources than will ever be marshalled at any one time in a zero growth world: "They involve interactions with nature on a scale so vast that the resources needed for their realization remain outside our economic reach in a world of finite resource-availability" (p. 250).

Rescher's economic argument for perpetual revolution in science is novel and enticing. And while we cannot here do justice to the many facets of the argument, something should be said by way of assessment even if a fuller discussion of the argument may find the argument beyond question. Given this, it should be noted that scientific progress could proceed indefinitely, whatever the cost, only if the number of questions in principle answerable by the scientific method is infinite. And the only apparent evidence Rescher gives for this is the appeal to the 'Kant-Proliferation Effect', or the belief that in the course of answering old questions, we constantly come to pose new ones.

It is questionable, however, that appeal to the 'Kant-Proliferation Effect' can establish that the number of questions in principle answerable by the scientific method is infinite. Appeal to it is nothing more than the assertion without proof of just what requires proof, namely, that there will always be questions to be answered. Indeed, appealing to the 'Kant-Proliferation Effect' to guarantee unending revolution in science seems to beg the question against final success in science by supposing that science can progress *ad infinitum* without ever reaching any final goal. As just noted, however, what is required to justify such a conception of science has not been justified.[98]

Certainly, in the process of answering *some* questions, we pose new ones. But there is no evidence that for each and every question answered by science, there is at least one empirically answerable question that is raised as a result of answering each question.[99] And, seemingly, this is precisely what is needed if appeal to the Kantian principle is to have the effect Rescher ascribes to it.

Incidentally, too, while space does not here permit an adequate discussion of it, there is good reason to think that, in spite of what Peirce said about the economy of research, Peirce's views on the economy of research do not imply the position Rescher here adopts and indirectly attributes to Peirce. For one thing, although Rescher is quite right in noting the extent to which Peirce's views on the economy of research have been sadly neglected, it is somewhat doubtful that these views imply that there are some true propostitions that will never be known. For various reasons, Peirce never tired of asserting that the unknowable does not exist. Indeed, it is arguable that what Peirce was driving at in his views on the economy of research is that there comes a point in the testing of hypotheses where the cost of testing one hypothesis, rather than another, is too high in the light of the likelihood of any significant advance. In that case, economic constraints require that we move in the direction of testing those hypotheses where there is more likelihood of theoretical advance (7.159; MS 678 (p. 28)). On this reading (which cannot be fully argued here) scientific progress can hardly be viewed as a process wherein the magnitude of the advance decreases in such a way that the final answer to any answerable question cannot be reached.[100]

Moreover, it might be objected that there must be an infinite number of questions in principle answerable by the scientific method because there are an infinite number of things in the world. And proof that there is an infinite number of things in the world appears to follow from the fact that mathematics tells us the way the world is, and mathematics must assume the existence of infinite series. In other words, if one assumes a realistic view of mathematics, a view easy enough to assume since classical mathematics with its allegedly Platonistic assumptions allows a maximum of prediction and control which would be hard to explain short of assuming that mathematics with its transfinite assumptions captures the nature of the real world, then it would follow that there must be an infinite number of things. And, presumably, there is at least one question that can be asked of each.

This sort of argument, however, assumes that in virtue of our success in utilizing classical mathematics, we must assume a realistic view of mathematics, or a view that mathematical statements are, when accurate, literally true of the world. But Phillip Kitcher has shown, I believe, that one can employ classical mathematics successfully without having to countenance the ontology of the Platonist. Very briefly, Kitcher's argument is that mathematics need not be construed as about the world at all.[101] Rather, we can, if we like, construe mathematics as being about a set of operations. Kitcher's proposal is not seemingly any more novel than instrumentalist views of mathematics. Whether those views of mathematics are correct need not detain us here since it seems patent that the assumption essential to this last objection is controversial and by no means clearly true, if true at all.

Furthermore, in opposition to the view that countenancing an infinite number of empirically answerable questions is quite counterintuitive, some will object that we can quite naturally generate an infinte number of empirical questions simply by taking the sentence form "Are the number of Xs Y?" and substitute any of the natural numbers for Y. And certaintly we can generate an infinite number of empirically answerable questions in this way. But the problem with this objection is that, for the purpose of determining whether scientific progress could continue indefinitely, the questions so generated are sufficiently trivial or uninteresting to warrant being excluded from the class of empirically answerable questions. If this sounds inconsistent and *ad hoc*, suppose then, for the sake of argument, that the questions so generated were the only kind of question asked in empirical science. In that case, all empirically answerable questions would be trivial or uninteresting since they could be answered simply by computing or measuring. In such a universe theoretical progress in science ends although, to be sure, progress by way of precision and refinement continues indefinitely. Hence interesting or non-trivial empirically answerable questions should not be identified with (or include as a proper sub-set) the class of empirically answerable questions generatable from the sentence-schema "Are the number of Xs Y?" In short, if by "empirically answerable question" we mean the sort of question science typically asks and the answering of which provides solid theoretical progress, and which is not trivially answered by quasi-mechanical or computational procedures, then we cannot generate an infinite number of empirically answerable questions from the sentence schema "Are the number of Xs Y?" by substituting any of the natural numbers for Y.

In arguing that we can indefinitely refine our knowledge and enhance our precision computationally although all empirically answerable questions will be answered, Peirce appears to have been restricting the class of empirically answerable questions to those that are not answerable simply by measurement or computation. And, along with Peirce, for the reason just mentioned, we can and should consider the class of empirically answerable questions as exluding those empirically answerable questions generated by substituting any natural number for Y in the sentence schemae "Are the number of Xs Y?" These latter questions are uninteresting and can exist in a universe wherein all important questions are answered. Certainly, for the remainder of this discussion it should be understood that when we speak of empirically answerable questions we mean to designate empirically answerable questions which are not trivially answerable by quasi-mechanical computational procedures.

Nor, incidentally, could we argue for the intuitive plausibility of infinitely many answerable questions by urging that we can generate an infinite number of such questions by employing the Law of Addition. On this objection, since every true sentence has an infinite number of consequences as a result of The Law of Addition, we need only ask for each disjunct added to a true sentence whether that disjunct is true: "Is it true that either P or Q?", "Is it true that either P or Q or R?" etc. This objection is unacceptable, however, because the infinitely many questions generated in this manner are not empirical questions. After all, if one member of the disjunct is known to be true, the infinitely many questions generated by the use of The Law of Addition are not empirical because answering them does not require any observation, experiment, or even measurement. Accordingly, every true statement may have an inifinite number of consequences and true sentences, but it does not thereby follow that there are infinitely many empirically answerable questions.

Finally, it might be thought that the whole issue of whether science would answer all questions in principle answerable by the scientific method depends on just how science progresses. There are, after all, different views on how science progresses, even among those who hold the traditional view on the objectivity of science. Consequently, it might be reasonable to believe that the way one construes the nature of scientific progress reflects strongly on whether we think science could answer all questions in principle answerable by the scientific method. On this item, some have argued that science progresses cumulatively because replacing theories better explain the questions explained by the previous theories and they explain more. Consequently, the replacing theory answers all the questions answered by the previous theory plus some more questions not answered by the previous theory. However, this view has been severely criticized (whether justifiable so is not at issue here) for failing to capture the sense in which science has in fact progressed.[102] Laudan has argued, for example, that science has progressed not because the replacing theory answers all the questions answered by its rival (or earlier theory) plus some more questions not answered by the previous theory, but rather because the replacing theory answers *more* questions although it may not answer all the questions answered by the previous theory.[103] At any rate, it is important to note that all that is required for science to answer every question in principle answerable by the scientific method is that the number of questions be finite and that science answer more and more questions in the course of time. So, it actually makes little difference where we stand on how science progresses as long as we ultimately construe the progress of science in terms of answering more and more questions in the course of time, and this latter point is not disputed as between the two different views just discussed.

Summarizing our results thus far, there would appear to be no argument establishing that the number of questions in principle answerable by the scientific method is infinite. Moreover, since objections to the supposition that the number of such questions must be finite seem inadequate, we have indirect evidence that if scientific progress were to continue indefinitely it would come to answer every question in principle answerable by the scientific method. At this point, the alleged reasons for believing the contrary are not at all persuasive.

More importantly, Peirce's attempt to synthesize both realism and idealism requires showing that scientific inquiry will continue indefinitely; and this position is considerably more difficult to defend. There can be no doubt that Peirce thought it would, but his reasons for so believing leave a bit to be desired. On one occasion, for example, he claimed that although it is *certain* that the human race will extirpate itself, it is also *certain* that other forms of extra-terrestrial intelligence will pick up the results and continue the process of inquiry *ad infinitum*:

> We may take it as certain that the human race will ultimately be extirpated; because there is a certain chance of it every year, and in an indefinitely long time the chance of survival compounds itself nearer and nearer zero. But, on the other hand, we may take it as certain that other intellectual races exist on other planets,—if not of our solar system, then of others; and also that innumerable new intellectual races have yet to be developed; so that on the whole, it may be regarded as most certain that intellectual life in the universe will never finally cease. (8.43)

He gave no evidence for the alleged 'certainty' of the claim that other intellectual races exist. Nor does he ever make it clear precisely *how* other intellectual races would 'pick up' the scientific results of an extirpated race.

In the end, however, Peirce came to the view that believing inquiry will continue forever, and thus that the final opinion will obtain, is an assumption which cannot be shown to be false and is further justified by its indispensableness for making any action rational. He said:

> This would serve as a complete establishment of private logicality, were it not that the assumption, that man or the community (which may be wider than man) shall ever arrive at a state of information greater than some definite finite information, is entirely unsupported by reasons. There cannot be a scintilla of evidence to show that at some time all living beings shall not be annihilated at once, and that forever after there shall be throughout the universe any intelligence whatever. Indeed, this very assumption involves itself a transcendent and supreme interest, and therefore from its very nature is unsusceptible of any support from reasons. This infinite hope which we all have (for even the atheist will

constantly betray his calm expectation that what is best will come about) is something so august and momentous, that all reasoning in reference to it is a trifling impertinence. We do not want to know what are the weights or reason *pro* and *con*—that is, how much *odds* we wish to receive on such a venture in the long run—because there is no long run in the case; the question is single and supreme, and All is at stake upon it. We are in the condition of a man ... (so circumstanced) that the only assumption upon which he can act rationally is the hope of success. So this sentiment is rigidly demanded by logic. If its object were any determinate fact, any private interest, it might conflict with the results of knowledge and so with itself; but when its object is of a nature as wide as the community can turn out to be, it is always a hypothesis uncontradicted by facts and justified by its indispensableness for making any action rational. (5.357. See also 2.654; 8.153; 5.160; MS 425 (Logic 88))

The intent of this passage is clear; but the argument isn't. Even if we grant (as we must) that believing inquiry will continue indefinitely is an assumption which cannot be shown to be false, still, it is difficult to see precisely how such an assumption is an indispensable condition for human rationality. Admittedly, we must and do hope that we will be successful in our inquiries. Deprived of such a hope it is unlikely that we would undertake any inquiry at all; and if this were so, it is equally unlikely that we would attain to any knowledge in terms of the final opinion. If there is no hope of success, there is no reason to inquire. Indeed, without the hope of success we would not make any inquiries. And Peirce's point seems to be that assuming inquiry will continue indefinitely is a necessary condition for any real hope of success. After all, if we were to assume that inquiry will not continue indefinitely, what real hope could we have that sooner or later we shall attain to the ultimate irreversible opinion?

There are at least two things wrong with this line of reasoning. In the first place, the argument quietly begs the question. The question at issue is whether inquiry will continue indefinitely, and the argument is that unless we assume that it will, we can have no hope of attaining the ultimate truth (as correspondence) embodied in the final irreversible opinion of the community. In other words, the argument assumes that there is an ultimate truth and opinion to which we must attain and assuming inquiry will continue indefinitely is a necessary condition for the attainment. But the whole point of determining whether or not inquiry will continue indefinitely is to ascertain whether there can be any ultimate truth and opinion which we can hope to attain. That inquiry will continue indefinitely is a necessary condition for there being the sort of truth and knowledge in question. To say that inquiry must continue indefinitely otherwise we cannot hope to attain to the ultimate truth simply repeats what is a necessary condition for there being such truth and knowledge, but it by no means establishes that inquiry will continue indefinitely. Secondly, even if assuming inquiry will continue indefinitely is a necessary condition for the hope of success without which hope the ultimate opinion cannot be attained, still, 'hoping' that we shall be successful, however much it be a requirement for human rationality, is consistent with not being successful in attaining to the ultimate irreversible opinion. In which case, even if the indefinite prolongation of inquiry is a necessary condition for 'hoping' for success, such success (and hence the existence of such truth and knowledge) need not obtain. Thus while it cannot be shown that inquiry will not continue indefinitely, Peirce's positive reason for believing that it will is unconvincing.

But we can remedy this deficiency (and provide Peirce with a helping hand) with the following argument:[104] The right to believe that inquiry will continue indefinitely can be purchased by appealing to the Jamesian doctrine that if a proposition recommends itself to our belief and if it is a proposition for which there is no systematic evidence one way or the other, then we have a right to believe the proposition if in so believing we are better able to create some moral value that would not otherwise obtain. In other words, by appealing to the Jamesian doctrine wherein evidence in favor of a belief can be supplied purely in terms of the positive moral value likely to occur as the result of accepting the belief we can justify the belief that inquiry will continue forever. For there is one notable advantage which accrues to the belief that inquiry will continue indefinitely but which does not accrue to the belief that inquiry will not continue indefinitely. Namely, in believing that inquiry will continue indefinitely we provide for the unlimited *hope* in the perfectability of the species. Without such hope it seems unlikely that the species will strive for moral and social improvement as strenuously as if it were to be deprived of such hope. The alternative would seem to be not necessarily moral despair but rather a self-conscious turning to some version of "eat, drink and be merry because tomorrow we die." This latter attitude would appear to be inconsistent with the attainment of the highest standards of morality where those standards are ultimately cashed-in for the happiness of the group. Presumably, the happiness of the group is not a moral value to be gainsaid willy-nilly. Thus, believing inquiry will continue indefinitely is more likely to provide the hope and optimism required for a strenuous moral enterprise whereas the lack of such hope and optimism is less likely to provide as beneficial results.

It might be objected that the most this shows is that it is probably best for us to believe that inquiry will continue indefinitely, but this has nothing to do with the truth of the matter. To such an objection it can only be replied that it is not difficult to construct examples such that even in science what is true would be undeniably a matter of what it is morally best for us to believe. Such an example would occur where the confirmation of a hypothesis depended on testing procedures which could not be employed because of the moral risk involved. A good example of this would be that we have constructed a bomb that can destroy the universe; and the only testing procedure available to confirm the hypothesis consists in dropping the bomb. In this case the claim that the hypothesis is unacceptable because not confirmed (or confirmable) would be true. The reason why the hypothesis is not confirmed (or confirmable) turns on the moral risk involved in testing the hypothesis; and since it is better for us not to test the hypothesis, the epistemic status of the hypothesis is ultimately a matter of what it is morally best for us to believe. Alluding to the distinction between what is true and what is morally best for us to believe seems vacuous if the point of the allusion is to suggest that we are rejecting a hypothesis that may be true; for, since the hypothesis cannot be tested, the sense in which it might be true amounts to nothing more than a mere logical possibility. As a matter of fact, it is true that the hypothesis would be unacceptable.

If these considerations fail to convince anyone that that, *ceteris paribus*, that hypothesis should be chosen which is best for us to believe, then at least it will not be denied that we have a right to believe, *ceteris paribus*, that hypothesis which is more likely to provide for the implementation of moral values that would not otherwise obtain. Even for Peirce, truth is a species of the good (MS 309 (p. 27)). In which case the hypothesis that inquiry will continue forever is an hypothesis we have a right to believe whereas we would not have the right to believe that inquiry will not continue forever. Moreover, we would not seem to have the right to suspend judgment on the matter either; for the right to suspend judgment obtains only when there is no forced option. And we can suggest that the strenuous pursuit of moral betterment (which pursuit is more likely to take place given the belief in the infinite perfectability of man) is not something we can turn our backs on, even if only temporarily.

It is quite unlikely that Peirce intended anything like the preceding when he argued that belief in the indefinite continuance of inquiry reduces to the sentiment of hope. But the question is whether these considerations render the theory independently credible. If they do, then we have good grounds for considering Peircean epistemology more seriously. If they do not, then it must be remembered that even in the absence of some good reason for believing that science will continue indefinitely, we cannot show that it will not.[105] But if we cannot show that science will not continue indefinitely, the proposal stated in assumption B back on p. 51 becomes an assumption which cannot be shown to be false. In which case the acceptability of B would turn not so much on our ability to show that science will continue indefinitely, nor even on the fact that the contrary view cannot be shown true. More fundamentally, the acceptability of B would then turn on the extent to which assuming that science will continue indefinitely is systematically more fruitful to adopt than the alternative assumption, namely, that science will continue indefinitely. Determining which of two competing assumptions would be systematically more fruitful to adopt is largely a matter of what we are willing to consider essentially problematic in the data to be systematized and this in turn is a function of how we initially characterize the data. Fortunately, how we shall initially characterize the data of epistemology is sufficiently controversial to warrant the conclusion that it is by no means obvious that assuming science will continue indefinitely is less fruitful than the alternative assumption.

One final point: There is something terribly wrong with the realist–idealist controversy. For one thing, the controversy feeds on the untested assumption that in the end one must be either an idealist or a realist. Indirectly this is usually taken to imply that one's theory of truth will either be a matter of correspondence or coherence but not both. Moreover, there is the all too pervasive tendency to infer that just as coherence theories of truth necessarily hook-up with idealism, correspondence theories of truth inevitably align themselves with realism. No doubt, the belief that truth must be uniquely defined is quite likely the culprit in all this. If our interpretation and extension of Peirce is correct, we are confronted with a novel and plausible attempt to bypass these venerable assumptions and distinctions. The novelty of the proposal consists in supporting a correspondence theory of truth by arguments which, if the proposal is correct, can be considered true only under a coherence definition of truth. In other words, if we accept Peirce's theory of truth and knowledge, we must consider the truth of the arguments in support of the proposal as nothing more than what we are fully authorized in writing down relative to our current conceptual framework; but this does not commit us radically to conceptual idealism since what we are fully authorized in writing down is that scientific inquiry on any given answerable question will continue indefinitely and terminate in a final irreversible answer which shall tell us how things really are independently of any relationship they may have to minds in being known.

Let us turn now to Peirce's views on common sense and the foundations of knowledge.

V. *COMMON SENSE AND THE FOUNDATIONS OF KNOWLEDGE*

Straightforwardly drawn, the distinction between non-basic and basic knowledge is the distinction which obtains between what we can and what we cannot justify by appeal to other known propositions. The distinction goes back at least as far as Aristotle who, in Book I of the *Posterior Analytics*, argues that we do have demonstrative knowledge, knowledge which is the product of inference from premises, but if there is to be any demonstrative knowledge there must also be non-demonstrative knowledge, knowledge which does not proceed by way of demonstration from other known premises. Aristotle reasoned that this must be the case because if one is to know the conclusion of a demonstration, he must also know the premises of the demonstration; and if the premises of any demonstration are knowable only if demonstrable, then in order to know the conclusion of any demonstration we would be obliged to pass through an infinite series of demonstrable premises. So, since we cannot traverse an infinite series and since we do have demonstrative knowledge, there must be some knowledge which is not demonstrable by appeal to other known premises. Otherwise there would be no demonstrative knowledge.[106] Hence the reason for the above distinction rests on the well-founded belief that if some knowledge is knowledge only because it can be justified by appeal to other known propositions, then there must be some knowledge which is knowledge but does not require justification by appeal to other propositions. It is important to note at the outset that in 2.27 Peirce repeats and endorses Aristotle's argument for the existence of basic knowledge as distinct from non-basic or demonstrative knowledge. And the argument is urged again in MS 425 and in MS 736 (p. 7).[107]

Notice that if we reject the distinction between basic and non-basic knowledge, then we must hold that all knowledge is basic or all knowledge is non-basic. But if *all* knowledge is basic, then it is *never* a necessary condition for knowing that one provide evidence for his knowledge claim; and if all knowledge is non-basic, then, since one must know the premises of a demonstration if he is to know the conclusion, he must pass through an infinite series of premises in order to know anything. Indeed, we can make a good claim to the effect that rejecting the distinction between basic and non-basic knowledge entails scepticism.

The sweet reasonableness offered in support of the distinction has, however, been eclipsed by the now familiar debate over the epistemic status of the non-derivative propositions which are basically known. Even among the most cerebral of empiricists it has been argued, following Aristotle's lead, that unless these foundational beliefs are absolutely certain, then no proposition inferred from them could even be probably true. Part of the reasoning behind *this* foundational view is that *if* knowledge is to obtain, one's evidence in favor of his beliefs must be ultimately unimpeachable because the data which support a genuine probability must themselves be certainties. Probability is essentially relative in character and no statement is probable *per se* but only in relation to its evidence, the presumed truth of some other statement.[108] And we are all by now familiar with standing objections to this latter view as an unwholesome and unnecessary return to Cartesian epistemology unworthy of any self-respecting empiricist. Some, like Wilfrid Sellars, have even argued that knowledge does not have any foundation of certainty and that "empirical knowledge, like its sophisticated extension, science, is rational not because it has a *foundation* but because it is a self-correcting enterprise which can put any claim in jeopardy though not all at once."[109] This is usually understood as a simple and outright rejection of any foundational view of knowledge. Others, like Popper and Price, do hold that knowledge must have a foundation but take exception to the claim that the distinguishing character of foundational beliefs is their certainty. On their view, foundational beliefs are as corrigible as any belief but are foundational simply in the sense that they are logically first in any line of inference. Popper has called these foundational beliefs 'conventions' which are to be accepted as long as there is no good reason to call them into doubt.[110]

But there are difficulties with both these attacks on the foundational metaphor. If we opt for the Sellarsian approach, we apparently commit ourselves to the view that either there is no knowledge at all or the truth of what we know is a matter of coherence. More importantly, on the Sellar's approach we can no longer endorse the distinction between basic and non-basic knowledge. And of course it is precisely the demonstrated need for this distinction which generates the foundational metaphor. On the other hand, if, with somebody like Popper, we grant that knowledge does have foundations but that the foundations represent ultimately and only impeachable conventions, we still seem to be at a loss to preserve the distinction between basic and non-basic knowledge since, presumably, a convention is more like an inference ticket than a true proposition; and if basic knowledge is to be knowledge at all, it must be of statements that are true. Without caring to go further into the myriad detail of the debate just now, the issue is important for any epistemology and I hope to show that Peirce's treatment of the problem represents a third view (not yet noted) and an independently compelling thesis which is central to, and consistent with, the general tenets of his epistemology.

As we shall see, Peirce's view is more like Popper's than Sellar's because Peirce can reasonably be construed as holding the view that knowledge does have foundations although the foundational beliefs are fallible and subject to revision. Unlike Popper, however, Peirce holds that although these foundational beliefs are fallible and subject to revision, they are nonetheless *true* and not mere conventions. This is clearly a third position and, if defensible, would have the merit of showing us how to reject the claim that knowledge rests on foundations of certainty without discarding the distinction between basic and non-basic knowledge. When this latter distinction is discarded, as it inevitably must be under either of the above attacks on the foundational metaphor, the consequences are sufficiently drastic to warrant our searching out a defensible way to keep the distinction and in some attenuated form the attending foundation metaphor *without* simultaneously finding ourselves saddled with the view that knowledge rests on foundation of unimpeachable certainly. In other words, it will not be necessary to reject the distinction between basic and non-basic knowledge simply to avoid foundational certainty if this third position, which we attribute to Peirce, is correct. After arguing that it is in fact the only plausible view to attribute to Peirce, we shall defend it although in the end it will become clear that the acceptability of the Peircean thesis will depend on our willingness to accept the unique features of Peirce's coherence theory of truth.

A. Common Sense Beliefs as Fallible, True, and Basically Known

Those propositions which are presupposed by the method of inquiry but cannot be established by it, and those propositions which we accept and believe simply because we do not (and never have had) any good reason to disbelieve them, Peirce calls propositions of common sense or instinct and claims that they are in some sense privileged. Indeed, there is a sense in which they must be regarded as infallibly true even for a fallibilist like Peirce:

Philosophers of very diverse stripes propose that philosophy shall take its start from one or another state of mind in which no man, least of all a beginner in philosophy, actually is. One proposes that you shall begin by doubting everything, and says that there is no one thing that you can not doubt, as if doubting were 'as easy as lying'. ... But in truth, there is but one state of mind from which you find yourself at the time you do 'set-out'—a state of mind in which you are laden with an immense mass of cognition already formed, of which you can not divest yourself if you would; and who knows whether, if you could, you would not have made all knowledge impossible to yourself? Do you call it doubting to write down on a piece of paper that you doubt? If so, doubting has nothing to do with any serious business. But do not make believe; if pedantry has not eaten all the reality out of you, recognize, as you must, that there is much that you do not doubt in the least. Now that which you do not at all doubt, you must and do regard as infallible absolute truth. Here breaks in Mr. Make Believe: 'What, do you mean to say that one is to believe what is not true, or that what a man does not doubt is *ipso facto* true?' No, but unless he can make a thing white and black at once, he has to regard what he does not doubt as absolutely true. ... All you have any dealings with are your doubts and beliefs, with the course of life that forces new beliefs upon you and gives you power to doubt old beliefs. If your terms 'truth' and 'falsity' are taken in such senses as to be definable in terms of doubt and belief and the course of experience (as for example they would be, if you were to define the 'truth' as that to a belief in which belief would tend if it were to tend indefinitely toward absolute fixity), well and good: in that case you are only talking about doubt and belief. But if by truth and falsity you mean something not definable in terms of doubts and beliefs in any way, then you are talking of entities of whose existence you can know nothing, and which Ockham's razor would clean shave off. (5.416)[111]

Moreover, he said:

> If you absolutely can not doubt a proposition—can not bring yourself, upon deliberation to entertain the least suspicion of the truth of it, it is plain that there is no room to desire anything more. (6.498)[112]

At first glance this is confusing. For Peirce characteristically seems to equivocate on the epistemic status of these propositions. He claims that we must regard what we do not really doubt as infallibly true, but in the response to Mr. Make Believe he concedes that what a person does not really doubt is not *ipso facto* true; and this suggests that these first propositions are merely inference tickets or conventions which are neither true nor false and so not actually *known*. He then appears to take it all back with the assertion that truth and falsity should be defined in terms of belief and doubt and that if by truth and falsity we mean something not definable in terms of doubt and belief, then we are talking about entities of whose existence we can know nothing and which Occam's razor would clean shave off. Further, if, as Peirce claims, there is nothing more to be desired than that our first propositions be free from all real doubt, then this would seem to imply (since the assertion of such propositions would satisfy every requirement for knowing) that they are true, and moreover, that their truth consists in their not being really doubted (MS 1 (p. 9); MS 427 (Logic II (pp. 16 and 40); MS 309 (p. 37)). Like Mr. Make Believe, we may be willing to concede the distinction between basic and non-basic knowledge; but if basic knowledge is to be defined in terms of what we do not really doubt antecedently to any inquiry, does this not mean that a proposition not really doubted antecedently to any inquiry is *true* and known simply because it is not really doubted? And Peirce apparently waffles his way through a no–yes answer.

Before trying to make sense of all this, at any rate it seems clear that, for Peirce, the sense in which propositions of common sense are 'infallibly true' is merely the sense in which they are not subject to criticism as long as there is no good reason to disbelieve them. Strictly speaking, they are not 'infallibly true' (although they must be *regarded* as infallibly true) if by 'infallibly true' we mean 'logically certain' or 'in principle unimpeachable.' They occupy the most privileged of epistemic position inasmuch as they are basic and not to be justified by inference through other known propositions. But this does not mean that they could not turn out to be false:

We have to acknowledge that doubts about them may spring up later, but we can find no propositions which are not subject to this contingency. We ought to construct our theories so as to provide for such discoveries: first, by making them rest on as great a variety of different considerations as possible, and second, by leaving room for the modifications which can not be foreseen, but which are pretty sure to prove needful. Some systems are much more open to this criticism than others. All those which repose heavily upon inconceivability of the opposite have proven particularly fragile and short-lived. Those, however, which rest upon positive evidences and which avoid insisting upon the absolute precision of their dogmas are hard to destroy. (5.376 #2N)

What we do not doubt today, experience may force us to doubt tomorrow, in which case what we do not doubt today may turn out to be false tomorrow. Stated differently, common sense beliefs are privileged as inferentially basic but are as fallible as any belief. Although fallible, they are the genetic product of the evolutionary process representing the wisdom of the ages and what we cannot help but believe:

If, with St. Augustine, we draw the inference 'I think; therefore, I am,' but, when asked how we justify this inference, can only say that we are compelled to think that, since we think we are, this uncriticized inference ought not to be called reasoning, which at the very least conceives its inference to be one of a general class of possible inferences on the same model, and all equally valid. But one must go back and criticize the premises and the principles that guide the drawing of the conclusion. If it could be made out that all the ultimate (or first) premises were percepts, and that all the ultimate logical principles were as clear as the principle of contradiction, then one might say that one's conclusion was *perfectly* rational. Strictly speaking, it would not be quite so, because it is quite possible for perception itself to deceive us, and it is much more possible for us to be mistaken about the undubitableness of logical principles. But as a matter of fact, as far as logicians have hitherto been able to push their analyses, we have *in no single case*, concerning a matter of fact, as distinguished from a matter of mathematical conditional possibility, been able to reach this point. We are in every case either forced by the inexorable critic, sooner or later, to declare, 'such and such a proposition or mode of inference *I can not doubt*! it seems perfectly clear that it is so, but I can't say why, or else the critic himself tires before the criticism has been pushed to its very end.

But again we must return to the question "Are these basic propositions true?" Peirce's apparent lack of clarity on the matter is fraught with difficulties. That they must be *regarded* as infallibly true is certainly not enough. For if basic knowledge is to be knowledge at all, the propositions of common sense must be true, otherwise they are merely belief assertions, conventions or inference tickets, and thus cannot properly function as evidence-bearers for non-basic knowledge. If they *are* true, how can Peirce get away with the claim that propositions not really doubted are not *ipso facto* true? And if they are true, how can they be true, basically known, and also fallible in the sense of being subject to revision in the light of future experience? In other words, even if we charitably suppose that Peirce intended to hold that these propositions are true, how could we reconcile the intended position with his explicit statement that propositions not actually doubted (common sense beliefs) are not *ipso facto* true and, moreover, if these propositions are true how can they also be fallible?

We can solve these problems for Peirce if we begin by noting what would count as adequate answers. To do this, let us repeat the three propositions argued earlier:

(A) The predicate 'is true' fundamentally designates a word–world relationship of semantic authorization relative to the rules of acceptance embedded in our present conceptual framework; and

(B) conceptual frameworks progressively evolve through ever more adequate systematizations of the universe in such a way that they will terminate in some final conceptual framework wherein what is semantically authorized as true also designates a word–world relationship of adequate, although not complete, correspondence; and, finally,

(C) we cannot ever be absolutely certain that we have attained to the final conceptual framework; so we must assume that whatever is authorized as true in our current conceptual framework is subject to overthrow in possible future and more adequate conceptual frameworks.

Given these three propositions, it would make perfectly good sense to note that propositions of common sense are true inasmuch as their not being really doubted renders them acceptable under the canons of our current conceptual framework although they are not thereby true in the correspondence sense of the term since we cannot be sure that we have attained to the final conceptual framework wherein what is semantically authorized as true also designates a word–world relationship of correspondence. In other words, given (A), (B) and (C) we would want to say that common sense propositions are true in the coherence sense of the term simply because these propositions are not really doubted, but this does not entail that they are true in the correspondence sense of the term since we have no way of being certain that what we do not presently doubt will in fact be authorized in the final conceptual framework where what is authorized as true also designates a world–world relationship of correspondence. Hence, propositions of common sense are true in the coherence sense because they are not really doubted, but they are not *ipso facto* true in the correspondence sense. Thus, given (A), (B) and (C), we could read Peirce as saying that propositions of common sense are true in the coherence sense of truth because they are not really doubted but they are not *ipso facto* true in the correspondence sense of true. And, moreover, with respect to common sense propositions and *all* propositions, we must regard as true what we do not really doubt relative to the canons of acceptance embedded in our current conceptual framework. In the second place, given (A), (B) and (C), propositions of common sense would be true but also fallible. This is because their truth consists in being completely authorized by the rules of our current conceptual framework and because we cannot be certain that what is presently authorized under our current conceptual framework will not be impeached in a possible future and more adequate conceptual framework. Since we cannot ever be certain that we have attained to the final conceptual framework on any given matter, we must consider the truth value assigned to any proposition in principle subject to revision in the light of future possible frameworks. So if one understands the truth of a proposition in terms of coherence (or warranted assertibility) within a present conceptual framework, and not in terms of correspondence with extra-linguistic fact, then there is no mystery as to how a proposition can be true and fallible since its being authorized at one time relative to a given conceptual framework does not entail that it will continue to be authorized under a possible future and more adequate conceptual framework. Hence, assuming that propositions of common sense must be true, and if we assume (A), (B) and (C), then there shouldn't be anything terribly perplexing about the claim that propositions of common sense are true simply because they are not really doubted although not thereby *ipso facto* true, and while such propositions are true they are also fallible.

We have already argued that propositions (A), (B) and (C) reflect in part the position that Peirce actually adopted. Moreover, we have argued that (A), (B) and (C) are internally consistent and that each is independently defensible as an element in any adequate theory of knowledge. We need not repeat those arguments here.

It is enough to note that we have strong reason for believing that, in the light of his general doctrine on the nature of truth, Peirce held that the propositions of common sense are true, basically known to be true, and fallible. We will discuss shortly some of the difficulties attending just such a view of basic knowledge; but for the moment let us look to the reasons Peirce gave for the acceptability of propositions free of all real doubt antecedently to any inquiry.

B. Reasons for Accepting Common Sense Beliefs as True and Basically Known

First of all, it is quite likely that Peirce knew the basic Cartesian argument against his thesis and rejected that argument on the grounds that such an argument leads to absolute scepticism. The Cartesian argument against Peirce's thesis consists in asserting that we should doubt all those propositions which we do not really doubt, since it is at least logically possible that they are false. It would not be much of a conjecture to say that Peirce rejected the Cartesian doubt on the grounds that its validity would presuppose a definition of knowledge which can not in principle be satisfied for the simple reason that, for Peirce, there are no propositions which are so true that they could never be false. Obviously, if one were to hold (as did Peirce) that there are no strictly analytic propositions and that all knowledge is a matter of synthetic inference, then one could not reasonably adopt the view that one should doubt a proposition simply because it is logically possible that the proposition in question is false. For if one were to adopt this latter view, he would be logically constrained to the view that we can know only those propositions which can not possibly be false—a view which, when combined with the denial of strict analyticity leads to absolute scepticism. Alternately put, had Peirce endorsed the validity of the Cartesian doubt and had he at the same time endorsed the thesis on Fallibilism, he would have been committed to absolute scepticism. He had to deny either the validity of the Cartesian doubt, or the possibility of knowledge. Hence if knowledge is to be possible, we must begin with propositions free of all actual doubt. This line of reasoning would not only explain why, but also justify Peirce's frequent claims to the effect that (a) the Cartesian doubt (calling into question a proposition which one does not really doubt on the grounds that it is logically possible that the proposition is false) is illegitimate;[113] (b) the Cartesian thesis is the thesis of scepticism;[114] and (c) if knowledge is to be possible, legitimate doubt must be external in origin.[115]

Secondly, Peirce envisaged another somewhat different objection to his thesis and his second argument stands as a refutation of that objection. The objection in question would be that it is unreasonable to accept any proposition without positive inductive confirmation. Whereas the Cartesian argument would insist on the legitimacy of doubting what we do not really doubt because of the logical possibility of error, this objection would insist on the legitimacy of doubting what we do not really doubt because of the unreasonableness of accepting any proposition without positive inductive evidence. Peirce attributed this sort of objection to Wundt and his followers.[116] And against such an objection Peirce argued that the requirement of positive inductive confirmation for all propositions would, once again, make knowledge impossible since such a demand cannot be satisfied with respect to the basic premises and principles which guide the drawing of our conclusions. That Peirce had such an argument in mind seems to be clearly implied in the passage previously noted, namely:

> If, with St. Augustine, we draw the inference 'I think; therefore, I am,' but, when asked how we justify this inference, can only say that we are compelled to think that, since we think we are, this uncriticized inference ought not to be called reasoning, which at the very least conceives its inference to be one of a general class of possible inferences on the same model, and all equally valid. But one must go back and criticize the premises and the principles that guide the drawing of the conclusion. If it could be made out that all the ultimate (or first) premises were percepts, and that all the ultimate logical principles were as clear as the principle of contradiction, then one might say that one's conclusion was *perfectly* rational. Strictly speaking, it would not be quite so, because it is quite possible for perception itself to deceive us, and it is much more possible for us to be mistaken about the indubitableness of logical principles. But as a matter of fact, as far as logicians have hitherto been able to push their analyses, we have *in no single case*, concerning a matter of *fact*, as distinguished from a matter of mathematical conditional possibility, been able to reach this point. We are in every case either forced by the inexorable critic, sooner or later, to declare, 'such and such a proposition or mode of inference *I can not doubt!* it seems perfectly clear that it is so, but I can't say why,' or else the critic himself tires before the criticism has been pushed to its very end. If you absolutely can not doubt a proposition—can not bring yourself upon deliberation, to entertain the least suspicion of the truth of it, it is plain that there is no room to desire anything more.[117]

Accordingly, it would be fair to say that for Peirce, unless the inductive process begins with propositions that are acceptable simply because they are not really doubted, then it would be impossible to inductively confirm any proposition. The method of science itself must presuppose some propositions which can not be established by the method.[118] For Peirce, knowledge has its foundation not in propositions so true that they can never be false, but rather in propositions we do not really doubt—otherwise there would be no knowledge (MS 425 (Logic 87 and 96)).

The third and final argument we can credit to Peirce has its roots in the fact that for Peirce, when a proposition is not really doubted, it is, by definition, a proposition which leads to modes of activity which are consonant with the course of experience. If a belief in a proposition did not lead to modes of activity consonant with the course of experience, if, in short, the belief in question led to the surprising or frustrating, then the evidence requisite for its being questioned would be present. But when the evidence required for questioning a belief is absent, it follows that the belief in question satisfies the end of inquiry, which is the establishment of beliefs leading to the avoidance of surprise and frustration. Such beliefs have the positive confirmation of leading to modes of activity which allows us to expedite our dealing with sense experience, and this is precisely why the evidence required for questioning such beliefs is absent. Peirce's first two arguments for accepting common sense beliefs show that the denial of his thesis leads to absolute scepticism, while this third argument of accepting common sense beliefs is that such beliefs satisfy the end of inquiry—otherwise they would be really doubtful.

Peirce did not simply plead for common sense beliefs. He carefully characterized them and provided arguments in defense of their acceptability without ever suggesting that there is some conflict between a thorough empiricism and commitment to common sense. Peirce's pragmatism is a thoroughgoing empiricism which fully endorses the necessity of appealing to the acceptability of what we do not really doubt (MS 425 (Logic 87 and 95); 5.423 and 6.496) without thereby suggesting that what we do not really doubt cannot become the subject of legitimate doubt. It is a pragmatism which insists that we should begin with common sense and appeal to science only when our common sense fails us (2.178) and even then, science will be based upon common sense in so far as the method of science presupposes some common sense beliefs which cannot be directly established by the inductive method. Let us consider objections to all this.

C. Objections

There are no less than three basic objections that can be raised against Peirce's doctrine on the nature and status of common sense beliefs. The first two deal with the independent plausibility of the thesis itself and the third deals with the justifiability of ascribing it to Peirce. In the first case it will be objected that Peirce's position can preserve the foundational metaphor and the distinction between basic and non-basic knowledge without entailing that the foundational beliefs are absolutely certain only if we are willing to endorse a coherence theory of truth. Secondly, if common sense propositions are true (in the coherence sense of the term) simply because, as Peirce claims; they are not really doubted or because they are propositions that we cannot help but believe, then basic knowledge and truth would apparently consist ultimately and only in the present inconceivability of mistake. And it will be urged that our inability to conceive of the possibility of mistake by no means entails the truth of what we profess to know. Finally, even if the position as stated were independently plausible, there is reason to think that Peirce may not have held it. Indeed, the common view on this matter is that Peirce was among the very first to attack the foundational metaphor and argue that knowledge has no foundation at all. This view is expressly asserted by D. M. Armstrong, for example, who apparently supports his claim by appealing to the fact that Peirce espoused the view that *all* knowledge is a matter of synthetic inference, and if *all* knowledge is a matter of synthetic inference, how could *any* knowledge be basic in the sense of not being the product of inferential reasoning. Obviously, it would appear, according to Armstrong, that if *all* knowledge is the product of synthetic inference, the very distinction between basic and non-basic knowledge would dissolve to be replaced by the view that justification involves an infinite, albeit virtuous, regress.[119] Moreover, Bruce Aune has argued that the Peircean position is in fact the same position subsequently argued for by Sellars and Aune himself. But Aune's reason differs from that of Armstrong's. For Aune apparently holds that the no-foundation view follows from Peirce's alleged definition of truth and knowledge as the *ideal* product of what the scientific community *would* agree to if scientific inquiry were to continue indefinitely and progressively. Stated differently, Aune's view is that the no-foundation view follows from the fact that for Peirce knowledge and truth are regulative concepts designating ideal and future states that *would be* attained if the scientific community did its job indefinitely. If knowledge and truth are ideal, then the rationality of science cannot consist in its being based upon known and certain propositions, but rather in its ability to grow more and more accurate by methodological procedures that are self-correcting.[120] We shall take these objections in the order of their appearance.

The point of the first objection is obvious: any pure coherence theory of truth will not wash. Philosophers most frequently argue that where coherence is the meaning of truth (and not simply the criterion) then there is no entailment between what one knows and the way the world is. In other words, where truth is only a matter of coherence, then one's knowing that p does not entail that there is any extra-linguistic state of affairs uniquely described by p, and hence knowing that p need not tell us anything at all about the way the world really is. On this view, the coherence theory of truth entails radical Idealism.[121] Where coherence is the meaning of truth some have even argued that we could never know what the real world is like since mutually exclusive hypotheses about the world can be independently and systematically coherent.[122]

But even if these objections succeed in something more than begging the question against the coherence theorist, still, they would not count against what I have called Peirce's coherence theory of truth. For although Peirce held that the predicate 'is true' primarily designates a word–world relationship of semantic authorization relative to a current conceptual framework, he also claimed that conceptual frameworks evolve and *will* terminate in some final framework wherein what is semantically authorized as true also designates a word–world relationship of adequate (although not complete) correspondence. Hence Peirce's espousal of a coherence theory of truth is not at all inconsistent with the view that knowledge and truth corresponds to a world of extra-linguistic fact. It's just that this latter kind of knowledge and truth (which will obtain) we cannot profess to have since we cannot know for certain that we have attained to the final framework. And since we cannot transcend the limitations of our present conceptual framework, we must consider truth as what we are fully authorized in asserting relative to the rules of our present conceptual framework. Admittedly, we cannot be certain at any given time that our knowledge captures the world as it really is, but that doesn't entail that it doesn't or that ultimately it won't. Whatever ills beset Peirce's novel doctrine on the nature of truth and knowledge, it cannot be laid to rest under the usual attacks on the coherence theory of truth since Peirce's doctrine does not entail the wholesale idealism which is envisaged by the usual attack on the coherence theory of truth.

Secondly, to suppose that the Peircean view is unacceptable because our inability to conceive of the possibility of mistake does not entail the truth of what we profess to basically know, is simply to assume that 'truth' in any sense must be defined in terms of correspondence. And this begs the question against the Peircean conception of truth in terms of warranted assertibility or coherence. Naturally, if truth is understood in terms of a relationship of correspondence between words and extra-linguistic fact, then, since truth so understood cannot be guaranteed by our inability to conceive of the possibility of mistake (witness the inability of the ancients to conceive of the universe as anything but flat) our inability to conceive of the possibility of mistake cannot be an adequate criterion of truth. But if the truth of what we basically know is a matter of coherence or warranted assertibility, then the fact that we cannot help but think what we do (cannot conceive of the possibility of being mistaken) could certainly stand as a criterion of truth since presumably we are not obliged to offer a criterion which guarantees truth in the correspondence sense of the term.

Moreover, it might be further argued that, no matter how we define truth, one's inability to conceive of the possibility of mistake cannot be an adequate criterion for the truth of what we basically know because people's ability to conceive of the possibility of error differs from person to person and from time to time depending on their intellectual abilities, training, heredity and even the strength of their eyesight. And this would make knowledge and truth a very subjective affair to be determined simply by ascertaining whether or not people are in a certain mental state characterized by 'feeling quite certain' that what they profess to know is true. On this score, defenders of the Peircean position may take refuge in the claim that it would certainly be a necessary condition for any proposition being basically known that it represent what all men would generally admit as something they cannot doubt. Every person, for example, cannot help but believe that he exists. If we came across a person who honestly and genuinely entertained the possibility that he did not exist, we would conclude that his problem is by no means philosophical but rather medical. Although Peirce thought that there was a list of specifiable common sense propositions, he failed to provide the list. The thesis at any rate does not require the actual specification of these basic propositions, but only that on some basic items all men will agree that they are propositions which they cannot help but believe.

Also, if all men honestly claimed that they could not help but believe that p, and if p is a proposition for which one could not provide evidence for or against by appeal to other known propositions, and if p is consistent with all their other beliefs, then not only could we not say that p is false but also, if coherence or warranted assertibility is the meaning of truth, we must say that what they profess to know is true. Although this is an admittedly psychological criterion of truth, still, with respect to basic knowledge claims where coherence is the meaning of truth, what other criterion could there be? Besides, it isn't an excessively or exclusively psychological criterion because our inability to conceive of the possibility of error, where acceptable as a criterion of truth, will be rooted in the overall consistency or coherence of the belief with the rest of our beliefs.

Thirdly, it is wrong to suggest along with Armstrong that Peirce did not hold to the foundational metaphor but rather opted for an infinite, albeit benign, regress in justification. Admittedly, Peirce did argue that all knowledge is a matter of synthetic inference and in "Questions Concerning Certain Faculties" he also argued for the view that there is no cognition not determined by a previous cognition (5.2.3ff). But the fact that there is no belief which is not the product of inference by no means entails that that there are no propositions which are first in the sense that they are not the object of criticism and not the product of *conscious* inference from other known propositions. For Peirce, common sense propositions are first not because they are not the product of inference but because they are not the product of conscious inference. In any line of conscious reasoning, epistemological justification does and must end in some premise or premises for which we cannot consciously provide justification in terms of other known propositions. Although these propositions themselves are the product of inference, the inferential processes involved in their establishment are unconscious and for that reason these propositions are not subject to conscious criticism. They are first on the conscious level, but as products of unconscious inference, they are psychologically derivative from other propositions. Accordingly, there is nothing *per se* inconsistent with the view that all knowledge is the product of inference and that knowledge must ultimately come to rest in propositions that cannot be justified by conscious appeal to other known propositions.

Indeed, to claim that knowledge admits of an infinite regress of justification (and that therefore knowledge cannot have a foundation) because there is no belief which is not the product of inference, would be to confuse the *psychology* of knowing with the *epistemology* of justification. It is only with respect to the epistemology of justification that knowledge can be said to have a foundation. And this means that in any line of conscious inference or justification we must ultimately come to some proposition which is first in the sense that it cannot be consciously justified (or criticized) by appeal to other known propositions. But this by no means implies that the first propositions which are epistemically basic by way of justification are also psychologically basic in the sense that they themselves are not the product of unconscious inference. As a matter of fact, Peirce held that these common sense propositions, although epistemologically basic (and therefore foundational) because not subject to conscious criticism, are also psychologically derivative since they must be thought to proceed from an infinite series of unconscious inferences (5.213ff). In other words, the foundational view of knowledge understood in terms of the epistemology of justification, does not at all entail that what is epistemologically basic relative to conscious justification is also psychologically basic in the sense of not being the product of unconscious inference. Thus, not only is there no contradiction between the foundational metaphor and the inferential nature of all propositions, but also, and more importantly, there is no reason to believe that Peirce was obliged to abandon the former because of his commitment to the latter.

Furthermore, Aune's reason for thinking that the Peircean position involves a total rejection of the foundation metaphor is no better than Armstrong's. For Aune's conclusion rests on the belief that Peirce defined truth and knowledge solely in terms of an ideal that *would be* attained by the scientific community if inquiry *were* pursued successfully and indefinitely. But, as we have argued above, in addition to defining truth and knowledge in terms of the opinion which will ultimately obtain, Peirce was *also* committed to a conception of truth and knowledge in terms of what is warrantedly assertible fully relative to the canons of acceptance embedded in our present conceptual framework. The ultimate truth about the world is what *will* be authorized in the final conceptual framework and *that* truth will be a matter of correspondence not to be approached simply as a mathematical limit. Short of the ultimate truth, there is knowledge and truth understood in terms of coherence and what we are fully authorized in asserting (or what is warrantedly assertible) relative to our present conceptual framework. It is this latter aspect of Peirce's doctrine on knowledge and truth which requires keeping the foundational metaphor and acknowledging that the foundations are revisable although nonetheless foundational. As I see it, Aune (like Quine and Scheffler) is simply asserting that Peirce was committed to a limit theory of truth. And although Peirce did frequently define truth as the property of the final opinion which the scientific community *would* agree upon if it *were* to continue inquiry indefinitely, he also asserted (as cited earlier on p. 65) in his later years that it was a mistake to define truth in terms of what *would be* rather than in terms of what will be (MS 289 (p. 16)). Besides, on Aune's view we should be obliged to hold that for Peirce there is, as a matter of fact, no knowledge and truth, that the body of knowledge we call science is merely warranted belief, and that sort of scepticism simply does not square with Peirce's frequent claims to the effect that knowledge requires truth and that science is a body of knowledge.[123]

In the end, the single most attractive feature of the Peircean position on basic knowledge is that it preserves the distinction between basic and non-basic knowledge, and retains the foundational metaphor without being forced to characterize basic knowledge in terms of unimpeachable certainties. Other philosophers, in their haste to eschew foundational certainties, have either denied the foundational metaphor altogether or have characterized basic propositions as mere conventions or inference tickets. Neither move is very desirable since they both achieve the avoidance of foundational certainty only by denying in the end the distinction between basic and non-basic knowledge. What Peirce has shown, I think, is that it is not necessary to reject this distinction simply to avoid foundational certainty. Moreover, if it be urged that the Peircean position gains its plausibility only under some form of coherence theory of truth, well, of course, that is true. But of itself this does not show that Peirce is wrong. It simply raises the question of the adequacy of Peirce's coherence theory of truth. Besides, if Peirce's position can be thought wrong simply because it entails a coherence theory of truth, then so too would be the positions of those who reject the foundational metaphor outright or characterize basic propositions in terms of conventions or inference tickets since these also entail a coherence theory of truth if there is to be any real knowledge at all this side of eternity. And this leaves the Peircean sitting very pretty if Peirce's theory of truth should turn out to be right.

VI. SUMMARY REMARKS ON PEIRCE'S EPISTEMOLOGY

There are three general impressions that should emerge from this discussion. The first is that the whole of Peirce's epistemology is largely a systematic development of the doctrine of synechism. If synechism is false, then so too is the justification provided for the indeterminacy of meaning which leads logically to wholesale fallibilism which in turn provides the conceptual foundation of his unique views on the nature and status of truth, knowledge and common sense beliefs. It is regrettable that even among American philosophers Peirce is usually thought to be a seminal thinker and anything but systematic. As a matter of fact, the truth of the matter seems to be that the whole of his epistemology (and metaphysics as well) will fall if the arguments which he provided in defense of his commitment to a synechistic universe fall. Those arguments, presented above, deserve more attention but seem to me compelling.[124]

The second impression is that Peirce has left us with a theory of knowledge which, if synechism is true, represents a unique and defensible synthesis of science and common sense. Rigorously empirical in its demand for truth, the theory does not repudiate what we want to accept most, namely, the validity of our common sense (MS 291 (p. 41)). Indeed, the theory not only specifies the domain of both common sense and science, but also the necessity for each, the limitation of each and the way in which they relate to one another.

Finally, the third impression we are left with is that Peirce pretty much failed to provide us with convincing reasons for thinking that scientific inquiry will continue indefinitely. And so he failed to avoid idealism since he did not establish the existence of the real as the object of the final opinion because he did not establish that the final opinion will come. And he did not establish that the final opinion will come because he did not establish what is necessary for this view, namely that science will go on indefinitely. I suspect that Peirce himself realized that his arguments for the indefinite continuation of science were weak;

and that this may be the reason why he sometimes defined truth as the product of the final opinion which the scientific community *would* reach if inquiry were to continue indefinitely. Moreover, it would also account for his later temptation to argue that belief that the final opinion will come reduces to the sentiment of hope, which sentiment reduces to an indispensable condition for human rationality.[125]

By the same token, however, I have been urging that there are good reasons for thinking that science will go on indefinitely and that if this is so, we can provide what Peirce needed to avoid idealism. In other words, I think there is a strong argument to the effect that although Peirce failed to successfully defend the thesis that science will continue indefinitely, the thesis is pre-eminently defensible. And if the considerations adduced above succeed in showing that science will continue indefinitely, I do not see how we can avoid the conclusion that Peirce's epistemology is in the main correct although he did not defend it as strenuously as he should have.

What I find particularly attractive about Peirce's epistemology, as herein reconstructed, is that it provides a healthy antidote to current forms of idealism in the recent empiricist tradition. Some empiricists (among whom we can number Quine, Goodman and Putnam[126]) are committed to the view that unto eternity there will be competing alternative theories, no one better in principle than the other; and hence what the real world is can never be known. This throwback to *Der Ding an Sich* carries with it the view that the real world is a world well lost, that truth in the end is a man-made product. That this sort of idealism hinges on the view that unto eternity there will not be any final theory explaining the world better than any other is obvious. If, however, Peirce is right, if, that is, science will terminate in some final theory explaining the world better than all conceivable others, then the basic reason for the idealism in question will be undermined. If Peirce's theory is not correct, it is by no means obviously wrong; and this in itself, given the status of contemporary empiricism, more than justifies a much more serious consideration of Peirce's theory than has generally been thought necessary. Naturally, a good deal more can be said here. For the moment, however, let us turn to a more detailed discussion of the ways in which Peirce defended his belief in the existence of an external world. Later on, after discussing his theory of perception, we shall examine views to the effect that Peirce was also an idealist.

NOTES

1. 5.374–5. See also MS 596 (pp. 3ff); MS 753 (pp. 1ff); MS 828 (Logic I ii, P. 1). Throughout the following we will conform to the standard method of citing references from *The Collected Papers of Charles Sanders Peirce*, ed. by C. Hartshorne and P. Weiss (vls. 1–6) and A. W. Burks (vls. 7–8) (Cambridge, Harvard University Press, 1931, 1935, 1958). Thus, for example, Volume One, paragraph 355 would read 1.355. Also, when referring to Peirce's unpublished papers, I shall simply refer to the manuscript number and place an MS in front of the number. Hence, references to the unpublished papers will be preceded by an MS and followed by the number and page (if numbered) of the unpublished paper. For example, MS 390 (p. 4), refers to page 4 of the unpublished paper numbered 390. The unpublished papers are available on a microfilm edition and can be obtained from the Widener Library at Harvard University, Cambridge, Mass.

2. In the following discussion (and elsewhere) I have cited sections from Peirce's essays "The Fixation of Belief" and "How to Make Our Ideas Clear" which, while they are initially written in 1877 and 1878 respectively, were revised in 1893. I have cited from the revised versions as they appear in the *Collected Papers*. Presumably, the substance of these essays as they appear in the *Collected Papers* reflect his mature opinion on the topics there discussed.

3. See MS 682 (p. 11). The methodological behaviorist insists that the only subject matter of psychology is human bodily behavior, but he need not demand that there are no mental states. Such a demand, when combined with methodological behaviorism, constitutes an instance of analytical behaviorism, which, as a form of reductive materialism, is inconsistent with mind–body dualism. On this point see Cornman and Lehrer, *Philosophical Problems and Arguments: An Introduction* (New York: Macmillan Company, 1968), p. 243. These observations, however, are not intended, and should not be understood to prejudice the case against Peirce's being a monist on the mind–body problem. Indeed, it may well be argued that, in the last analysis, Peirce's apparent dualism dissolved into an idealistic monism asserting that matter (body) is simply a form of mind. More on this in Chapter IV below.

4. See also MS 1 (D.M. 43 Draft 4). On Peirce's dispositional analysis of belief see also Israel Scheffler's *The Conditions of Knowledge: An Introduction to Epistemology and Education* (Glenview, Illinois: Scott, Foresman and Company, 1965), p. 89. See also 5.27–8.

5. See pp. 13ff below.

6. On the well-known objections to *analytical behaviorism*, see Cornman and Lehrer, *Philosophical Problems and Arguments, An Introduction*, pp. 249–53.

7. See R. M. Chisholm's *Preceiving* (Ithaca, New York: Cornell University Press, 1957), pp. 168–73.

8. 5.370ff; 5.400; 5.480; MS 596 (pp. 12ff).

9. 5.417; 5.373; 5.398; 5.371 and 5.510.

10. 5.443. See also MS 280 (p. 82); L75; MS 300 (p. 16); 5.512; 5.498; 5.589; 5.51 and 5.57–8.

11. See 7.186; 5.158; MS 362; MS 366.

12. 5.375. See also 5.394; 5.400; 6.485; 5.372–5; 2.173; 2.167; 5.198; 5.377; 2.160 and 5.197.

13. 5.372 n. 2; 2.176–7 and 8.211.

14. Insert mine.

15. 5.563–4. See also 2.4–5; 4.523; 3.430; 5.587; and 8.209. Moreover, that the true is not simply that which it pleases us to believe (in the sense that belief need not be established by scientific method) see 5.377 and note 1.

16. In MS 473 (p. 26), after noting that induction cannot guarantee the truth of its conclusion, Peirce goes on to say of induction:

"And yet, it has to conclude that a hypothesis is true because certain predictions based upon it have been verified. Under what modification is it warranted in asserting that? Without exhausting the inexhaustible future, it certainly cannot be justified in asserting that absolutely. It can, however, assert this subject to such modification as further quasi-experimentation may make."

And in MS 473 (p. 40) he asserts that we are warranted in accepting inductive conclusions as true even though there is no entailment relationship between the evidence and the conclusion.

Apart from providing (as we shall see) good evidence for the view that Peirce was committed to at least two different characteristics of the nature of truth, these texts sustain the view that beliefs established by inquiry are to be considered true. See also MS 426 (Logic II, p. 51); MS 362; MS 366; MS 473 (p. 40); MS 502 (p. 1); more on this below.

17. *From a Logical Point of View* (New York: Harper and Row, 1961), pp. 44–5.

18. See the footnote to 5.283, where Peirce argues that the *a priori* philosophers (especially Descartes) are those who deal in figments. See also MS 333 (pp. 5ff assorted pages); MS 407; MS 628 (p. 1N).

19. 5.384 and 5.406.

20. See 3.430.

21. Bertrand Russell, "Dewey's New Logic," *The Philosophy of John Dewey*, ed. Paul Schilpp, p. 149 (New York, Tudor Publishing Company, 1939). Now published by the Open Court Publishing Company, La Salle, Illinois.

22. In his book, *The Origins of Pragmatism* (San Francisco, Calif.: Freeman, Cooper, and Company, 1967), Professor A. J. Ayer claims that Peirce persistently rejected the thesis that the truth of a proposition consists in its being believed. Professor Ayer, however, gives no textual evidence to support his claim. His main reason for claiming this is that "firmly believing a proposition is consistent with that proposition being false," and hence Peirce could not have made such a mistake. What Professor Ayer overlooks is that for Peirce, belief is not simply a mental state, characterized by feeling sure about a proposition. Belief (as the result of Inquiry) is a habit of activity which allows one to expedite one's dealings with experience as the result of scientific inquiry, and hence, believing a proposition as a result of Inquiry is sufficient for the truth of the proposition. The proposition may turn out to be false, but this is a contingency which, for Peirce, affects all propositions firmly believed because of the fallible nature of all knowledge. Nor, as we shall see, does this imply that truth is not a necessary condition for knowledge. Had Professor Ayer read Peirce somewhat more closely he would not have foisted upon Peirce a purely mentalist notion of belief which (as Ayer rightly points out), entails the falsity of the thesis that firmly believing a proposition is sufficient for its truth. Given Peirce's notion of belief, there is no distinction between what is true and what we firmly believe to be true as the result of inquiry, although what we firmly believe to be true as the result of inquiry may turn out to be false (5.98). On this point, see also 7.335 and 5.510.

23. See pp. 80ff below.

24. 5.373; see also 8.270.

25. 5.402 (revised for publication in 1902). See also 5.2; 5.9; 5.18; 5.427; MS 327.

26. See 5.18; 4.453; 5.480–3; 3.440; 3.472; 4.572; 8.194–5; 8.359–61; 2.330; 3.440; MS 817 (p. 3).

27. It is important to note that initially (as noted in 5.18 and suggested in 2.330), Peirce had insisted that the meaning of any positive assertion consists in a corresponding conditional, the antecedent of which is of the form "If you do x, then etc." rather than "If you *were* to do x, then etc." The initial formulation led Peirce to the following question: suppose a diamond crystallized in the middle of the earth and was accidentally consumed by fire before one could verify that it was hard. Was

that diamond *really* hard? Peirce initially answered the question by saying that it was simply a matter of linguistic convenience to say that the diamond was really hard (5.403). Much later, however, he changed his mind on this question and argued that the hardness of the diamond does not accrue to it in virtue of the actual employment of the experimental method. Indeed, to say that a diamond is hard, is to say that if one *were* to perform certain operations, then certain sensible results *would* ensue (5.457). See also 5.480–2; 8.380–4; 1.420; 6.327; 8.216; 4.546; 4.580ff; 8.208; 5.453; 8.359–61; 5.457; MS 289 (p. 11).

28. 2.330 This example was put forth before the problem of the diamond was solved. See also 5.529.

29. 5.553. See also 5.467; 2.407 n. 1; 5.412.

30. Peirce identified the concept of law with the concept of habit. The laws of the universe are the habits which the universe takes on. Hence if the meaning of any proposition is fundamentally a statement of the laws which govern and account for the properties of objects, then it would follow that what a proposition means is simply what habits it involves (5.400). See also 5.18; 2.148; MS 289 (p. 4).

31. See 5.491 and MS 318. In his book, *The Development of Peirce's Philosophy*, Professor Murphey argues (as against Buchler and Gentry), that the logical interpretant *cannot* be the meaning of any proposition; rather the meaning of any proposition is what the logical interpretant expresses, namely, the law or habit which the adoption of the given statement as a belief would imply (pp. 315ff). Actually, however, the truth of the matter seems to be that for Peirce, the meaning of a proposition is expressed by a set of conditional statements which express a law so that ultimately the meaning of a proposition derives from the existence of laws (habits). Meaning for Peirce is not law; rather law is the foundation of meaning or accounts for the existence of meaningful propositions. 'Meaning' is a property of utterances (5.427).

32. On the indeterminacy of meaning see also 2.428; 1.549; 2.357; 5.569; 6.494; 5.505–6; 1.339; 2.646; 8.208; 6.496; 5.157; 5.183; 5.480; 5.447–8; 5.554; MS 432 (Logic IV, p. 193); MS 9 (p. 5).

33. For a very interesting defense of the view that conceptual inexactness is a necessary feature of empirical concepts. See R. G. Swinburn's "Vagueness, Inexactness and Imecision," in *The British Journal for the Philosophy of Science*, XIX, No. 4. See also the opposing view as expressed Marvin Kohl in "Bertrand Russell on Vagueness," *Australasian Journal of Philosophy* (May, 1969), pp. 31ff. Furthermore, it should be noted that, for Peirce, it is not the case that a term is vague because the *extent* of its application is essentially doubtful.

34. 1.175; 3.93ff; MS 886; MS 949 (pp. 2ff); MS 950. See also M. G. Murphey's *The Development of Peirce's Philosophy* (Cambridge: Harvard University Press, 1963), last chapter.

35. For reasons which cannot be discussed here, I would add, however, that Peirce's views on the nature of universals and numbers did not incline him to construing either as real platonic abstract entities. See Chapter V below.

Incidentally, it has been argued that Peirce's commitment to a belief in abstract entities is inconsistent with his obvious espousal of naturalism, and that this bespeaks an unfortunate inconsistency which runs throughout his philosophical world-view (see T. Goudge's *The Thought of Charles Sanders Peirce*. Toronto: University of Toronto Press, 1950). It can be argued, however, that this criticism assumes that naturalism, by definition, is a doctrine which asserts that only physical objects exist; and while this may be true for many naturalists, it seems clear that Peirce's naturalism is not to be construed in this way. Rather it is the thesis that only with the employment of the method of the natural sciences can we determine the truth of what is asserted to exist. On this latter contrual of naturalism, if it can be argued, as Peirce did, that belief in the existence of abstract entities can have conceivable practical or observable effects which would verify the belief, then there is no reason to assume that naturalism implies repudiating an ontology of abstract entities.

36. The second branch is *Critic*, which classifies arguments and determines the validity and degree of force of each kind. And the third branch is *Methodeutic*, which studies the method that ought to be pursued in the investigation, in the exposition, and in the application of truth (1.191).

37. For other definitions of the sign see 2.92; 2.303; 8.332; MS 278 (p. 10); see also Volume IV of the *Collected Papers* and MS 7 (pp. 14ff); MS 510 (p. 14); MS 142; MS 278a (p. 10); MS 483 (pp. 105ff); MS 284 (p. 59); MS 293 (p. 18); MS 293 (p. 76); MS 478 (p. 45).

38. Pointing fingers, photographs of existing objects and personal pronouns are also examples of the index.

39. See also 1.558.

40. See also 4.531; 2.315; 2.321; 2.292; 4.536; 2.235 n.

41. See MS 949 (pp. 2ff).

42. See also 2.203; 4.536; 5.475.

43. 2.292; 8.332.

44. 8.332ff.

45. 8.184; MS 318.

46. For a fuller discussion of these difficulties and the participants involved see Douglas Greenlee's *Peirce's Concept of Sign* (The Hague: Mouton, 1973); John Fitzgerald's *Peirce's Theory of Signs as Foundation for Pragmatism* (The Hague: Mouton, 1966); M. G. Murphey's *The Development of Peirce's Philosophy* (Cambridge: Harvard University Press, 1961), p. 314ff, and *The Transactions of the Charles S. Peirce Society: A Quarterly Journal in American Philosophy* (Spring 1976).

47. "The Pragmatist's Place in Empiricism". At present this paper is unpublished but was read at a Symposium on Pragmatism at the University of South Carolina in 1975. In referring to this essay I am referring to a copy of the paper obtained at the Colloquium. The proceedings of the Symposium will soon be published by the University of South Carolina and will include Quine's paper.

48. P. 12. Quine also argues that the limit theory of truth is distinctive of Peirce and could perhaps best be construed anthropocentrically as a sort of idealism or social Protagoreanism, representing scientific method as dictating to reality.

49. See 2.511 n. 1; 2.639; 2.640; 2.511 n.; 5.203; 5.198; 5.402 n. 2 and 5.423.

50. Curiously enough, Quine frequently identifies *verificationism* as a view about the meaning of sentences, a view which he contrasts with *holism*. So construed, of course, *verificationism* is a doctrine Quine rejects in favor of *holism*. But when he identifies it as a theory about sentence meaning, a theory which allows one to purge some (but not all) reference to abstract entities, it is not a doctrine which he rejects; and I am arguing that if, as Quine urges, *verificationism* has the virtue of supporting the nominalist's stance, it could only achieve that end only if *narrow verificationism*, as I have construed it, is true. And this is to say that Quine's endorsement of the virtue of *verificationism* is inconsistent with his adopting an ontology that allows for belief in *any* abstract entities. Presumably, these considerations will dispell the charitable suggestion that there is nothing at all inconsistent with adopting verificationism as a technique for purging reference to some abstract entities and countenancing an ontology that allows for belief in abstract entities.

51. "Indeterminacy of Translation and the Underdetermination of the Theory of Nature," *Dialectica*, vol. 27, no. 3–4 (1973), pp. 289–301.

52. 5.426; 5.467; 7.78; 5.424; 5.506; 2.762; 2.407ff; 2.637; 2.709; 2.717; 2.732. In arguing, as we have, that the pragmatic maxim is a criterion for the meaning of sentences, it need not be thought that the adoption of the pragmatic maxim is inconsistent with the adoption of holism. Holism, I take it, is *not* the view that *sentences* do not have meaning; rather, it is the view that the meaning of the

sentence is issued in terms of the conditions for the whole theory in which the sentence is embedded.

53. For a detailed examination of Peirce's theory of truth and various objections against it, see my "Fallibilism and the Ultimate Irreversible Opinion," *The American Philosophical Quarterly Monograph*, vol. 9, 1975, pp. 33–54, and "Science and Idealism," *Philosophy of Science*, vol. 40, no. 2, June 1973, pp. 242–54.

54. 7.419; 1.171–2; 7.566ff; 6.13; 6.553ff; 5.296ff; 1.103ff and 7.95.

55. See 2.77; ME 334 E2; 5.567–9; 7.566.

56. See also 2.81; 1.145; 1.149; MS 334 E2; MS 426 (Logic II, p. 71): MS 425 (Logic 86).

57. 2.447; 1.140; 2.693; 4.237; 4.478; 4.531; 5.376 n. 2, n. 1; 1.630; 7.108; 1.248; 2.216; 2.30; MS 16 (p. 7); MS 334 E2; MS 606 (Liy 28).

58. For other texts bearing on Peirce's rejection of the analytic–synthetic distinction, see 5.187; 2.192; 2.176; 2.162; 2.171ff; 3.527; 4.71; 2.173; 2.158; 1.633; 1.661; 2.151; 2.192; 5.506; 5.560; 5.183; 5.480; 4.447; 6.496; 5.554; 4.487; 1.441ff MS 955 (p. 4); MS 200 (MME 82); MS 200 (MME 96); MS 1 (p. 4); MS 355.

59. Quine, Willard Van Orman, "Whither Physical Objects" in Cohen, Feyerabend, and Wartofsky (eds.), *Essays in Memory of Imre Lakatos*. Dordrecht: D. Reidel, 1976, pp. 303–10.

60. "Quine in Perspective," *The Journal of Philosophy*, vol. lxix, no. 1 (Jan. 13, 1972), pp. 5–14.

61. "The Pragmatist's Place in Empiricism," p. 21.

62. "Epistemology Naturalized" in *Empirical Knowledge*, ed. by Chisholm and Swartz (New York: Prentice-Hall, 1972).

63. "The Origins of the Indeterminacy Thesis," *The Journal of Philosophy*, vol. lxii, no. 62 (1975), pp. 370ff.

64. "Quine vs. Peirce," *Dialectica*, vol. 30, no. 1 (1976), pp. 7–8.

65. We need not suppose that these considerations militate against the holism attributed to Peirce on page 38ff above. For while one needn't take negative instances as disconfirming or falsifying a proposition, still, *ordinarily*, negative instances will count as falsifying the proposition just as the truth of a proposition requires that what is virtually predicts "should *ordinarily* be fulfilled" (8.192; emphasis not mine).

66. Peirce had a good deal to say about the nature and problems of probability theory. Much of what he said in this regard is not relevant to our present purposes; but the reader should consult "Peirce on Probability" by E. H. Madden in *Studies in the Philosophy of Charles Sanders Peirce*, Series II, eds. Moore and Robin (Amherst, Mass: University of Mass Press, 1964) pp. 122ff. Also in the same volume see "Peirce's Two Theories of Probability" by A. Burks. See also MS 703 (Notes Art. III, p. 16); MS 356[R].

67. See 3.527; 4.71; 2.173; 1.633; 1.661; 2.151; 2.192; 5.506; 2.158; 5.560; 5.183; 5.480; 5.447; 6.496; 5.554; 1.441ff; MS 955 (p. 4); MS 200 (MME 82); MS 200 (MME 96); MS 1 (p. 4); MS 335; MS 661 (AR 114); MS 703 (notes, Art. III 11).

68. 7.119.

69. 1.171–2.

70. 7.566ff; 6.13; 6.553ff; 6.296ff; 1.103ff and 7.95.

71. See also 2.192 and 2.216.

72. See also 1.140; 2.693; 4.237; 4.478; 4.531; 5.376, n. 2, n. 1; 2.447; 1.630; 7.108; 1.248; 2.216; 2.30; MS 16 (p. 7); MS 334 E2; MS 426 (Logic II, p. 71); MS 606 (Liy 28); MS 425 (Logic 86).

73. See Lewis's treatment on the pragmatic conception of the *a priori* in *Mind and the World-Order* (New York: Dover Publications, Inc., 1956), pp. 230–74. See also Peirce's claim that the analytic-synthetic distinction is not very clear (5.187) and 2.192; 2.176; 2.162; and 2.173.

74. This familiar argument is offered by (among many others) Arne Naess in

Scepticism, New York: Humanities Press, 1969, p. 138, footnote 3. See also Austin's "Other Minds."

75. 7.495; 3.374; 2.70; 2.222; MS 279; MS 425 (logic 97).

76. 2.86; 2.532; 7.55; 1.232.

77. This is another way of saying that truth is a matter of warranted assertibility or that the predicate 'is true' as it applies to sentences means 'warrantly assertible relative to our current conceptual framework.' Because there is no entailment relationship between propositions warrantedly assertible and truth understood in terms of word–world relationship of correspondence, in arguing (as I will) that Peirce endorses (A), I shall therefore be ascribing to Peirce a coherence theory of truth although that is only half of Peirce's theory of truth.

Also, I realize that the concept of 'conceptual framework' is vague and that there are some who will consider it hopelessly vague. To forestall any difficulties that may arise in this regard, let it be understood that by 'conceptual framework' I will mean simply 'theory.' Although this is not quite correct (since I think theories are generated *from* conceptual frameworks) it will suffice for present intents and purposes.

78. Given this, 'I know that p' would not offer a guarantee which saying 'but I may be mistaken' withdraws. It would merely tell us what sort of a guarantee is being offered by 'I know that p'; namely, that p is true and p's being true consists in the fact that assertion (or inscription) of p is fully authorized by the rules of confirmation in our present conceptual framework which can be replaced by a future framework in which the inscription of p may not be authorized. The value of endorsing (A), (B) and (C) is that it allows the fallibilist to say 'I know that p but I may be mistaken' without inconsistently implying that p is true and possibly it isn't. No one can say 'I know that p but I may be mistaken' if so saying amounts to asserting that p is true and possibly it isn't. But, given the above assumptions, the sense in which the fallibilist may be mistaken in what he knows does not at all impugn the truth of what he knows.

79. 1.578; 2.652; 2.135; 7.659; 8.144; 5.549; 8.126.

80. MS 409 (p. 182).

81. There is, however, a view to the effect that Peirce defined truth and knowledge in terms of an ideal limit which inquiry asymptotically approaches as a mathematical limit. The inadequacy of this view is demonstrated below on pp. 62ff.

82. This, as previously noted, is what I mean when I say that Peirce was committed to the view that the predicate 'is true' designates a word–word relationship of semantic authorization in addition to the view that the predicate designates a word–world relationship of correspondence.

83. Incidentally, when Peirce characterizes science in this way he usually makes it clear that in this regard he is characterizing science as an activity (and not as a body of beliefs) which feeds on dissatisfaction with existing knowledge (MS 965 (p. 1); MS 1269 (p. 7); 5 50). Hence the rationale for his claim that inductive conclusions are not quite true, a claim which means, I believe, that inductive conclusions needn't be thought to represent what will be thought in the final opinion wherein what is warrantedly assertible bespeaks a relationship of correspondence between language and the world. Still, for all that, they can still be true inasmuch as they are warrantedly assertible relative to one's current conceptual framework. It's hard to see how we can reconcile Peirce's frequent claims to the effect that inductive conclusions are true and provide us with knowledge (MS 473 (p. 26); MS 473 (p. 40); MS 430 (Logic III, p. 8); MS 502 (p. 1); MS 931 (p. 25); MS 1148 (p. 6) and his equally frequent claims to the effect that they are not quite true and do not provide us with knowledge (MS 841 (p. 48); MS 409 (p. 182); MS 345; MS 764 (p. 46); MS 345; MS 473 (pp. 36 and 39)); unless we suppose that he was committed to two different but mutually consistent characterizations of 'true' and 'knows'. And the evidence (to be stated forthwith) suggests strongly that he was so committed.

84. Peirce's rejection of the doctrine of the "mutability" of truth in 6.486 I take to be a rejection not of the view that what is true today may not be true tomorrow but rather of the view that what is true today may not be true tomorrow *and* there may never be an ultimate irreversible opinion on any matter. In other words, Peirce rejected the view that would not allow for a final irreversible opinion and not the view that what is true today may not be true tomorrow. In the absence of what Peirce clearly meant by the doctrine on the 'mutability' of truth, this is the only reading consistent with the rest of what he said.

85. Roughly, the intuitive point here is that if we must consider the truth value assigned to any proposition in principle subject to revision, then we cannot infer from a proposition's being properly assigned 'is true' that the proposition necessarily describes a non-linguistic state of affairs. But that is precisely what we must infer if 'is true' means any variant of 'corresponds with the facts.' In other words, if it is a *conceptual* matter that 'is true' means 'corresponds with the facts,' then the satisfaction of the conditions which allow for the proper application of the predicate 'is true' should *entail*, as a conceptual truth, that the proposition assigned 'is true' accurately describes the non-linguistic facts. But if the truth value assigned is in principle subject to revision, then, barring changes in the world, there is no entailment between a proposition's being true and its describing the facts. Hence where truth–value revision is in order, we need not think that the proper application of the predicate 'is true' *designates* a word–world relationship of correspondence; and so, 'is true' must mean 'warranted assertibility' (designating rather a word–word relationship of semantic authorization) if the predicate is to admit of instantiation in our language.

86. As H. S. Thayer has recently pointed out in his book, *Meaning and Action* (New York: Bobbs-Merrill, 1968), pp. 107ff, the 'law of large numbers' was initially Bernoulli's theorem (in *Ars Conjectandi*, 1713) and can be restated in the following way: 'Let p be the probability of the occurrence of some event E in a single trial (such as a coin landing heads when tossed). Now in a series of trials Tr, in which E may or may not occur, the most probable proportion, or frequency of occurrences of E to the total number of Tr (i.e. $E/E+Tr$), is p. Moreover, the probability of the frequency of E's deviating from p will be less than any small positive number e, no matter how small e may be, provided that the number of trials is large. As the number of Tr is increased, the probability of the frequency of E deviating from p by less than e increases.'

87. 8.12; 2.769; 2.729 and 2.693.

88. Israel Scheffler, *Conditions of Knowledge* (Glenview, Ill.: Scott, Foresman and Company, 1965), pp. 42–3.

89. Willard Van Orman Quine, *Word and Object* (New York: M.I.T. Press 1960), p. 23.

90. Bertrand Russell, "Dewey's New Logic," *The Philosophy of John Dewey*, ed. Paul Schilpp, pp. 143–56.

91. Quine is also opposed to Peirce's definition of truth because the definition apparently assumes a final organon of scientific method and appeals to an infinite process. In the interest of completeness, these observations are equally unacceptable. Peirce did not assume a final organon of scientific method. Rather, he *argued* that the inductive method could not fail as a legitimate source of knowledge in any conceivable universe (5.435). Secondly, Peirce argued (as we shall see) that science will continue indefinitely.

92. See p. 91ff below where Bruce Aune's endorsement of the same view is discussed in another context.

93. See 2.150 and 5.494.

94. For a recent and provocative defense of the thesis that there is no good reason for believing that there will always be competing alternative theories purporting to systematize our surface irritations. See William Kneale's "Scientific Revolutions Forever?" in *The British Journal for the Philosophy of Science*, XIX, No. 1 (1968).

95. "Scientific Revolutions Forever?", *The British Journal for the Philosophy of Science*, 19 (1967), pp. 27ff.

96. *Scientific Progress* (Basil Blackwell, 1978).

97. This argument is also developed by Rescher in his book *Peirce's Philosophy of Science* (Notre Dame Press, 1978).

98. Kant never proved it either; for he made his point in terms of a rhetorical question. He never in fact established that there will always be questions to be answered. See *Prolegomena To Any Future Metaphysics* (1783), section 57.

99. It should be noted that appeal to the 'Kant–Proliferation Effect' could sustain eternal revolutions in science if no less than one question were raised with *every* question answered.

100. In *Peirce's Philosophy of Science* (Notre Dame Press, 1978), pp. 25ff, and in other publications, Rescher has criticized Peirce for adopting the mistaken view that scientific progress proceeds by way of *cumulative accretion*—like the growth of a coral reef. I would urge, however, that while Peirce claimed that science progresses steadily by feeding on previous lessons (7.88; 7.51), this should not be construed as a process of cumulative accretion similar to the growth of a coral reef. Indeed, Peirce claimed that thought advances and grows by violent breakup of habits (7.267; 2.159; 1.174; 2.770; 6.311; 7.77; 7.88) and that science advances by great revolutions (5.587; 1.107; 1.122; 6.311; 2.770; 2.769; 2.157; 2.97; 2.150; MS 953 (pp. 5 and 6). Peirce even spent a good deal of time refuting the sort of incremental view Rescher attributes (questionably citing 2.157 as supportive evidence) to Peirce (6.311; 2.159; 6.313; 1.138; 1.174; 2.664; 5.376 no. 2, n. 2; MS 427 (p. 46, Logic II ii); MS 955 (p. 37); MS 956 (p. 2); MS 959 (p. 19)).

101. Phillip Kitcher, "The Plight of the Platonist," *Nous* (May 1978).

102. See, for example, Adolf Grunbaum's "Can a Theory Answer more Questions than One of its Rivals," *British Journal for the Philosophy of Science* (vol. 27, 1976), pp. 1–22.

103. L. Laudan, "Two Dogmas of Methodology," *Philosophy of Science* (vol. 43, no. 4, Dec. 1976), pp. 585–97. See also his *Progress and its Problems* (Berkeley: University of California Press, 1978).

104. For a more detailed discussion of the view that scientific inquiry pursued indefinitely will terminate in a single theoretical framework better than all conceivable others, and that there is some evidence for believing that science will continue forever, see my "Science and Idealism," *Philosophy of Science* (June 1973).

105. As against the view that science will continue indefinitely, most physicists now claim that it is only a matter of time until the sun burns out thereby ending the possibility of indefinite survival on our planet and on all other planets in our solar systems. But this shouldn't be thought to imply that science will not continue indefinitely; for it seems likely that, before the Cassandrian prediction comes to pass, we will have mastered the skill of interstellar travel. Indeed, depending on which physicists one may consult, there is every reason to suppose that we are on the threshold of interstellar travel. So, there is as much reason to think the species will survive the eclipse of our sun as there is that the sun will burn out.

Incidentally, Peirce seems to have envisaged the substance of such an objection when he argued that although the human race will be extirpated, science will continue on in the hands of vastly more intelligent creatures who inhabit other planets and who will 'pick up' our results (5.409; 5.587; 8.43; MS 596 (L 29)). For Peirce, rational life in this universe will never cease, although it is certain that human life will come to an end. Curiously enough, however, Peirce had little by way of solid evidence for any of these claims. Saying that it is virtually certain that the human race will extirpate itself because "there is acertain chance of it happening every day (8.43)," overlooks the fact that, inductively speaking, the evidence supports the opposite view. Moreover, how does Peirce *know* that other planets are inhabited by creatures vastly more intelligent than we are? And even if he knew the latter, why would such creatures (being vastly more intelligent than we are) have any need to 'pick up' *(sic)* the body of science after we are gone? Indeed, Peirce's reasons for thinking science will go on indefinitely are sufficiently weak and *ad hoc* to render them likely reasons why Peirce sometimes wanted (and in the end came) to argue that belief in the indefinite continuation of science (and the reaching of the final opinion) reduces to the sentiment of hope, which sentiment reduces to an indispensable condition for human rationality. And it might also account for Peirce's claim (MS 682 (p. 17)), that his earlier belief (MS 596 (L 29)) that a superior race will 'pick up' the results of our science was a mere dream. More on this later.

106. *Posterior Analytics*, Book 1, Chapter 1–3 in *The Oxford Translation of Aristotle* (Cambridge: Clarendon Press, 1958).

107. See also MS 425 (Logic 87); MS 473 (p. 8 and p. 24); MS 628 (p. 5).

108. See for example C. I. Lewis, *An Analysis of Knowledge and Valuation* (LaSalle: Open Court, 1946), Chapter II.

109. Wilfrid Sellars, *Science, Perception and Reality* (London: Routledge and Kegan Paul, 1963), p. 170.

110. K. Popper, *The Logic of Scientific Discovery* (New York: Harper and Row, 1959), Chpater 5; H. H. Price, *Truth and Corrigibility* (Oxford: Clarendon Press, 1936).

111. See also 8.91; 5.445; 6.500; 5.265; MS 362; MS 366.

112. See also 5.419; MS 1 (p. 9); MS 309 (p. 37); MS 606 (Liy 26).

113. 5.392; 5.416 and 5.525.

114. 5.416.

115. 5.443.

116. See 5.505; 5.52 and 5.603.

117. 6.498. See also 5.419.

118. I think this is the argument that Peirce was attempting to state against Wundt in 5.521. It should also be noted that in 5.522 of Peirce argues for the acceptability of common sense on the grounds of the general reliability of instinct. In so doing, he maintains that science, without being aware of it, virtually presupposes a host of common sense propositions and would not be able to survive if it did not.

119. D. M. Armstrong, *Belief Truth and Knowledge* (Cambridge: Cambridge University Press, 1973), pp. 155–6.

120. Bruce Aune, "Two Theories of Scientific Knowledge," *Critica* (Vol. 5, #13, 1971), pp. 15–16.

121. See N. Rescher, *The Coherence Theory of Truth* (Oxford: Oxford University Press, 1973), pp. 27ff.

122. B. Russell, *The Problems of Philosophy* (London: Home University Library, 1912), p. 191.

123. See pp. 67–9 above.

124. See MS 949 (p. 2ff); MS 950. For an interesting defense of Peirce's synechism as a necessary condition for any valid philosophy of science, see E. C. Moore's "On the World as General," *The Transactions of the Charles S. Peirce Society: A Quarterly Journal in American Philosophy* (Spring 1968) and also J. Aronson's "Connections: A Defense of Peirce's Category of Thirdness," also in the same journal (Summer 1969).

125. It is sometimes suggested that late in life Peirce gave up the idea that scientific inquiry *will* answer any answerable question and instead opted for the view that we can only hope that science will answer any answerable question. However, textual considerations indicate that Peirce seemed to be torn between the two views. In the following texts (all of which were written after 1890 and ranging up to 1903) Peirce holds out for the view that we can only *hope* that science will answer the answerable question: 8.113 (1900); 8.153 (c. 1902); 3.432 (1896); 2.114 (1902); 5.161 (1903); 5.608 (1900); 6.610 (1893) and 2.654. But, by the same token, in the following texts (all of which were written after 1890 and range up to 1906) Peirce asserts the view that science *will* come to answer any answerable question: 7.78

(1900); 8.127 (1902); 4.547 (1906); 2.269 (1897); 5.170 (1903); 5.384 (1903); 5.430 (1905); 5.420 (1905); 5.494 (1906); 5.608 (1900).

Hence, it would appear that Peirce vacillated on this item and (as just suggested) I suspect that the ambivalence was rooted in his realization that his arguments for the indefinite continuation of science were weak. In the end, however, I think he came to the view (as noted above) that our belief that science *will* answer the answerable question is a necessary condition for hoping we will be successful is an indispensable condition for being rational. But, for the reasons mentioned above, this final position did not provide Peirce with what he needed.

126. See Quine's "On Empirically Equivalent Systems of the World" and Goodman's "Words, Works, Worlds" in *Erkenntnis* (vol. 9, May 1975). See also H. Putnam's 1976 APA Presidential Address "Realism and Reason" in *The Proceedings of the American Philosophical Association* (vol. 50, August 1977).

Chapter II

Peirce's Epistemological Realism

I. INTRODUCTION

In addition to justifying his belief in the existence of an external world, an epistemological realist must also specify an acceptable criterion for determining the externality of any perceived object. Any commitment to epistemological realism which fails to provide such a criterion effectively renders the external world unknowable; and presumably the epistemological realist will not want to defend the claim that his external world is unknowable or incapable of being distinguished from those mental objects not external in origin.

Fortunately, Peirce was aware of the necessity to provide *both* a justification for belief in the existence of an external world *and* criteria for determining which objects of our experience fall into the class of external objects. In this chapter I shall reconstruct and partially defend Peirce's justification for the belief in the existence of an external world. I say 'partially' because it would be pretentious to think that this defense of the thesis could be anything but open-ended. And this will become obvious as we progress. In the end I shall discuss and evaluate Peirce's criteria (tests) for externality.

II. ARGUMENTS FOR THE EXISTENCE OF AN EXTERNAL WORLD

In his essay "The Fixation of Belief," after insisting that the method of science is the only objective method for the determination of truth within the context of inquiry, Peirce said:

> Such is the method of science. Its fundamental hypothesis, restated in more familiar language is this: There are real things whose characters are entirely independent of our opinions about them; these reals affect our senses according to regular laws, and though our sensations are as different as are our relations to the object, yet, by taking advantage of the laws of perception, we can ascertain by reasoning how things really and truly are; and any man, if he has sufficient experience and he reasons enough about it, will be led to the one true conclusion. The new conception here involved is that of reality. It may be asked how I know

that there are reals. If this hypothesis is the sole support of my method of inquiry, my method of inquiry must not be used to support my hypothesis. The reply is this: (1) If investigation can not be regarded as proving that there are real things, it at least does not lead to a contrary conclusion; but the method and the conception upon which it is based remain ever in harmony. No doubts of the method, therefore, necessarily arise from its practice, as is the case with all others. (2) The feeling which gives rise to any method of fixing belief is a dissatisfaction at two repugnant propositions. But here already is a vague concession that there is some one thing which a proposition should represent. Nobody therefore can really doubt that there are reals, for if he did, doubt would not be source of dissatisfaction. The hypothesis therefore is one which every mind admits, so that the social impulse does not cause men to doubt it. (3) Everybody uses the scientific method about a great number of things, and only ceases to use it when he does not know how to apply it. (4) Experiences of the method has not led us to doubt it, but, on the contrary, scientific investigation has had the most wonderful triumphs in the way of settling opinion. These afford the explanation of my not doubting the method or the hypothesis which it supposes; and not having any doubt nor believing anybody else whom I could influence has, it would be the merest babble for me to say more about it. If there is anybody with a living doubt upon the subject, let him consider it. (5.384)[1]

Peirce intended in the above passage to provide a justification for the general belief in the existence of an external world. But the passage is perplexing. After claiming, in effect, that the objectivity of the method of science presupposes the existence of a world of objects whose properties are entirely independent of our opinions about them, he then points out in apparent response to the question "How do we know that the hypothesis is acceptable?" that the hypothesis cannot be established inductively without begging the question. So far, so good. After this, however, the confusion begins to enter. For when he starts citing reasons in defense of the hypothesis, he cites four reasons which are such that the third and the fourth do not differ significantly and, moreover, are apparent repetitions of the last part of the first which is apparently not one but two different reasons. Further, Peirce's second reason seems to be inscrutable as a defense of the hypothesis in question. In spite of all this confusion, however, I would like to suggest that if we simply do not consider Peirce's third and fourth reason we are left with two distinct truncated arguments in defense of the hypothesis in question.

The first argument is suggested in Peirce's first reply. Noting that the method of science cannot demonstrate the contrary of the hypothesis in question, Peirce then says that "the method and the conception upon which it is based remain ever in harmony. No doubts of the method therefore necessarily arise from its practice". If we combine this brief reply with Peirce's claim that science actually presupposes the hypothesis in question we can derive the following argument:

P1. The inductive method as it is actually employed presupposes the existence of a world of objects whose properties are entirely independent of our opinions about them.

P2. We have no good reason to call into question the legitimacy of inductive inference as a source of knowledge.

P3. If the inductive method presupposes a world of objects whose objects are entirely independent of our opinions about them, and if there is no good reason for calling into question the legitimacy of inductive inference, then there is no good reason for calling into question the legitimacy of the hypothesis which the inductive method presupposes.

Therefore: There is no good reason for calling into question the legitimacy of the hypothesis which the inductive method presupposes, namely, that there is a world of objects whose properties are entirely independent of our opinions about them.

This argument is sound and, I suggest, an explicit formulation of what Peirce meant when he gave as a reason in defense of the hypothesis in question that "the method and the conception upon which it is based remain ever in harmony". After all, P3 is nothing more than a statement to the effect that if A presupposes B and A is true, then B cannot be false; and where such a relationship obtains it would be legitimate (although not very precise) to observe in defense of the truth of B that A and B are in harmony which would mean, of course, that the falsity of B would be inconsistent with the truth of A.

Before discussing Peirce's second argument it is important to point out that while the above argument is deficient in one significant respect, Peirce elsewhere provided another argument which supports the same hypothesis but which is not obviously subject to the same deficiency.

The respect in which the above argument is significantly defective is reasonably clear. At most, the argument shows only that the existence of an external world is a sufficient condition for the legitimacy of inductive inference. It does not show that the hypothesis in question is a necessary condition for the validity of inductive knowledge. Indeed, we can all recall the familiar thesis that science does not determine between realism and phenomenalism: any physical-object statement can be paraphrased into a purely phenomenalistic statement without loss of truth value thereby rendering the ontic commitment of science neutral with respect to realism and phenomenalism. This thesis entails, of course, that in the absence of being able to show that the existence of physical objects is a necessary condition for the validity of inductive inference, the physical-object language which science employs represents merely a convention or a choice of a convenient linguistic framework no better in principle than the choice of a purely phenomenalistic language.

Apart from the questionable claim that physical-object statements can be translated, *salva veritate*, into a *purely* phenomenalistic language, in opposition to the above objection we can note that Peirce provided another argument showing that the existence of an external world (physical objects) is a necessary and not simply a sufficient condition for the legitimacy of inductive inference. For in the second section of the second chapter of an incompleted and unpublished book entitled "Minute Logic" (written in 1902), Peirce said:

> You certainly opine that there is such a thing as truth. Otherwise reasoning and thought would be without a purpose. What do you mean by there being such a thing as truth? You mean that something is So—is correct, or just—whether you, or I, or anybody thinks it is so or not. Most persons, no doubt, opine that for every question susceptible of being answered by *yes* or *no*, one of these is true and the other false. Perhaps that is carrying the doctrine to an extravagant pitch. At any rate the mere fact that you wish to learn logic would not prove that you go so far as that. It only shows that you think that *some* question—some interesting question, what one, perhaps, you are not just now prepared to say—has one answer which is decidedly right, whatever people may think about it. The essence of the opinion is that there is *something* that is So, no matter if there be an overwhelming vote against it. So you plainly opine. For if thinking otherwise is going to make it otherwise, there is no use in reasoning or in studying logic. (2.135)

Without stretching this passage very much it seems that Peirce's intention here is to provide an argument to the effect that if there were no external objects (physical objects), there would be no truth—a claim Peirce often made.[2] Notice too that *in this context* Peirce is talking about truth as a property of propositions (statements) such that if a proposition is true we can infer that it describes a non-linguistic state of affairs. As we have seen, this sort of truth (usually Peirce spells it with a capital T) Peirce defined in terms of correspondence and reckoned it the destined product of the final opinion, the final conceptual framework, of the scientific community. It is what the scientific community *will* reach when the final conceptual framework is attained.[3] And if we make two small additions to what is either explicitly asserted or implied in the passage, the intended argument emerges. What is explicitly asserted in the passage is the following:

P1. We assume (opine) that there is such a thing as Truth in virtue of the fact that we conduct inquiries.

P2. In assuming that there is such a thing as Truth we assume that something is the case whether anyone thinks it so or not.

P3. If the truth of a proposition consists in our thinking it to be true, then there would be no reason (use) in conducting an inquiry on any given question.

If, in addition to these assertions, we add what seems to be implied by P2, namely,

P4. To say that "something is the case whether anyone thinks it so or not" is to say "there is a world of objects whose properties are neither logically nor causally dependent upon the noetic act of any number of finite minds" which is to say that there is a world of external (physical) objects.

and what seems to be implied in the last statement in the passage, namely,

P5. If it is not the case that there are external realities (physical objects), then the truth of a proposition would consist merely in our thinking it to be true.

then we would need to supply only two additional propositions to derive a valid argument. The propositions in question would be:

P6. If there is no use (reason) in conducting an inquiry on any given question, then we could not legitimately assume that there is such a thing as Truth.

and

P7. We rightly assume that there is such a thing as Truth.

While P7 is an addition to the above text, it is an addition for which Peirce argued in a section following the above text where he claimed that we rightly assume that there is such a thing as Truth or that something is the case regardless of how we think about it because we find our opinions constrained by the force of experience. He said:

> The very opinion entertained by those who deny that there is any Truth, in the sense defined, is that it is not force, but their inward freedom which determines their experiential cognition. But this opinion is flatly contradicted by their own experience. They insist upon shutting their eyes to the element of compulsion, although it is directly experienced by them. The very fact that they can and do so shut their eyes confirms the proof that fact is independent of the opinion about it. (2.138)[4]

I suggest, then, that the argument intended in the above passage is the following valid argument:

P1. We assume (opine) that there is such a thing as Truth in virtue of the fact that we conduct inquiries.

P2. We *rightly* assume (opine) that there is such a thing as Truth.

P3. In assuming that there is such a thing as Truth we assume that something is the case whether anyone thinks it so or not.

P4. If the Truth of a proposition consists merely in our thinking it to be true, then there would be no reason (use) in conducting an inquiry on any given legitimate question.

P5. To say that something is the case whether anyone thinks it so or not, is to say that there is a world of objects whose properties are neither logically nor causally dependent upon the noetic act of any number of finite minds which is to say that there is a world of external (physical) objects.

P6. If it is not the case that there are external (physical) objects, then the Truth of a proposition consists merely in our thinking it to be true.

P7. If there is no reason (use) in conducting an inquiry on any given legitimate question, then we could not legitimately assume that there is such a thing as Truth.

Therefore: It is false that it is not the case that there are external (physical) objects.

We can also derive from these premises the conclusion that if there are no physical objects there is no Truth. And all this seems to follow almost trivially from the fact that if we define Truth as a relationship of correspondence between language and extra-linguistic fact, then there could be no Truth, in the sense defined, if there were no extra-linguistic fact bespeaking a world of objects cognitively independent in origin. As a matter of fact, this seems to be the best way to restate the thrust of the above argument. And if we combine this argument with the preceeding argument, we have a reasoned defense for the view that not only does science legitimately assume the existence of an external world, it could not do otherwise and still guarantee the objectivity of its results. The existence of an external world is not only a sufficient condition for the validity of inductive inference, it is also a necessary condition if there is to be anything like the Truth we ordinarily and justifiably understand as a relationship of correspondence between language and extra-linguistic fact.

It might be urged that this last argument begs the question against the phenomenalist and the adherents to the thesis that science does not determine between realism and phenomenalism. For presumably, if the argument is sound it is only because it assumes that what we *must* mean by truth is a relationship of correspondence between language and extra-linguistic fact. And obviously the phenomenalist will not grant this assumption since it makes the existence of Truth dependent on the existence of an external world. Rather his claim is that the objectivity and Truth of science can just as easily be construed in terms of the conformity of experiment to hypothesis both of which can be described in purely phenomenalistic language without loss of what is usually meant by explanatory, predictive and control power. And the phenomenalist can further urge that it won't help to accuse him of solipsism since that not only begs the question against him but also misconstrues his claim. For his claim is *not* that there is no external world, but simply that if there is, science cannot show it. Science can *assume* the existence of an external world and the language of physicalism along with truth understood in terms of word–world correspondence, but as a working hypothesis the assumption is no better in principle than the phenomenalistic assumption since any physical-object statement can be translated without loss of *truth* into purely phenomenalistic terms.

Peirce was not in a position to deal with these sorts of objections. He was long dead when they first began to appear. But there is enough in the literature now to show that physical object statements *cannot* be translated *salva veritate* into purely phenomenalistic terms. Moreover, phenomenalistic expressions presuppose and are parasitic upon the physical-object language in such a way that the language of phenomenalism turns out at best to be merely an extension of the physical object language indispensable for even sensible phenomenalistic discourse.[5] On this sort of reasoning, the language of physicalism is anything but an expendable assumption and thus to suggest that a phenomenalistic language for science could be ontically neutral with respect to the existence of physical objects is sheer folly. But it's obvious that we can do science without the language of phenomenalism.

Secondly, Peirce's justification for the statement that we rightly assume that there is such a thing as Truth (entailing the existence of external objects) rests, here at any rate, upon his contention that we cannot deny that our opinions are constrained by the force of experience. Unfortunately, however, some philosophers have argued, and continue to argue, that we *can* deny that our opinions are constrained by the force of independent experience. Feyerabend and Kuhn, for example, question the standard view of science as objective by appealing to certain facts of psychology, semantics and the history of science. If their view is correct, it would follow that the notion of Truth to which Peirce and many others appeal does not admit of any instantiation and hence could not be utilized to provide for our belief in the existence of an external world.

Here again, however, although we cannot enter into the details of the Feyerabend–Kuhn thesis (as was the case with the previous objection). I hope it will be enough for the moment to point to the literature in which the objection can be generally thought defused.[6]

These then are two major objections that could be raised against Peirce's second argument, and at the moment there wouldn't seem to be any stronger objection that we might want to raise. So, with respect to Peirce's second argument (the belief in the existence of an external world is a necessary condition for science since without such a belief there would be no truth as we ordinarily understand it) we can certainly conclude the following: Barring the thesis that science does not determine as between phenomenalism and realism, and barring the Feyerabend–Kuhn thesis, science, as we ordinarily understand it, does and must assume the existence of an external world. Let us turn to the next argument.

Returning to the original passage in question (and our claim that Peirce's second reply can be construed as a truncated argument in defense of the realistic hypothesis) we noted that Peirce gave as the second part of his reply the following rather mysterious reasoning:

> ... (2) The feeling which gives rise to any method of fixing belief is a dissatisfaction at two repugnant propositions. But here already is a vague concession that there is some one thing that a proposition should represent. Nobody therefore can really doubt that there are reals, for if

he did, doubt would not be a source of dissatisfaction. The hypothesis therefore is one which every mind admits, so that the social impulse does not cause men to doubt it.

What is mysterious here is that Peirce apparently leaps from the argument purporting to show that there is some one thing which a proposition should represent (otherwise doubt would not be a source of dissatisfaction) to the conclusion that nobody can really doubt that there are reals (external things). The most that would seem to be established by this argument is that we have good reason for believing that there is some one thing that a proposition should represent otherwise doubt would not be a source of dissatisfaction. Now if the reply is intended as an argument in defense of the hypothesis in question, something is tacitly assumed. And it is not difficult to imagine what is missing if we keep in mind that in the same passage in question Peirce defined the real not only as that whose properties are independent of our opinions about it,[7] but also as the object of the final opinion which the community will ultimate agree upon. This latter definition of the real is found throughout the whole of Peirce's thought both early and late.[8] Given this latter definition of the real, Peirce need only establish that for any answerable question there will be an ultimate opinion in order to derive the existence of the real. This, I suggest, is precisely the point behind the mysterious reply. For in providing us with an argument in favour of there being some one thing which a proposition should represent, Peirce is providing us with an argument supporting his thesis that for any given question which admits of an answer, there will be an ultimate opinion. Allowing this and the alternate characterization of the real as the object of the ultimate opinion, it would follow that nobody can really doubt that there are reals. Explicitly stated, then, the intended argument would appear to take the following form:

P1. The real (that which is independent of our opinions about it) is the object of the ultimate opinion which the community will reach.

P2. If the ultimate opinion will be reached on some given question, then the real exists.

P3. If there is some one thing that a proposition should represent, then the ultimate opinion will obtain.

P4. If it were not the case that there is some one thing that a proposition should represent, then doubt would not be a source of dissatisfaction.

P5. Doubt is a source of dissatisfaction.
Therefore: The real exists.

This argument is valid but, on the face of it, not sound. For even if we grant that there is some one thing which an answerable proposition should represent, it does not thereby follow that there is some one thing which an answerable proposition *will* represent. Put differently, what the argument needs for soundness is some other argument (or set of arguments) showing that for any answerable question there *will* be a final opinion but this is hardly guaranteed by the "vague" concession that there is some one thing that a proposition *should* represent. In other words, the problematic premise is P3 which, if it is true, is by no means established by anything Peirce says in the above passage.

At any rate, if this argument is not sound because of the third premise, still, we have seen that in many places Peirce argued for the existence of the real external world on the grounds that for any given answerable question there will be an ultimate answer; and since the real is the object of the ultimate opinion which the community will reach, the real exists.[9] The soundness of this latter type of argument depends not only upon the legitimacy of the arguments which Peirce proposed in defense of his thesis that for any given question susceptible of being answered there will be an ultimate opinion, but also upon the acceptability of his definition of the real external world as the object of the ultimate opinion of the community. With respect to the legitimacy of the arguments in defense of the thesis that for any answerable question there will be an ultimate answer, we have already argued that these seldom-noted arguments are not only not to be rejected for the reasons alleged by Quine, Scheffler, Russell and others, but also, they are capable of independent establishment.[10]

With respect to Peirce's definition of the real external world as the object of the ultimate opinion of the community, however, we seem faced with a problem. For in defining the real as the object of the ultimate opinion of the community, it would appear that the real depends for its existence upon the mind of the community in the sense that if there were no ultimate opinion then the real would not exist. But how can such an alternate characterization of the real be rendered consistent with the definition of the real as that whose properties are independent of our opinions about it? If we are to accept both characterizations of the real, it would seem to follow that the real both is and is not independent of mind.

Moreover, if both characterizations of the real are to be accepted, then it also apparently follows that Peirce's basic argument for the existence of the real based upon the thesis that inquiry will lead to an ultimate destined opinion is an argument in support of an idealistic thesis which is at once inconsistent with the two arguments cited earlier purporting to show respectively that the existence of an external (independent) world is legitimately assumed and must be assumed for the validity of inductive inference. Or so it might be urged.

But this is not a serious problem. For we can argue, as Peirce did, that *what* is known is independent of mind in the sense that the mind does not always create the objects of its experience; and yet since the real independent world must be *knowable*, it depends upon the existence of minds for its knowability. Thus there need be nothing inconsistent about asserting that the external world is independent of thought and also that it is dependent on mind for its being known. As a matter of fact, the sense in which the real external world is dependent on mind turns out to be trivially true and necessary for any epistemological realism wherein it is a necessary condition that the external world be knowable.[11]

Finally, we should not end this discussion without noting that some philosophers seem fully convinced of the sceptic's claim that we cannot *know* that there is an external world because it is always logically possible that we are mistaken about the origin of our sense experience. It is, they urge, certainly conceivable that an evil deceiving demon provides us with those sensations and beliefs which we would have if there were an external world. In which case we can imagine our experience being precisely what it is without there being an external world. Under such an hypothesis it is logically possible that we be mistaken in our belief about the existence of an external world, and so (since knowing precludes any possibility of mistake) we cannot know that there is an external world. As a consequence of taking the sceptic's claim seriously, some have conceded that indeed we cannot know that there is an external world. They then proceed to argue that in spite of all this, still, our belief in the existence of an external world is a very reasonable belief worthy of rational acceptance.[12]

It is obvious that the sceptic's strategy can be re-employed to defend wholesale scepticism and not merely scepticism with respect to the existence of the external world.[13] Of itself, this does not show the sceptic wrong. But it does show that we cannot accept his strategy without simultaneously accepting the view that knowledge requires grounds which preclude the *logical* possibility of error. In other words, the sceptic's strategy proceeds on the assumption of the strongest possible sense of 'knows' when at the very least there is no good reason to believe that this is the most important or even the only sense of 'knows.' Peirce, it will be recalled, went even further in rejecting the presupposition behind the sceptic's claim when he effectively argued that *all* knowledge is fallible because based upon synthetic inference which always admits of some possibility of error.[14] And we may infer from this that, for Peirce, the sceptic can achieve his desired end only by fostering a sense of 'knows' which, for all its apparent familiarity in ordinary usage, does not and cannot reflect the sort of knowledge which we actually possess. As a matter of fact, Peirce frequently observed that if we begin with the sceptic's sense of 'knows' (which sense he correctly saw behind the Cartesian doubt and the evil demon hypothesis) then not even an infinitely intelligent Descartes could logically avoid scepticism.[15] Thus, for anyone who, like Peirce, can muster arguments to the effect that knowledge does not require the preclusion of the logical possibility of error, the sceptic's prime objection will not work. For the sceptic will stand convicted of begging the question against his opponents by tacitly assuming a sense of 'knows' which cannot in principle be satisfied. Only if we accept the sceptic's sense of 'knows' as the only appropriate sense of 'knows', which Peirce never did, can the sceptic's objection get off the ground.[16] Let us summarize the discussion up to this point.

We began this chapter with a passage from Peirce's essay on "The Fixation of Belief" and in the course of our discussion we have noted that, in defense of epistemological realism, Peirce put forth at least four distinct arguments which fall into two separate categories. The first argument (reconstructed from the first reply in the passage from the "Fixation of Belief") in conjunction with the second argument (reconstructed from the essay on "Minute Logic") urge respectively that science assumes the existence of an independent world, and also that it *must* if the standard view of science as objective is correct. Together, these two arguments do not, I believe, show conclusively that an external world exists. But they do have the effect of casting the burden of proof back on the sceptic who will need to show that the standard view of science as objective is not correct or that our opinions are not constrained by the force of experience in the way that Peirce suggests. These two arguments fall into the category of arguments purporting to show the existence of the real as that which is independent of our opinion about it. The third argument (reconstructed from the second reply in the passage from the "Fixation of Belief") and the fourth argument (referred to as Peirce's general argument for the existence of the real based upon the assertion that for any given answerable question there will be an ultimate answer) purportedly show that the existence of the real follows from the fact that there will be an ultimate answer to any answerable question. In the end, however, these latter two arguments are only as good as the basic assumption behind the standard view of science, namely, that truth is to be defined in terms of a relationship of correspondence between language and extra-linguistic fact. But defining truth in this way makes no sense unless we can prove that there is a world of extra-linguistic fact, or that our opinions can be constrained by a force outside ourselves for the reasons urged by Peirce. So, these latter two arguments can be sound only if the former two arguments are sound. And this is to say that the ultimate force of Peirce's general argument for epistemological realism consists in the fact that he places the burden of proof back on the shoulders of the sceptic who must now show that our opinions are never constrained by a force independently of ourselves. Unless people like Feyerabend and Kuhn can succeed in showing us that none of our opinions are so constrained, that indeed the standard view of science is a myth, I think we should conclude that Peirce has done as much as anybody has, or can, to defend the view that there is a world of extra-linguistic fact. These latter two arguments fall into the category of arguments attempting to show the existence of the real as the object of the ultimate and destined opinion of the community. While more can be said on the topic, this fairly represents the way in which Peirce defended his general belief in the existence of an external world and, in addition, the extent to which the defense in question is deserving of extended consideration if not qualified acceptance.

III. *PEIRCE'S TWO CRITERIA FOR EXTERNALITY*

As noted earlier, given that the knowability of the external world is essential to the thesis of epistemological realism, any general defense of epistemological realism will fail if it fails to provide an acceptable criterion for determining which objects of our experience are external. For if there is no acceptable way of determining which objects of our experience are external, then the external world would not be knowable because indistinguishable from the 'internal' world.

In turning to Peirce's thought on this issue, we are beset with a number of textual difficulties and hence it might be well at the outset to provide a brief outline of what will follow. I will begin by showing that Peirce, in his treatment of the category of Secondness, maintained that the compulsiveness (or Secondness) of our perceptual experience guarantees the externality of the object which we perceive. This implies that in Peirce's thought we find an immediate criterion for externality (Secondness, compulsiveness) and that Peirce held in some way the famous common sense doctrine on the immediate perception of the external world. We will also see that Peirce held at the same time with equal emphasis the view that the only way we can know whether or not anything is external to us is by inductive inference (the method of prediction and confirmation). In the face of such a seeming incompatibility with regard to the criterion for externality and in the face of a number of Peirce scholars who simply choose one criterion over the other, I shall propose an interpretation (based upon the doubt–belief theory of inquiry) attempting to show that Peirce consistently held both criteria for externality, neither one to the exclusion of the other but both within well-qualified contexts It will be seen that Peirce's first criterion for externality (compulsiveness, Secondness) falls within the domain of his commitment to the validity of common sense beliefs which are said to be infallibly true (in the sense specified in the preceeding chapter) simply because they are not doubted, whereas Peirce's second criterion for externalty (inductive inference) falls within the domain of his commitment to the scientific fixation of belief given a real doubt about the externality of a perceived object. In effect, we will show that, for Peirce, the compulsiveness of our perceptual experience is ordinarily a sufficient condition for externality, but if any real doubt should arise with respect to the externality of any perceived object the first criterion fails and we must appeal to the way of prediction and confirmation to settle the question. Whichever criterion is applicable will be a function of whether or not there is entertained any real doubt about the externality of the perceived object. The acceptability of Peirce's teaching on the question of externality will depend, of course, upon the acceptability of the doubt–belief theory of inquiry and the way in which he argued for the validity of common sense beliefs along with the conditions under which common sense is to be eschewed in favor of inductive inference. After pointing to a number of considerations which justify this interpretation and the value of it, I will end by suggesting that the one basic deficiency in Peirce's doctrine can be readily patched-up thereby rendering Peirce's discussion on externality quite forceful given the legitimacy of the doubt–belief theory of inquiry and the acceptability of the way in which Peirce reconciled both common sense and science.

In a work entitled "A Detailed Classification of the Sciences" (written in 1902), Peirce introduced a new method for the purpose of deriving the fundamental categories of experience. The method consists in a simple (and presuppositionless) phenomenological analysis of the data of consciousness. Peirce called the method the science of phaneroscopy (or phenomenology) and he insisted that if we employ the method by simply turning to our phenomenal experience and describing what we see, we will find the fundamental categories of being, categories which are applicable to, and derivable from all experiences, namely, the categories of Firstness, Secondness and Thirdness.[17]

The first category the phenomenological analysis manifests is the category of Firstness which is the purely qualitative aspect of our experience. A First is the simple unanalyzable quality of our immediate perceptual experience. It is that which is simply experienced and cannot be conceptualized. A pure phenomenal suchness more properly felt then conceived of.[18] The second category manifested in the phenomenological analysis, namely, Secondness, is the category of 'otherness,' or "the non-ego acting upon the ego" which is manifested in our experience of action and reaction. Peirce most often described the category of Secondness phenomenologically in terms of our experience of it; hence, Secondness is the category of 'shock,' 'interruption,' 'compulsion (compulsiveness),' 'vividness,' 'intrusion.' Moreover, Secondness is that category of our experience which Peirce (in 1896) identified with the Scotistic principle of individuation—haecceitas. Hence, Secondness is the brute (un-get-overable), compulsive element of otherness in our experience. That which is not created by the ego as other.[19] The third category derived from the phenomenological analysis of our perceptual experience, namely, Thirdness, is the category of mediation, generality, continuity, habit or law. Thirdness is that element of our experience which accounts for the law-like nature of our experience. Thirdness is our phenomenal experience as subject to law which accounts for the intelligibility or meaningfulness of our experience.[20] For Peirce, these, and only these three, are the basic categories of experience and while they can be considered separately they can not be experienced in isolation from each other. Every object of our experience manifests these three categories which can exist separately only in thought.

In further characterizing the nature of Secondness, Peirce maintained that it is the category of fact, individuality, existence, and externality. The last two characterizations of Secondness are important if we are to understand the sense in which Peirce can be said to provide a criterion for externality.

Peirce claimed that Secondness is the category of individual existence in so far as: "Existence is that mode of being which lies in opposition to another. ... A thing without opposition 'ipso facto' does not exist" (1.435). 'The mode of being of an individual thing (Secondness) is existence and existence lies in opposition merely" (1.458). In 1903 Peirce quite clearly identified the Firstness of true Secondness with existence:

> We may say with some approach to accuracy that the general Firstness of all true Secondness is existence—though this term more particularly applies to Secondness in so far as it is an element of the reacting first and second. If we mean Secondness as an element of the occurrence, the firstness of it is actuality, but actuality and existence are words expressing the same idea in different applications. (1.532)[21]

And finally, some time after 1900, he said:

> When we say that a thing exists, what we mean is that it reacts upon other things. That we are transferring to it our direct experience of reaction is shown by our saying that one thing acts upon another. (7.534)

The brutality or 'haecceity' manifested in our experience of Secondness stands as the criterion of existence. Unfortunately, however, there are texts which seem to indicate that Peirce used the term "existence" broadly enough to cover hallucinations and illusions in such a way as to imply that the experience of Secondness is no guarantee for the externality of our experience but only for individuality or existence which can be either internal or external:

> There are different kinds of existence. There is the existence of physical actions, there is the existence of psychic volition, there is the existence of all time, there is the existence of material things, there is the existence of the creations of one of Shakespeare's plays, and for aught we know there may be another creation with a space and time of its own in which things may exist. Each kind of existence consists in having a place

among the total collection of such a universe. It consists in being a second to any object in such a universe taken as a first. (1.433)

This text, combined with some others in which Peirce characteristically insisted that the only way to distinguish an hallucination from a true perception is ultimately a matter of inductive inference, has led many to believe that for Peirce the criterion for externality is not a matter of compulsiveness (Secondness) immediately perceived, but rather of inductive inference. The question, of course, is crucial and it is by no means as clear as Peirce ought to have made it. Before analyzing the view that externality for Peirce was a matter of inductive inference and the reasons in behalf of that position, it might be well to point to some of the numerous texts written after 1896 in which Peirce held that externality, is a matter of Secondness and as such is immediately perceived rather than inductively inferred. At one time after establishing that Secondness is the Category of fact, Peirce insisted that facticity is a matter of externality:

> Whenever I've come to know a fact, it is by its resisting us. A man may walk down Wall Street debating within himself the existence of an external world; but if in his brown study he jostles up against somebody who angrily draws off and knocks him down, the sceptic is unlikely to carry his scepticism so far as to doubt whether anything besides the Ego was concerned in that phenomenon. The resistance shows that something independent of him is there. When anything strikes upon the senses the mind's train of thought is interrupted, for if it were not, nothing would distinguish the new observation from a fancy. (1.431)[22]

And elsewhere he said:

> One of the simplest and for that reason one of the most difficult of the ideas which it is incumbent upon the author of this book to endeavor to cause the reader to conceive is that the sense of effort and the experience of any sensation are phenomena of the same kind, equally involving direct experience of the duality of the without and the within. The psychology of the sense of effort is not yet satisfactorily made out. It seems to be a sensation which somehow arises when striped muscles are under tension. But though this is the only way of it, yet an imagination of it is by association called up, upon the occasion of other slight sensations even when muscles are uncontracted; and this imagination may sometimes be interpreted as a sense of effort. But though the sense of effort is thus merely a sensation like any other, it is one in which the duality which appears in every sensation is specially prominent. A sense of being resisted. Exertion can not be experienced without resistance, no resistance without exertion. It is all one sense but a sense of duality. 'Every sensation involves the same sense of duality though less

prominently. This is the direct perception of the external world of Reid and Hamilton ...' (5.539)

And again, when talking about the compulsiveness of Secondness he asserted:

> An idealist need not deny the existence of the external world any more than Berkeley did. 'For the reality of the external world means nothing except that real experience of duality.' Still many of them do deny it—or think they do. Very well; an idealist of that stamp is lounging down regent street, thinking of the utter nonsense of the opinion of Reid, and especially of the foolish 'probatio ambulandi,' when some drunken fellow who is staggering up the street unexpectedly lets fly his fist and knocks him in the eye. What has become of his philosophical reflections now? Will he be so unable to free himself from prepossessions that no experience can show him the force of that argument? There may be some underlying unity beneath the sudden transition from mediation to astonishment. Grant that: does it follow that the transition did not take place? Is not the transition a direct experience of the duality of the inward past and the outward present? A poor analyst is he who cannot see that the Unexpected is a direct experience of the duality, that just as there can be no effort without resistance, so there can be no subjectivity of the unexpected without the objectivity of the unexpected, that they are merely two aspects of the one experience given together and beyond all criticism. If the idealist should pick himself up and proceed to argue to the striker saying: "you could not have struck me because you have no independent existence, you know," the striker might reply: "I dare say I have not separate enough existence for that; but I have separate existence enough to make you feel differently from what you were expecting to feel." Whatever strikes the eye or the touch, whatever strikes the ear, whatever strikes the nose or palate contains something unexpected. Experience of the unexpected forces upon us the idea of duality. Will you say, "Yes, the idea is forced upon us, but it is not directly experienced"? The reply is that experience means nothing but just that of a cognitive nature which the history of our lives has forced upon us. (5.539)[23]

This rather lengthy text, written in 1903, is much like the preceeding text, written in 1897, and both texts were written in the context of a discussion on the nature of Secondness in so far as it is the compulsive element of our experience. Both texts argue for the claim that we have an immediate perception of the existence of external objects. Indeed, even as late as 1907 Peirce still held that the brutality or compulsiveness of our personal experience (which compulsiveness is characteristic of Secondness) suffices as an immediate criterion for externality and distinguishes the external from the internal world:

> It is that every man inhabits two worlds. These are directly

distinguishable by their different appearances, but the greatest differences between them by far is that one of these two worlds, the Inner world, exerts a comparatively slight compulsion upon us, though we can by direct effort so slight as to be hardly noticeable, change it greatly creating and destroying existent objects in it; while the other world, the Outer World, is full of irresistable compulsions for us and we can not modify it in the least except by one peculiar kind of effort, and but very slightly even in that way. (5.474)[24]

Peirce had made the same point a year earlier in 1906:

Every sane person lives in a double world, the Outer world and the Inner world, the world of percepts and the world of fancies. What chiefly keeps these from being mixed up is (besides certain marks they bear) everybody's well knowing that fancies can be greatly modified by a certain nonmuscular effort while it is muscular effort alone (whether this be "voluntary" that is, preintended, or whether all the intended endeavor is to inhibit muscular action, as when one blushes, or when peristaltic action is set up on experience of danger to one's person) that can to any noticeable degree modify percepts. (5.487)

When talking about Secondness and perception Peirce says:

But the important point (is) that the sense of externality in perception consists in a sense of powerlessness before the overwhelming force of perception. (1.334)[25]

It seems, then, that if Secondness is the immediate criterion for externality, Peirce ought to have espoused the doctrine of the immediate perception of the external world. And, as a matter of fact, Peirce often said that we immediately perceive the external world and that he himself held the doctrine of immediate perception of the external world.[26] In no fewer than twenty-three texts ranging from 1897 to 1910 (with the exception of one which was written in 1871, namely, 8.16) Peirce has made a rather strong case on behalf of the view that it is the Secondness of our perceptual experiences which guarantees the externality of what is perceived.[27] Moreover, since the experience of Secondness or compulsiveness is not inferred, then this Secondness would stand as an immediate criterion for externality which would further imply that the criterion proposed in this way comes to the doctrine of the immediate perception of externality which the Scotch school, among others, taught and which Peirce said that he himself held.[28]

Unfortunately, however, there are a number of texts that could well be cited in defense of the view that, for Peirce, the only way we know whether anything is external is by inductive inference. And the reader need only glance at 7.655; 2.142; 8.149; MS 200

(MMF 40) and 8.144 to see the extent to which Peirce held this view.[29]

In the light of these considerations we seem to be faced with the conclusion that either Peirce was quite inconsistent in simultaneously espousing two different criteria for externality or that there must be some sense in which both are compatible. Simply to choose one criterion over the other is either to ignore the corroborative evidence supporting the other or to maintain that Peirce did not mean to put forth both criteria. Neither alternative is critically acceptable. There is good evidence in favor of the view, however, that Peirce consistently held both criteria, neither one to the exclusion of the other but both with serious qualification. Let me say why.

It is within the context of the doubt-belief theory of inquiry that we find the key to understanding the sense and extent to which Peirce consistently proposed both criteria for externality. I propose that his first criterion for externality (compulsiveness, Secondness) was intended by Peirce to be applicable only within the context of his commitment to common-sense indubitables in such a way as to imply that the compulsiveness (Secondness) of our perceptual experiences suffices as a criterion for externality when the percipient entertains no real doubt about the externality of what he perceives; whereas, the second criterion for externality (inductive inference, or the method of prediction and confirmation) was intended by Peirce to be applicable only within the context of the critical fixation of belief when the percipient really doubts the externality of what he perceives. In effect, the compulsiveness (Secondness) of our perceptual experiences constitutes a sufficient condition for externality if there is no real doubt about the externality of the object perceived. If, however, there exists a real doubt about the externality of the object perceived, then our knowledge of externality becomes a matter of inference, but not otherwise.

And, indeed, there are a number of considerations which support this interpretation. First, consider the following texts in which Peirce states the conditions under which externality becomes a matter of inference:

> The percepts, could I make sure what they were, constitute experience proper, that which I am forced to accept. But whether they are experience of the real world or only experience of a dream, is a question which I have no means of answering with absolute certainty. I have, however, three tests which, though none of them is infallible, answer

very well in ordinary cases. 'The first test consists in trying to dismiss the percepts. A fancy or day-dream can commonly be dismissed by a direct effort of the will. If I should find that the flow of percepts persists consistently in spite of my own will, I am usually satisfied. Still it may be an hallucination. If I have reason to suspect that it is so, I apply the second test which consists in asking some other person whether he sees or hears the same thing. If he does and if several people do, that will ordinarily be taken as conclusive. Yet it is an established fact that some hallucinations affect whole companies of people. There remains, however, a third test that can be applied and it is by far the surest of the three. Namely, I make use of my knowledge of the laws of nature (very fallible knowledge confessedly) to predict that if my percept has its cause in the real world, a certain experiment must have a certain result which in the absence of that cause would not be a little surprising. I apply this test or experiment. If the result does not occur, my percept is illusory, if it does it receives strong confirmation. For example, if I and all the company are so excited that we think we saw a ghost, I can try what an imaginative kodak would say to it. So MacBeth made the experiment of trying to clutch the dagger. (8.144)[30]

I see an inkstand on the table. That is a percept. Moving my head I get a different percept of the inkstand. It coalesces with the other. What I call the inkstand is a generalized percept, a quasi-inference from percepts, perhaps I might say a composite photography of percepts. In this physical product is involved an element of resistance to me, which I am obscurely conscious of from the first. Subsequently when I accept the hypothesis of an inward subject for my thoughts, I must yield to that consciousness of resistance and admit the inkstand to the standing of an external object. Still later, I may call this in question. But as soon as I do that, I find the inkstand appears there in spite of me. If I turn away my eyes, other witnesses will tell me that it still remains. If we all leave the room and dismiss the matter from our thoughts, still a photographic camera would show the inkstand there, with the same roundness, polish and transparency, and with the same opaque liquid within. Thus or otherwise I confirm myself in the opinion that its characters are what they are, and persist at every opportunity in revealing themselves regardless of what you or I, or any man or any generation of men, may think that they are. (8.144)

In these texts (written after 1900) Peirce talks of both criteria for externality. For in all of them the first test consists in trying to suppress the apparition which implies that the first criterion for externality is compulsiveness (Secondness), and ordinarily the inability to suppress the apparition is taken as a sufficient indication that the object perceived is external. But if there is a real doubt about the externality of what is perceived after one cannot suppress the apparition, then we must appeal to the criterion of inductive inference. Second, under this interpretation it would follow that we have a 'direct' and an 'indirect' method of ascertaining externality and whichever method we use is a function of whether or not there is any doubt about the externality of the object perceived. And Peirce quite clearly says this (1.431). Third, Peirce not only maintained that he held the doctrine of the immediate perception of externality which is implied by the first criteria (8.261), but also that it was impossible to deny it (5.56), and that it was a doctrine justifiable within the context of common sense (5.462; 5.444; 7.639; 8.16). Clearly, then, Peirce held the first criterion for externality (which he identified with the doctrine of immediate perception) to be a matter of common sense and in the absence of real doubt to constitute a sufficient criterion for externality.

Moreover, the first criterion implies nothing more than the doctrine of immediate perception taught by the Scotch common-sense Realists. Indeed, it can only be within this context that Peirce insists that the most conclusive of all single tests for externality is that of making a direct inward effort to suppress the apparition (6.334) which, as we said, implies that the criterion for externality is compulsiveness or Secondness. On the other hand, it is within the context of a commitment to the scientific fixation of belief that Peirce's second criterion is valid. For when one can not suppress the perceptual object and there persists a real doubt about the externality of what is perceived, then externality becomes a matter of inductive inference. And indeed, it can only be within this second context that Peirce insists that the surest test for externality is one of prediction and confirmation (2.142).

Apart from indicating the nature of Peirce's commitment to both common sense and critical philosophy in the light of his famous Doubt–Belief theory of inquiry, the value of this inter-pretation lies in the fact that it does not force us to accept one criterion for externality to the exclusion of the other. Those who hold that for Peirce externality was exclusively a matter of inductive inference can do so only by ignoring many texts in which he insists that externality is a matter of compulsiveness or Secondness, thus also ignoring Peirce's commitment to common sense and the doctrine of immediate perception in the absence of real doubt. On the other hand, those who hold that for Peirce externality was exclusively a matter of compulsiveness (Second-ness) or that Peirce held exclusively the common sense doctrine of the immediate perception of externality can do so only by ignoring the many texts in which Peirce maintains that externality in the face of real doubt is a matter of inductive inference, thus also ignoring Peirce's commitment to the scientific fixation of belief in the presence of living doubt.

Given that the above is a reasonably accurate account of Peirce's thought on how we are to justify our belief in the externality of any perceived object, one might well be tempted to argue that, from the viewpoint of the doubt-belief theory of inquiry, Peirce's first criterion is not necessary for justifying our belief in the externality of a perceived object. After all, if the compulsiveness (Secondness) of our perceptual experience suffices as a criterion for externality only in those cases where there is no real doubt about the externality of what is perceived, and if (as Peirce's discussion of the nature of common sense clearly indicates) our not really doubting a proposition is sufficient for the acceptability of the proposition, then would it follow that in those cases where we do not really doubt the externality of what we perceive, our belief in the externality of the object derives simply from the fact that we do not doubt and not from the compulsiveness of the perceptual experience. In short, if Peirce's teaching on the acceptability of propositions not really doubted is valid, then in those cases where we do not really doubt the externality of what we perceive there is no need for a criterion for externality. Within the context of its applicability as a criterion for externality, compulsiveness (Secondness) would be superfluous. This objection is telling and points to a rather serious deficiency which can be patched-up if we are willing to grant Peirce the following proposition:

A. Antecedently to any inquiry, in those cases where we do not really doubt the externality of what we perceive it is the compulsiveness (Secondness) of the perceptual experience which affords the reason for our not really doubting the externality of what we perceive.

If we grant Peirce this proposition, then, of course, compulsiveness (Secondness) would be necessary for our not really doubting the externality of what we perceive antecedently to any inquiry. Given this, the justification of our belief in the externality of what we perceive (when we have no real doubt about the externality of what we perceive) would derive from the fact that we do not really doubt without thereby casting aspersions on the necessity of compulsiveness (Secondness) as the criterion for externality when there is no real doubt about the externality of what is perceived. Given the above proposition, it would still be true to say that compulsiveness (Secondness) is ordinarily a sufficient criterion for externality when there is no real doubt about the externality of what is perceived. In short, given the above proposition, compulsiveness (Secondness) would still be necessary for the justification of our belief in the externality of what we perceive when we have no real doubt about the externality of what we perceive since the compulsiveness of our perceptual experience affords the reason for our not really doubting the externality of what we perceive. Hence the context in which the first criterion is applicable need not indicate that the criterion itself is not necessary. While we have no immediately obvious textual reasons for claiming that Peirce would (or intended to) endorse the above proposition, we have no good reason for believing that he would not endorse the above proposition. If, in granting Peirce the above proposition, we are thereby able to present his view in the most favorable light possible, there would seem to be no good reason to withhold the grant, especially when such a small grant plugs the hole in the rather coercive doctrine.

IV. *CONCLUDING REMARKS*

By employing rather standard techniques of reconstruction and interpretation there emerges from Peirce's later thought a forceful statement in defense of epistemological realism. Without suggesting that Peirce's defense of epistemological realism is conclusive, it seems that at least two basic observations can be made.

First, Peirce's arguments (as here reconstructed) in defense of the thesis that there is an external world are neither standard nor obviously lacking in merit. If anything at all, it has here been shown that the arguments taken together represent a unique effort deserving of extended and cautious consideration for those who would defend or attack the same thesis. Our apparent reluctance to grant the final seal of approval derives less from any feeling that Peirce somehow failed than from an instinctive sense of caution when presented with arguments the soundness of which presupposes a number of controversial issues (central to Peirce's theory of knowledge) which demand more detailed scrutiny than has here been possible. At any rate, pending the results of Chapter IV and pending the validity of Peirce's controversial thesis on the ultimate convergence of opinion, it cannot be denied that Peirce's arguments in defense of the thesis that there is an external world probably represent as unique and as persuasive a defense of that thesis as has ever been proposed. If this latter statement sounds too excessive, we should keep in mind that the whole generation of realists who were to follow Peirce established nothing more than that our belief in the existence of an external world cannot be disproved.[31] That generation established realism as an article of faith thereby rendering the thesis not much stronger than it had been in the age of faith when opposition to the thesis was non-existent. This generation, if I may be allowed a generalization, does not seem to have done much better.[32]

Secondly, in answer to the question 'how do we know that any perceived object is a member of the class of external objects?' Peirce has provided us with a challenging synthesis of two divergent theses heretofore not clearly reconciled. Let us call the two divergent theses in question the thesis of common sense and the thesis of science respectively. The thesis of common sense maintains that the externality of any perceived object is a matter of common sense, that common sense is an unerring source of knowledge and that any thesis which contravenes the testimony of common sense is proof positive of the falsity of that thesis. The thesis of common sense is ordinarily attributed with a good deal of justification to such men as J. L. Austin, G. E. Moore, Thomas Reid, Roderick Chisholm and others. While the strength of this thesis is obvious (although not always well argued for), the major limitation of the thesis is ordinarily pointed out by the adherents to the thesis of science. They maintain that since common sense is not an unerring instinct (physics has proven common sense false or at least unreliable), the existential import of perceptual judgments is always an empirical matter. This latter thesis can be attributed to such men as Wilfrid Sellars, Don Locke, and, in general, to those who maintain that all perceptual claims are virtual predictions and therefore to be justified in the same way as any empirical assertion. The major limitation of the thesis of science (as ordinarily pointed out by the adherents to the thesis of common sense) is that it is in principle impossible to provide verification for all perceptual claims without ultimately appealing to some propositions which are not empirical questions. There must be some direct or non-inferential knowledge presupposed by the process of verification—otherwise the method of verification would not get off the ground. It seems fair to say that, in general, the adherents of the common sense thesis overlook what the adherents of the thesis of science never cease to argue for, namely, the inherent liability of any appeal to common sense as a source of knowledge not subject to criticism. Likewise, it seems fair to say that the adherents to the thesis of science overlook what adherents to the thesis of common sense assert, namely, the inherent impossibility of confirmation without appeal ultimately to propositions which can not be established by the method itself. For those of us who acknowledge the force and the limitations of each thesis, Peirce's solution to the problem would seem to be quite attractive in so far as it acknowledges the force of each thesis without countenancing their respective limitations. In claiming that if we do not really doubt the externality of what we perceive (given the compulsiveness of the perceptual experience) then our belief is justified, and in claiming that if there is some good reason to doubt the externality of what we perceive we must appeal to the method of prediction and confirmation to settle the issue, Peirce clearly endorsed the necessity of appealing to common sense without repudiating the necessity of science just as he endorsed the necessity of appealing to science without repudiating the necessity of appealing to common sense. Needless to say, Peirce's answer to the question is simply a logical extension of the way in which he reconciled his commitment to common sense and science thereby indicating the systematic relation that obtains between Peirce's epistemology and his espousal of epistemological realism. Hence, for those who acknowledge the force of the two theses in question, but who are reluctant to accept exclusively either one because of the aforementioned limitations, Peirce's solution (or something very similar to it) would seem to be quite forceful. It constitutes an endorsement of both common sense and science without maintaining either that common sense cannot err or that the method of verification should always be employed. If Peirce's general thesis to the effect that we should reject neither common sense nor science but rather state the conditions under which the deliverance of each are to be accepted is valid (and I have suggested that it is), Peirce's answer to the above question is not only challenging, but it is also probably correct.

Let us turn now to what has been conspicuously absent throughout the whole of the discussion thus far, namely, Peirce's views on the nature of perception. Thus far, I have argued that Peirce was strenuously committed to epistemological realism and the question before us is whether or not this commitment is consistent with his views on the nature of perception. If it is, then we shall have stronger evidence for reading Peirce as a consistent realist; if it is not, then we will need to conclude that Peirce's view

on the nature of perception render his commitment to epistemological realism quite inconsistent with his theory of perception. Some
people have suggested that Peirce's theory of perception is a clear
instance of phenomenalism and hence should be taken as strong
evidence for the view that Peirce was as committed to idealism as
he was to realism, and that, in the end, this twofold commitment is
downright inconsistent. So, if we are to answer the question of
whether Peirce was *both* a realist *and* an idealist, we must look
closely at what he said about perception. And when this is done we
shall then turn directly to examining evidence to the effect that, in
spite of what we have said thus far, Peirce was an undaunted
idealist.

NOTES

1. See also 5.351ff and 5.405ff.

2. See 7.659; 6.328.

3. See pp. 62ff above.

4. As we have seen, this is by no means the only argument Peirce offers in
defense of the view that Truth, understood in terms of correspondence between
language and extra-linguistic fact, exists as the destined product of the final opinion
of the scientific community. But it is certainly an important argument since it also
provides Peirce with a *criterion* for externality. See also 1.431; 1.334; 7.534; 1.325;
MS 141; MS 200 (M.M. E79); MS 289 (p. 30); MS 717; MS 860 (p. 6); MS 309
(p. 58).

5. See, for example, R. J. Hirst (ed.) *Perception and the External World* (New
York: Macmillan, 1965).

6. For a complete summary and alleged refutation of the Feyerabend–Kuhn
thesis see at least I. Scheffler's *Science and Subjectivity* (Bobbs-Merrill Co., New
York, 1967). See also Richard Hall's "Kuhn and the Copernican Revolution,"
British Journal for the Philosophy of Science, Vol. 21, 1970.

7. For other passages in which the real is defined as external and independent of
thought, see pp. 150ff below.

8. See pp. 148ff below.

9. See pp. 95ff above and also 5.357; 2.654; 8.153; 5.160.

10. Hence, even if the second argument reconstructed from Peirce's reply is
unacceptable because of P3, we would still be obliged to consider the general type of
argument Peirce presumably had in mind (and explicitly stated elsewhere) and the
different arguments in support of the thesis that for any answerable question there
will be an ultimate opinion.

11. 5.431; 6.327; 7.337–40 and 5.311. For a fuller discussion see Chapter IV
below. Unfortunately, there is good reason for thinking Peirce believed that the
thesis of idealism amounts to no more than the claim that real objects cannot exist
without being related to minds. In granting this as well as the view that real objects
also exist independently of any relationship to mind, Peirce apparently felt that he
was synthesizing realism and idealism (see 5.494; 5.539). As I shall argue below,
however, realism and idealism, as traditionally conceived, are logically incompatible.

12. See, for example, M. A. Slote's *Reason and Scepticism* (New York:
Humanities Press, 1970).

13. The general strategy is adopted by K. Lehrer in one of his earlier defenses of scepticism. See "Why Not Scepticism?", *Philosophical Forum* (Boston, Spring, 1971).

14. See pp. 49ff above and also 1.145; 2.141; 7.82; 6.523; 7.55.

15. 5.416. See also 5.392; 5.525 and 5.443.

16. See my "Defeasibility and Scepticism," *The Australasian Journal of Philosophy* (December 1973).

17. 1.284–353. See also MS 284 (p. 47); MS 298; MS 478; MS 717; MS 1335.

18. 1.304; 2.85; 1.357ff; 8.264.

19. 8.266; 1.521; 1.528; 8.330; 7.548; 1.333; 7.531–43; 8.267.

20. 7,532; 7.535–7; 8.331.

21. See also 1.527; 7.534.

22. See also 1.334; 7.534; 1.325; and texts cited in note 4 above.

23. See also 5.45–8; 1.332. See also the texts cited in note 4 above.

24. See 5.493; and 1.321 for the same point.

25. See also 1.337; 8.148; and 1.175 for the same point.

26. See MS 934 (p. 26); 8.16 (where Peirce defends the doctrine of immediate perception as a realistic doctrine); 7.561 n. 25 and 7.639.

27. 5.56. See also 5.239 where Peirce maintains that we have a faculty for immediately distinguishing between dreams and reality.

28. For a fuller discussion of the relationship between the doctrine of the Scotch common sense realists and Peirce's views see my "The Epistemological and Metaphysical Realism of Charles S. Peirce," Ph.D. Dissertation, University of Pennsylvania, 1968.

29. In *The Development of Peirce's Philosophy* (pp. 310–11) M. G. Murphey urges that judgments asserting the externality of things are, for Peirce, always a matter of inductive inference; and this view is shared by W. P. Haas who urges the same thesis in *The Concept of Law and the Unity of Peirce's Philosophy* (Notre Dame, Indiana: University of Notre Dame Press, 1964), pp. 41 and 50. On the other hand, the view that, for Peirce, judgments assertive of externality are not a matter of inductive inference rather than immediate perception is argued by Richard Bernstein in "Peirce's Theory of Perception," *Studies in the Philosophy of Charles Sanders Peirce*, Second Series, eds. Moore and Robin (Amehurst: University of Massachusetts Press, 1965), p. 179, and by Isabel Stearns in "Firstness, Secondness, Thirdness," *Studies in the Philosophy of Charles Sanders Peirce*, eds. Wiener and Young (Cambridge: Harvard University Press, 1952), p. 202. For a fuller exposition and discussion of each position see my "Charles Peirce and the Existence of the External World," *The Transactions of the Charles S. Peirce Society: A Quarterly Journal in American Philosophy* (Spring 1968).

30. See also 5.117.

31. This, of course, is the final verdict of one of the most outstanding members of the movement, namely, William Pepperell Montague. His thesis is convincingly argued in "The Story of American Realism," *Philosophy*, vol. 12, no. 46, pp. 140–61.

32. By way of example, it might be noted that in his recent book *Science and Subjectivity*, Israel Scheffler attempts to defend the standard view of science by showing that there is an external world which is manifested in the fact that experience constrains our opinion as to which theories are acceptable. As far as I can see, the acceptability of the standard view of science presupposes the existence of an external world and nowhere does Scheffler argue very convincingly for that presupposition.

Chapter III

Peirce's Theory of Perception

1. INTRODUCTION

Perhaps because a great deal of what Peirce said on the nature of perception seems at first glance incomplete, inconsistent, and hardly relevant to contemporary discussion, not very much has been written about Peirce's views on perception.[1] And certainly it also seems fair to say that without a clear understanding of Peirce's theory of perception it is improbable that we will be able adequately to assess the nature of Peice's metaphysics. After all, if, as Peirce claims, all knowledge begins with perception, then *what* it is that one perceives, and *how* one perceives it, will determine what it is that one can know about. And if we are unclear about the nature of perception, it is difficult to see how we can be very clear about what it is that we know, or even *how* we can know, what we claim to know when we hold forth on the nature of reality. In the following few pages, then, I hope to reconstruct the basic elements of Peirce's theory of perception in order to shed some light on the nature of his metaphysics. In doing this, I also hope to show that Peirce's doctrine on the nature of perception is quite consistent with his espousal of epistemological realism and in no way consistent with a theory of perception proper to idealism classically understood. Moreover, since it is also my purpose to examine a particular theory which has merit independently of the fact that Peirce proposed it, my examination will take the following shape: Firstly, since Peirce claimed that what we directly and immediately perceive in any act of perception is the percept, I will discuss his apparently contradictory assertions on the ontic status of percepts. On this point, I shall argue that there is no contradiction at all, and that what Peirce meant by a percept is simply a physical object perceived in the perceptual act. Secondly, as so delineated, Peirce's realistic doctrine on the ontic status of percepts naturally leads to the observation that such a doctrine is valid only if (among other things) the doctrine is embedded in a theory of perception which is such that it (a) provides independent arguments for the justification of our belief in the existence of physical objects, and (b) can counter arguments for the introduction of sense-data theories by providing an answer to the question "What did you perceive when you were hallucinated, illuded, etc?" without appealing to sense data. Since we have already noted at length the generally reliable nature of Peirce's arguments for the existence of physical (external) objects, I will only discuss (b) in order to emphasize the overall merit of Peirce's theory of perception. Thirdly, with respect to (b), after reconciling Peirce's apparently conflicting claims with respect to the epistemic status of perceptual judgments by reviewing in part his criteria for distinguishing between veridical and non-veridical perceptions, I will urge that Peirce provided a rather contemporary answer to the question formulated in (b). The answer in question is perhaps the only one consistent with his realistic characterization of the percept. In the end, I shall offer a few critical remarks on the value of the theory in question.

II. *THE PERCEPT*

Peirce very broadly defined the percept as that which we directly perceive in any act of perception.[2] The definition, of course, tells us nothing about the ontological status of what we perceive. We can still ask the following traditional sorts of questions. Is the percept some sort of nonphysical representative entity, image, appearance, or copy through which we infer the nature and existence of that which it professes to represent or copy? Is the percept *merely* a psychic entity or mental construct of the data of sensation such that percepts do not exist apart from the acts of perception? Is the percept itself an object (say, a physical object) such that percepts exist when nobody is perceiving them? What, in short, is it that we directly perceive in any act of perception? A partial answer to these questions is found in a work entitled "Telepathy and Perception" which Peirce wrote in 1903. In this essay Peirce stated that he did not believe in anything that he did not perceive. He then continued on to say:

> Only, the question arises, What do we perceive? It would not serve our turn to answer scholastically with an arbitrary definition which might be ill-considered. Let us rather set out from familiar instances, and having noticed what their relation is to the formation of scientific opinions, found upon a definition which shall cover all that is so related to knowledge and shall cover nothing else.
>   Let us say that, as I sit here writing, I see on the other side of my table, a yellow chair with a green cushion. That will be what psychologists call a "percept" *(res percepta)*. They also frequently call it

an "image". With this term I shall pick no quarrel. Only one must be on one's guard against a false impression that it might insinuate. Namely, an "image" usually means something intended to represent,—virtually professing to represent,—something else, real or ideal. So understood, the word "image" would be a misnomer for a percept. The chair I appear to see makes no professions of any kind, essentially embodies no intentions of any kind, does not stand for anything. It obtrudes itself upon my gaze; but not as a deputy for anything else, not "as" anything. It simply knocks at the portal of my soul and stands there in the doorway.

It is very insistent for all its silence. It would be useless for me to attempt to pooh-pooh it, and say, "oh come, I don't believe in the chair." I am forced to confess that it appears. Not only does it appear, but it disturbs me, more or less. I can not think the appearance is not there, nor dismiss it as I would a fancy. I can only get rid of it by an exertion of physical force. ...

Such is the percept. Now what is its logical bearing upon knowledge and belief. This may be summed up in three items, as follows:

1st, it contributes something positive. (Thus the chair has is four legs, seat and back, its yellow color, its green cushion, etc. To learn this is a contribution to knowledge.)

2nd, it compels the perceiver to acknowledge it.

3rd, it neither offers any reason for such acknowledgment nor makes any pretension to reasonableness. ... The percept, on the contrary, is absolutely dumb. It acts upon us, it forces itself upon us; but it does not address the reason, nor appeal to anything for support.

Let us say, then that anything is, for the purposes of logic, to be classed under the species of perception wherein a positive qualitative content is forced upon one's acknowledgement without any reason or pretension to reason. There will be a wider genus of things partaking of the character of perception, if there be any matter of cognition which exerts a force upon us tending to make us acknowledge it without any adequate reason. ...

A visual percept obtrudes itself upon me in its entirety I am not therein conscious of any mental process by which the image has been contructed. The psychologists, however, are able to give some account of the matter. Since 1709, they have been in possession of sufficient proof (as most of them agree) that, notwithstanding its apparent primitiveness, every percept is the product of mental processes, or at all events of processes for all intents and purposes mental, except that we are not directly aware of them; and these are processes of no little complexity. The psychologists very reasonably argue that the first impressions made upon sense must have been feelings of sense qualities,—say colors, sounds, etc.—disconnected from one another, and not appearing to stand over against a self as objects; and it would seem that this must have been true of the very first impressions ever made upon sense in the history of mental development, however far the sense of the individual man of today may have been rendered capable of immediatly apprehending the complex. But this is quite inferential. We are, of course, directly aware of positive sense-qualities in the percept (although in the percept itself they are in no wise separate from the whole object); but as for their being at first disconnected and not objectified, that is a psychological theory.[3]

In the light of this rather lengthy text it is evident that, for Peirce, the ontological status of the percept should not be construed in any way amenable to the representational hypothesis or causalistic theory of perception. The percept is not an image, appearance or any intermediary entity through which we infer the nature of something beyond. Peirce is quite willing to let the psychologist talk about percepts as images, but he is careful to caution that this sort of talk is only a way of speaking and should not be taken to imply the philosophical thesis that percepts profess to represent something beyond.[4] Moreover, in the above text Peirce talks about percepts as though they are psychic entities in so far as they are mental constructs of sensory experience and the products of cognitive elaboration. Indeed, in many places Peirce seems to vacillate between a physicalistic description of the percept and a mentalistic description.[5] I submit, however, that the sense in which Peirce talks about percepts as mental entities makes it quite impossible to claim that either he is contradictory with respect to the ontological status of percepts or that what Peirce means by a physical object is actually no more than a psychic entity which would suggest that the physicalistic language employed is a thin disguise for what is really some type of phenomenalistic commitment. Let me explain why I think this is so.

It has been suggested that what Peirce meant by his frequent claim that percepts are mental products is that the percept represents an unconscious synthesis of sensory or qualitative elements which must be taken as the evidence of our senses. In short, it has been suggested that for Peirce our sensory experience comes to us already synthesized unconsciously into percepts by an unknown mental function strangely reminiscent of Kant's synthesis in intuition.[6] The suggestion is clearly supported in the above text and elsewhere.[7] It is important to note, however, that for Peirce, while the percept is a mental construct, it is a construct of elements which are not mental in origin which accounts for the fact that it cannot be dismissed as a fancy and can only be gotten rid of by physical exertion. In short, for Peirce, there is a *given* element in experience which is unconsciously *interpreted* by unknown processes. This *given* element *as interpreted* is the percept or what we directly perceive in any act of perception. It would seem, that if one were to ask "What is the ontological status of percepts in

Peirce's theory of perception?" the answer would be that they are not either physical or mental but both. Nor is this a contradiction. I suggest that, given Peirce's definition of the percept as that which we directly perceive in any act of perception and given the way in which he talks about a percept as a mental construct *of* sensory elements, his apparent vacillation between physicalistic and mentalistic description of the percept is simply an attempt to emphasize the fact that the percept is both a *what* which is given to the perceptual act and a *what-as-interpreted* in the perceptual act. In both cases, it is the same object but enjoys a different ontological status depending on whether or not we consider it apart from its relationship to the perceptual act. If we emphasize the *what* which is given to the perceptual act, then given the fact that for Peirce the sensory content of the percept is not of mental origin, we would be forced to talk about the percept in physicalistic terms. If we emphasize the *what-as-interpreted*, then it would seem clear that the *what* does not exist independently of the perceptual act and we would then be forced to talk about the percept as a mental entity. Apart from the inherent plausibility of this suggestion, we have the evidence that what is seemingly implied by the suggestion Peirce clearly endorsed. For if the suggestion is correct and if the original definition of the percept is not ambiguous (that is, if *both* the above senses of the percept are implied by the definition—rather than either one or the other), then it would seem to follow, given the existence of physical objects as objects of perception, that physical objects enjoy an ontological status apart from their relationship to the mind in being perceived; nevertheless, if they are to be known or knowable they cannot exist independently of the perceptual act. In short, if the suggestion is correct, then Peirce would be committed to the thesis that physical objects *insofar as they are known or knowable* depend for their existence upon the perceptual act and the mental processes necessary for bringing any object to perceptual awareness, but insofar as they are physical objects they enjoy an ontological status apart from their relationship to the mind in being perceived.[8] And, moreover, he claims that physical objects cannot exist apart from some dependency upon the perceptual or cognitive act—if they could, they would not be knowable and hence would not be real objects since the real must be knowable.[9] Hence, while it would be quite true that, for Peirce, what we directly perceive in any act of perception is a mental construct of the data of sensation, or, if you will, a physical *object-as-perceived*; nevertheless, it would be quite false to claim that what we directly perceive is not a physical object just as it would be false to claim that what we directly perceive is not a mental entity. For Peirce, what we directly perceive is a physical object appearing in a certain way and the way in which it appears is causally dependent upon psychological processes.

If all this is taken to imply that there is in Peirce's theory a clear distinction between objects as they are in themselves and objects as they appear, I think the inference is sound. But if the inference is taken to imply that what we directly perceive is the appearance of things rather than the *thing-as-appearing-in-a-certain-way*, then the inference is obviously unsound since the inference would clearly commit Peirce to the thesis that percepts are not physical objects, or to the thesis that what we perceive does not enjoy any ontological status apart from its relationship to the mind in being perceived. To the question, then, "What do we perceive?" Peirce would answer "percepts." To the question "What is a percept?" Peirce would answer "a physical object as perceived in a perceptual experience." Finally to the question "Does Peirce endorse a sense data theory of perception?" the answer is apparently a resounding "no."

Needless to say, one might suggest that Peirce's theory as so far discussed presupposes two very crucial points which must be proven if the theory is to have any force. On the one hand, the theory presupposes an independent argument for the existence of physical objects, while on the other hand, the ultimate acceptability of the theory would depend upon whether or not the theory is sufficiently strong to counter contemporary arguments for the introduction of sense-data theory. We have already discussed Peirce's arguments for the existence of an external world and hence we need only discuss whether or not the theory is sufficiently strong to counter the ordinary arguments for the introduction of sense-data theory.[10]

The arguments for the introduction of sense-data are primarily the arguments from illusion and hallucination. These arguments are sufficiently well known not to need detailed restatement. Suffice it to say that the arguments appeal to the fact of hallucinations and illusions or to the fact that what we claim to see is very often not the case. In these cases what we directly perceive is not an object as it really is. Rather what we directly perceive is something else—an appearance of an object or, more strictly, a sense datum.[11] In order to see how Peirce would counter these arguments we must say something about his doctrine on the nature of perceptual judgments.

The percept is not of itself knowledge. Knowledge enters into perception only through the mediating function of the perceptual judgment which Peirce defined as a proposition asserting what the nature of the percept is or was.[12] There is, however, some ambiguity in Peirce's thought with respect to the epistemic status of perceptual judgments. Sometimes he maintains that perceptual judgments are infallibly true statements about the nature of what is perceived.[13] At other times, as we have seen, he maintains that there are no infallibly true propositions and hence perceptual judgments are as fallible as any judgment about a matter of fact.[14] This stress in Peirce's thought can be resolved if we return for a moment to Peirce's position on the nature of determining externality.

It will be recalled that for Peirce if we simply have no real doubt about the externality of what we perceive, then our belief is perfectly justified as a matter of common sense whose reports are said to be 'infallibly true' for the simple reason that in the absence of real doubt they must be accepted and are not subject to critical inquiry. However, if there is some real doubt about the externality of what we perceive, then our perceptual judgment must be looked upon as virtual prediction whose truth value is to be ascertained in accordance with the method of prediction and confirmation. Given this, Peirce's apparently conflicting claims on the nature of perceptual judgments would seem to be resolved. For if we have no real doubt about the externality or nature of what we perceive, then the perceptual judgment may be said to be infallibly true (in the sense specified above) simply because it is not subject to criticism (MS 137 (Topic 12); MS 309 (p. 41)). It is what we must accept. But if there is some real doubt about the externality or nature of what we perceive, then the perceptual judgment would be as fallible as any judgment about a matter of fact.[15] In this latter case, for instance, if we have some real doubt about the externality of a perceived object even when it is compulsive, say, a dagger floating in the air, then there are a number of operations (implied by the meaning of the proposition if true) which I may perform upon the object of this percept which would inductively confirm its externality or internality. What would it take to confirm that the dagger which I see really is an external dagger floating in the air and not merely an hallucinatory one? If it really is an external dagger, then if I grasp it, I will feel resistance; if I should so desire, then I should be able to cut something with it; if this is a real dagger, then under normal conditions I should be able to take a photograph of it and find a representation of the dagger on the developed film; etc. Theoretically, there is an infinitely long list of consequent physical states that would occur as the result of performing the operations if the proposition asserting that there is a real dagger is true. This way of determining the externality of any perceived object does not constitute a logically sufficient criterion for externality. Peirce merely intended it to be one which works generally but not infallibly so.[16] All of this brings us back to the question of whether or not Peirce's theory is sufficiently strong to counter arguments for the introduction of sense-data theories.

In the light of Peirce's doctrine on the nature of the perceptual judgment and the way in which we are to determine the veridicality of perceptual claims implying the externality of what is perceived, the question which immediately comes to mind is: If we actually do doubt the externality of what we perceive, and if we employ the method of prediction and confirmation only to find that the object which we claimed to perceive did not exist, what then did we perceive? This, of course, is the classical question for which the introduction of sense data is supposed to provide an answer. Peirce's answer to the question is quite interesting and quite contemporary. For while he often maintains that we do perceive hallucinatory objects, he is equally emphatic in insisting that, strictly speaking, in cases of hallucination (illusion, simple perceptual mistakes) to claim that one perceives anything at all is a very inexact way of speaking.[17] Peirce's answer agrees in substance with the view of many contemporary philosophers who, for various reasons, insist that in cases of hallucination (illusion and simple perceptual mistakes) one cannot be said to perceive anything at all for the simple reason that 'perceiving verbs' can be used legitimately only in cases of veridical perception.[18] In cases of nonveridical perception one 'thought,' 'mistakenly believed,' or 'seemed' to perceive something, but one did not *really* perceive what he claimed to perceive for the sufficient reason that what he claimed to perceive did not exist. In such cases the question "What did you perceive?" becomes a request for a description of the mental state or processes which one undergoes when having such a perceptual experience. It is not my point to argue here the legitimacy of such an answer.[19] It is, however, my point to urge that if the sense-datum theory can be said to be unacceptable on the grounds that one need not introduce sense data in order to answer the question "What did you perceive when your perceptual claims were nonveridical?" then Charles Peirce showed (much ahead of his time) that the introduction of sense-data theory is not necessary to answer this question. Moreover, Peirce's answer to the above question not only agrees with the position taken by a number of contemporary common-sense philosophers, but is also perfectly consistent with his doctrine on the percept, a doctrine in which he maintains that we perceive physical objects appearing in a certain way and not the appearances of physical objects.

A good deal more than this can (and should) be said about Peirce's theory of perception. I have merely tried to outlines briefly as possible the major elements of that theory in order to show the extent to which that theory entails and is entailed by his views on the nature of knowledge and his commitment to the thesis that there is a world of physical objects which are objects of perception. The theory as stated is realistic and purports to provide against the introduction of sense-data theory without naively overlooking the possibility and fact of perceptual errors. Our perceptual claims, in the absence of reasons to the contrary, are to be accepted as statements about a world of physical objects directly and immediately perceived. Where there is some real doubt about the truth of our perceptual claims, then Peirce provides us with the techniques for ascertaining the veridicality of our perceptual claims without thereby endorsing the thesis that in cases of perceptual error what we perceive are unique non-physical entities, sense data. Regardless of the truth of what he has said, there are no grounds for attributing to Peirce any phenomentalistic thesis inconsistent with his commitment to epistemological realism. And that, of course, will undermine any thesis to the effect that Peirce's theory of perception provides more evidence for the view that Peirce was an idealist than does for the view that Peirce was a realist.

Finally, if the theory of perception which we have been discussing is false or unacceptable because of some irremediable defect, it is certainly not obviously so. This done, let us now turn to the question of the consistency of Peirce's epistemological realism with his apparently idealistic definition of the real and his continual espousal of an idealistic thesis.

NOTES

1. For interesting discussions on the topic, however, see especially R. Bernstein's

"Peirce Theory of Perception" in *Studies in the Philosophy of Charles Sanders Peirce*, eds. Moore and Robin (Amherst: University of Massachusetts Press, 1961), pp. 165–89, and S. Rosenthal, "Peirce's Theory of Perceptual Judgment: An Ambiguity," *Journal for History of Philosophy* (Sept. 1969).

2. See 5.53; 7.659; 7.630; 1.532; 7.538; 1.324.

3. 7.618ff.

4. See also 5.300–304.

5. See 8.144; 8.261; and 8.153.

6. Murray G. Murphey, *The Development of Peirce's Philosophy* (Cambridge: Harvard University Press, 1961), pp. 369–72.

7. See 8.144; 8.261; 8.153; 7.643.

8. See 8.129; 8.16; 8.311; 5.408; 5.431; 6.95; 6.327; 7.337–40.

9. See 5.311; 5.408; 6.95. It should be noted that late in life Peirce came to the conclusion that there are some real things which will never be cognized. Indeed, according to Peirce the true continuum is made up of an infinite number of real but unactualized points which implies that there are some incognizable realities. Peirce's bout with the status of real possibility is notorious, but it should not be taken to imply that his work on the nature of continuity necessarily committed him *in toto* to a Kantian universe of unknowable things-in-themselves. Rather, his work on the nature of continuity and real possibility suggests that the thesis that the real must be knowable is limited to the domain actualized possibilities and does not apply to the domain of real but unactualized possibilities. By implication it would follow that the universe of real but unactualized and unactualizable possibilities is not knowable, and hence is not real in the same sense that actualized possibilities are. I suggest, then, that for Peirce the term 'real' when applied to unactualized and unactualizable possibilities does not have the same meaning that it has when applied to actualized possibilities. Hence the interpretation we are here suggesting is applicable only when the term 'real' designates actualized possibilities. In short, the fact that for Peirce there are some real things which are not knowable does not imply the falsity of the claim that all real things are knowable. There is a perfectly legitimate sense in which Peirce's claim that the real must be knowable is consistent with his claim that there are real things which will never be cognized and the consistency is a function of noting the different senses of the term 'real' and the sense in which the term must be used to justify the above interpretation.

10. For Peirce's arguments for the existence of the external world see Chapter II above.

11. See A. J. Ayer, *The Problem of Knowledge* (Oxford: Penguin Books, 1966), Chapter I.

12. 5.568; MS 596 (p. 43); 4.541; 5.54; 7.626.

13. 2.192; 5.264; 5.157; 1.150; 2.75; 4.478; 5.577; 2.147; 5.311; 5.419; 1.661; 2.248; 5.53–6; 7.620–1; 5.570; 8.261; MS 137 (Topic 13); MS 309 (p. 41).

14. See 5.506; 5.157; 5.560; 5.183; 5.480; 5.447; 6.496; 5.554.

15. The problem of the epistemic status of the perceptual judgment is further complicated by the fact that Peirce sometimes describes the perceptual judgment as a statement asserting how the percept *appears* rather than what it is or was. When he describes it in this way he most often insists that it is infallibly or indubitably true which indicates that for Peirce the perceptual judgment sometimes serves the function of a protocol statement. And, indeed, if the perceptual judgment is taken in this narrow sense, Peirce is quite correct in saying that it is infallibly true. But this usage seems to be less frequent than the usage to the effect that the perceptual judgment is a statement as to what the percept *is or was*. Therefore the problem only remains to state in what sense the perceptual judgment (as assertion of what the percept *is* or *was*) can be both infallible and fallible. In any case, Peirce ought to have introduced a different term to describe the perceptual judgment in its function as a protocol. See S. Rosenthal's "Peirce's Theory of Perceptual Judgment: An Ambiguity" in *The Journal for The History of Philosophy* (June 1969).

16. See MS 200 (MME 66); MS 200 (MME 40).

17. For those texts in which Peirce claims that we do perceive hallucinatory objects, see 7.543; 6.492; 7.639; 7.647. For the text in which Peirce maintains that strictly speaking, one does not perceive anything at all in cases of hallucination and illusion, see 7.639–40.

18. See A. J. Ayer, *The Problem of Knowledge* (Oxford: Penguin Books, 1966), pp. 90–1; R. J. Hirst, "The Difference Between Sensing and Observing" in *The Philosophy of Perception*, ed. by G. J. Warnock, (London: Oxford Univ. Press, 1967) pp. 25–32; Gilbert Ryle, *The Concept of Mind* (London: Hutchinson, 1949), p. 238.

19. H. H. Price, for example, has argued strenuously against this view when he urged that in cases of hallucination one still 'sees' something, i.e. sense datum. See "Appearing and Appearances," *The American Philosophical Quarterly* (vol. 1), 1964.

Chapter IV

Peirce's Idealism

I. INTRODUCTION

In the last two chapters, and especially in Chapter II, we have argued that Peirce's later thought manifests a commitment to the thesis that there is a world of physical objects whose existence and properties are neither logically nor causally dependent upon the noetic act of any number of finite minds.[1] These arguments, however, sidestep a number of texts which might well be cited to support the claim that, for Peirce, the existence and properties of physical objects are causally, and therefore logically, dependent upon the noetic act of the sum of finite minds identified as the community of scientific inquirers. If this latter claim can be substantiated it would seem to follow that either (a) Peirce was fundamentally inconsistent in simultaneously espousing two mutually exclusive doctrines or (b) in his later writings Peirce was not an epistemological realist at all and that the whole doctrine on externality can be subsumed into an epistemological idealism in which the notion of 'external object' does not imply causal or logical independence of the noetic act but rather the experience of duality or otherness. In other words, if the claim that the later Peirce was an epistemological idealist can be supported then Peirce was either hopelessly inconsistent or merely trying to account for realistic distinctions within an idealistic framework such as to imply that the doctrine on externality does not satisfy the classical definition of epistemological realism.

In this chapter I would like to show that (a) in spite of many indications to the contrary, the later Peirce did not endorse the thesis of epistemological idealism (as classically understood) and hence the claim that the later Peirce was hopelessly inconsistent or merely trying to account for realistic distinctions within an epistemologically idealistic framework is false, (b) while it is quite clear that the later Peirce did not espouse the tenets of epistemological idealism, nevertheless he did espouse the thesis of *objective* idealism which he considered to be quite consistent with his final endorsement of epistemological realism—which is to say that Peirce's final thought represents a *purported* synthesis of

epistemological realism and objective idealism, and finally (c) the
co-tenability of epistemological realism and objective idealism
demands that a clear distinction be made between finite minds and
the mind of the Absolute. In the end I will suggest that such a
distinction cannot be maintained and that therefore Peirce failed to
successfully synthesize both epistemological realism and objective
idealism.

II. *EPISTEMOLOGICAL IDEALISM*

There are a number of texts in which Peirce apparently defines
the real as that which is dependent upon the mind of the
community for its existence and so is incapable of existing
independently of mind. These are typical texts which might be
cited to show that Peirce was an epistemological idealist:

> The real, then, is that which, sooner or later, information and reasoning
> would finally result in, and which is therefore independent of the
> vagaries of me and you. Thus, the very origin of the conception of reality
> shows that this conception essentially involves the notion of a *Com-
> munity*, without definite limits, and capable of a definite increase of
> knowledge. And so those two series of cognitions—real and the unreal—
> consist of those which, at a time sufficiently future, the community will
> always continue to re-affirm; and of those which, under the same
> conditions, will ever after be denied.[2]

Also:

> Occam's great objection is, there can be no real distinction which is not
> *in re*, in the thing-in-itself; but this begs the question for it is itself based
> only upon the notion that reality is something independent of represen-
> tative relation.[3]

Moreover:

> The question is "Whether corresponding to our thoughts and sensations,
> and represented in some sense by them, there are realities, which are not
> only independent of the thought of you, and me, and any number of
> men, but which are absolutely independent of thought altogether." The
> objective final opinion is independent of the thoughts of any particular
> man, but is not independent of thought *in general.*[4]

And finally:

> Finally, as what anything really is, is what it may finally come to be
> known to be in the ideal state of complete information, so that reality
> depends on the ultimate decision of the community.[5]

All these texts would seem to reflect the thesis of epistemological idealism which would seem to imply that our defense of Peirce's epistemological realism is incapable of complete corroboration.

On the other hand, however, there are a plethora of texts in which Peirce insists that real objects enjoy a mode of being causally independent of the noetic act and that this thesis is repugnant to the idealistic world view:

> All reasoning goes upon the assumption that there is a true answer to whatever question may be under discussion, which answer can not be rendered false by anything the disputants may say or think about it; and further, that the denial of that true answer is false. This makes an apparent difficulty for idealism. For if all reality is of the nature of an actual idea, there seems to be no room for possibility or any lower mode than actuality, among the categories of being.[6]

And:

> What is meant by calling anything *real*? I can tell you in what sense I always use the term. ... Any objects whose attributes, i.e. all that may truly be predicated, or asserted, of it, will, and always would, remain exactly what they are, unchanged, though you or I or any man or men should think or should have thought as variously as you please, I term *external*, in contradistinction to *mental*.[7]

Also:

> A real is anything which is not affected by man's cognitions *about it*; which is a verbal definition, not a doctrine. An external object is anything that is not affected by any cognitions, whether about it or not, of the man to whom it is external.[8]

And:

> Objects are divided into figments, dreams, etc., on the one hand, and realities on the other.
>
> The former are those which exist only in as much as you or I or some man imagines them; the latter are those which have an existence independent of your mind or mine or that of any number of persons. The real is that which is not whatever we happen to think it, but is unaffected by what we may think of it. The question, therefore, is whether *man, horse*, and other names of natural classes correspond with anything which all men, or all horses, really have in common, independent of our thought, or whether these classes are constituted simply by a likeness in the way in which our minds are effected by individual objects which have in themselves no resemblance or relationship whatsoever. ... Where is the real, the thing independent of how we think it, to be found? There must be such a thing, for we find our opinions constrained; there is something, therefore, which influences our thoughts, and is not created by them. ... These thoughts, however, have been caused by sensations, and those sensations are constrained by something out of the

mind. This thing out of the mind, which directly influences sensation, and through sensation thought, because it *is* out of the mind, is independent of how we think it, and is, in short, the real.[9]

And, when attacking Royce's idealism he argues against the view that the real is causally dependent upon the mind for its existence:

> ... a true proposition corresponds to a *real matter of fact*, by which is meant a state of things, definite and individual, which *does not consist merely in being represented (in any particular representation) to be as it is* (8.126). ... The realist simply says that B is not constituted by its being represented in R; that is, he says that the fact that B is as it is, would be logically consistent with R's representing it to be otherwise. ... Professor Royce is blind to a fact which all ordinary people will see plainly enough; that the essence of the realist's opinion is that it is one thing to be and another thing to *be represented*; and the cause of this cecity is that the professor is completely immersed in his absolute idealism, which precisely consists in denying that distinction.[10]

In the face of Peirce's apparently inconsistent espousal of both epistemological realism and epistemological idealism, the first observation to be made is that many of these texts cited to support the claim that Peirce was an epistemological idealist were written before 1885 and hence represent an aspect of his earlier thought, while the texts cited to support the claim that Peirce was a epistemological realist were all (with one exception) written after 1885. The safest conclusion to draw would seem to be that the early Peirce was an epistemological idealist but that late in life, for some reason, he abandoned that thesis and unequivocally endorsed epistemological realism. This conclusion suggests the falsity of the claim that in the last analysis Peirce was either inconsistent or not an epistemological realist at all. Although this interpretation seems safe, I submit that it is false in so far as a good case can be made for the claim that Peirce *never* espoused the doctrine of epistemological idealism. Indeed, both early and late, Peirce labored to articulate a distinction purporting to show that the sense in which the real is dependent upon the mind of the community is not the same sense in which one would infer that the real is dependent for its existence or properties upon the noetic act of any number of finite minds.

I submit that the distinction amounts to this: Real objects must be considered to exist in two ways. On the one hand, a real object must exist with its existence not so causally dependent upon the noetic act as to imply that knowledge is creative of the being of objects. On the other hand, since it is essential to the definition of real object that it be knowable, it could not exist as an object of knowledge apart from a relationship to the mind. In short, the being of real objects is not constituted by the noetic act, but these objects cannot be considered of as having no relationship whatsoever to mind for otherwise they could not be known and we would be committed to a realm of unknowable things-in-them-selves.[11] The sense in which all real objects are dependent upon mind is the sense in which without mind there would be nothing known or knowable which, in effect, is to say that there would be no reality for us. And, indeed, Peirce seemed to be striving to make such a distinction when he insisted rather paradoxically that the real is and is not independent of mind. After espousing the doctrine of common sense realism he said:

> The realist will hold that the very same objects which are immediately present in our minds in experience really exist just as they are experienced out of the mind; that is, he will maintain a doctrine of immediate perception. He will not, therefore, sunder existence out of the mind and being in the mind as two wholly improportional modes. When a thing is in such a relation to the individual mind that the mind cognizes it, it is in the mind; and its being in the mind will not in the least diminish its external existence. For he does not think of the mind as a receptacle, which if a thing is in, it ceases to be out of. To make a distinction between the true conception of a thing and the thing itself is, he will say, only to regard one and the same thing from two different points of view; for the immediate object of thought in a true judgment *is* the reality.[12]

Moreover, when commenting on Royce's understanding of the realist position as implying that the real can have no relationship to mind whatsoever, Peirce said:

> ... there is no thing which is in-itself in the sense of not being relative to mind, though things which are relative to mind doubtless are, apart from that relation.[13]

And, after stating that the real is the object of the ultimate opinion of the community, Peirce claimed:

> One is struck by the inexactitude of thought even of analysts of power, when they touch upon modes of being. One will meet, for example, the virtual assumption that what is relative to thought can not be real. But why not, exactly? Red is relative to sight but the fact that this or that is in that relation to vision that we call being red is not *itself* relative to sight; it is a real fact.[14]

And:

> Nothing can be more completely false than that we can experience only

our ideas. That is indeed the very epitome of all falsity. Our knowledge of things in themselves is entirely relative, it is true; but all experience and all knowledge is knowledge of that which is, independently of being represented. ... At the same time no proposition can relate or even pretend to relate to any object otherwise than as that object is represented.[15]

Finally:

Whatever is relative to sight is not mental. ... It is true that all colors are relative to the sense of sight. Yet there is a difference between color and the sensation of color. For a color is a quality of a thing which remains the same whether it be seen by a normal or color-blind eye.

Hence it becomes evident that when Peirce attacked idealism he attacked absolute idealism or the view that knowledge constitutes the being of the objects known, and that when he espoused what is apparently epistemological idealism he was simply espousing the view that the real is knowable which is to say that the real is dependent for its being known (or knowable) upon the minds of the community. This latter determination, however, is not such as to constitute the *being* of the objects known rather than the being-known of those objects. Moreover, given the above, Peirce's apparently idealistic definition of the real is not only not idealistic (in the epistemological sense of the term), but also, it is trivially true and necessary for a realism which insists upon a world of *knowable* external objects. This we have already seen in Chapter II above. Hence Peirce's definition of the real as the object of the ultimate opinion of the community in no way conflicts with his definition of the real as that which is independent of what we think about it. Rather, such an alternate definition is a necessary adjunct for a realism which maintains that the real external independent world is knowable.[17] For these reasons I believe that a good case can be made for the claim that Peirce was never an epistemological idealist.

This interpretation, of course, differs somewhat from the view of Murray Murphey. Professor Murphey maintains that the early Peirce was an epistemological idealist but the later Peirce abandoned this doctrine, as we shall see, for an objective idealism not to be confused with the early doctrine.[18] It is important to note that if Murphey's interpretation is correct, it is at least consonant with our interpretation on the nature of Peirce's later thought. Whichever interpretation we accept, we must conclude in any event that the later Peirce was not an epistemological idealist. This conclusion accounts for those late texts in which Peirce openly repudiates the claims of absolute idealism.

III. *OBJECTIVE IDEALISM*

These results should not be taken to imply that the later Peirce was in no sense an idealist (as some have suggested) but only that he was not an epistemological idealist. Indeed, it is quite clear that along with his denial of epistemological idealism the later Peirce strenuously endorsed the thesis of *objective* idealism which he held to be quite consistent with his final endorsement of epistemological realism. Consider the following texts in which the later Peirce claimed to be an objective idealist:

> The old dualistic notion of mind and matter, so prominent in Cartesianism, as two radically different kinds of substance, will hardly find defenders today. Rejecting this, we are driven to some form of hylopathy, otherwise called monism. Then the question arises whether physical laws on the one hand and the psychical law on the other are to be taken—(a) as independent, a doctrine often called *monism*, but which I would name *neutralism*; or (b) the psychical law as derived and special, the physical law alone as primordial, which is *materialism*; or (c) the physical law as derived and special, the psychical law alone as primordial, which is *idealism*.
>
> The materialistic doctrine seems to me quite repugnant to scientific logic as to common sense; since it requires us to suppose that a certain kind of mechanism will feel, which would be a hypothesis absolutely irreducible to reason—an ultimate, inexplicable regularity; while the only possible justification of any theory is that it should make things clear and reasonable.
>
> Neutralism is sufficiently condemned by the logical maxim known as Ockham's razor, i.e., that not more independent elements are to be supposed than necessary. ...
>
> The one intelligible theory of the universe is that of objective idealism, that matter is effete mind, inveterate habits becoming physical laws.[19]

And:

> I have begun by showing that *tychism* must give birth to an evolutionary cosmology, in which all the regularities of nature of mind are regarded as products of growth, and to a Schelling-fashioned idealism which holds matter to be mere specialized and partially deadened mind.[20]

And:

> I have thus developed as well as I could in a little space the synechistic philosophy, as applied to mind. I think that I have succeeded in making it clear that this doctrine gives room for explanations of many facts which without it are absolutely and hopelessly inexplicable; and further

that it carries along with it the following doctrines: first, a logical realism of the most pronounced type; second, objective idealism; third, tychism, with its consequent thoroughgoing evolutionism.[21]

In an essay entitled 'Man's Glassy Essence', written in 1891, Peirce began with a discussion on the molecular constitution and properties of matter. He then proceeded to catalogue the general properties of the class of substances called life-slimes or protoplasm. The most wonderful and indubitable property of protoplasm is, according to Peirce, that it feels or is conscious. It exercises all the functions of mind. But what, asked Peirce, is to be said of the property of feeling? If consciousness belongs to all protoplasm by what mechanical constitution is this to be accounted for? By what element of the molecular arrangement would feeling be caused? Peirce's answer was that the attempt to deduce it from the three laws of mechanics is futile. It can never be explained, unless we admit that physical events are but degraded or undeveloped forms of psychical events. Accordingly, Peirce claimed that initially everything was mind, that matter is effete mind, that through chance reactions to certain stimuli matter takes on habits or certain uniform ways of acting which constitute the laws of the universe. At first, matter reacts in terms of pure chance but gradually it takes on uniform ways of acting and continually evolves under the influence of ever more specific and complex modes of habit-taking that cannot be explained in a purely mechanical theory of life.[22] The elements then, of Peirce's cosmology include what he calls *objective idealism, tychism*, and *synechism*. The only plausible theory that can account for the properties of feeling and intelligence in the universe is the theory which postulates that all that is is mind and that matter is effete mind. This is *objective idealism*. Secondly, matter in its initial state responds at random to stimuli in a purely fortuitious way, which is to say that its initial responses are governed by absolute chance. This is *tychism*. Finally, although the initial responses of matter are governed by absolute chance, matter tends to take on habits of activity which accounts for law, generality, and continuity in the universe. This is *synechism* or the thesis that all that is is general. Hence, by postulating the theory that matter is effete mind which takes on law-like activities through initial responses that are governed by absolute chance, Peirce has provided an idealistic metaphysics which incorporates an evolutionary cosmology that can be explained in terms of purely mechanical theory of life. This is why Peirce insisted that an idealist need not fear a purely mechanical theory of life. Rather, such a theory, fully developed, is bound to call in a tychistic idealism as an indispensable adjunct.[23] In the last analysis, it would follow that for Peirce physical objects are bits or chunks of the Absolute Mind and exist as parts of the Absolute Mind in an undeveloped state. The property of human intelligence is an evolutionary characteristic of matter and, hence, it too, must be considered as a part of the Absolute Mind. The ordinary dualistic distinction between mind and matter is rejected for a monism of objective idealism. All this, of course, has been clearly well stated by Professor Murphey in a more detailed fashion and it is unfortunate that some of his critics still do not see that this, and only this, is the sense in which the later Peirce was an idealist.[24]

Peirce's endorsement of objective idealism late in life accounts for all those texts in which he claims to be an idealist, while his endorsement of epistemological realism accounts for all those texts in which he claims to repudiate the thesis of idealism. Clearly, his later repudiation of idealism is the repudiation of epistemological rather than objective idealism. Moreover, Peirce felt that there was nothing contradictory in his espousal of both epistemological realism and objective idealism. In Peirce's later thought, then, there are physical objects the existence and properties of which do not depend either logically or causally upon the noetic act of any number of finite minds, but these physical objects are themselves of the nature of mind; they are bits or chunks of the Absolute Mind. This also accounts for Peirce's apparently contradictory statements to the effect that even an idealist need not deny the existence of an external world.[25]

IV. *CONCLUSION*

In the last analysis, however, the espousal of both epistemological realism and objective idealism is very questionable. If, on the one hand, real external objects are causally and logically independent of finite minds, but are not causally or logically independent of the Absolute Mind (since they are of its nature and since without the Absolute they would not exist), then there must be a real distinction between finite minds and the mind of the Absolute—otherwise the union of epistemological realism and objective idealism is impossible. For, if the aggregate of finite minds (Community) is, in fact, identical to the Absolute Mind (as Peirce sometimes suggests), then either there really are no finite minds or the Absolute mind is finite, being simply the collection of finite minds; but if there are not finite minds, then it is nonsense to defend the thesis of epistemological realism, and if the Absolute Mind is finite, then it would be nonsense for an epistemological realist to claim that physical objects do not exist independently of the Absolute Mind. If, on the other hand, the aggregate of finite minds is not identical to the Absolute Mind, then the thesis that one can be an epistemological realist and an objective idealist seems tenable. But this, of course, only raises the question as to how it is possible to assert that there is an Absolute Mind which is the sum total of all being while at the same time asserting that there is something which the Absolute is not. This is a classical problem which must be faced if one is to hold the existence of an Absolute being endowed with the quality of mind and at the same time hold the existence of finite minds and physical objects which are not identical with the Absolute in the sense of being something or having some properties which the Absolute does not possess. Hence, if the aggregate of finite minds is identical to the Absolute Mind, then the thesis that one can consistently be both an epistemological realist and an objective idealist would seem to be untenable; if, on the other hand, the aggregate of finite minds is not identical to the Absolute Mind, then one must explain how there can be an Absolute and something which the Absolute is not. Needless to say, I am urging that one cannot consistently be both an epistemological realist and an objective idealist. No doubt, Peirce should have said more on the matter. More on this later.

Finally, bypassing for now the difficulties involved in reconciling epistemological realism and objective idealism, it is important to note that, in arguing for the doctrine of objective idealism, Peirce relied upon the claim that the property of feeling is irreducible to a property of matter. But it can hardly be said that Peirce provided very much argumentation for his latter claim. As a matter of fact, in the light of standard materialistic rejoiners, if the acceptability of the doctrine of objective idealism rests ultimately upon the claim that the property of feeling is irreducible to a property of matter, then it is difficult to see how the doctrine can be successfully defended in any quick way. By the same token, however, given the contemporary status of the mind–body problem, it is difficult to see how the doctrine can be successfully refuted.

In sum, the main conclusions that we have here reached are: (a) It is clear that the later Peirce was unequivocally committed to the denial of epistemological idealism while equally committed to both epistemological realism and what he termed *objective* idealism. This indicates that Peirce was not simultaneously espousing the mutually contradictory doctrines of epistemological realism and epistemological idealism in the later period; and this also indicates that his realism cannot be subsumed into an epistemological idealism. (b) The co-tenability of epistemological realism and objective idealism demands that a clear distinction be made between finite minds and the mind of the Absolute. It seems evident that the delineation of such a distinction involves certain classical difficulties which Peirce was either reluctant or impotent to discuss. Until someone can show that Peirce espousal of objective idealism is independently arguable and that the view is consistent with epistemological realism, I don't see how we can escape the conclusion that in the end Peirce's metaphysics took an unfortunate turn. But we can reflect on this later when we draw our conclusions. For the moment, let us turn now to the question of Peirce's *Logical* Realism.

NOTES

1. For similar views, see B. Gresham Riley's "Existence, Reality and Objects of Knowledge" in *Transactions of the Charles S. Peirce Society: A Journal in American Philosophy* IV, No. 1 (Winter 1968), pp. 34ff; and John E. Smith's "Community and Reality" in *Perspectives on Peirce*, ed. by R. J. Bernstein, Yale University Press, New Haven: 1965, pp. 92ff; and A. J. Ayer's *The Origins of Pragmatism* (San Francisco: Freeman, Cooper and Co., 1968), pp. 19ff.

2. 5.311 (1868). See also 5.356 (1868); 2.654 (1877); 5.352 (1868).

3. 5.312 (1868).

4. 7.336 (1873). See also 7.339 (1873).

5. 5.316 (1868). See also 8.13 (1877).

6. 8.126 (1902). See also MS 200 (MME 35); MS 317R; MS 322R; MS 371.

7. 6.327 (1908). See also 5.118 (1903); 5.457 (1905); 5.565 (1901–6); 5.503 (1905); 6.453 (1908); 5.96 (1903); 6.349 (1902); 5.431 (1905); 6.95 (1903); 5.535 (1905); 5.56–8 (1903); and 7.564 (1893).

8. 5.525 (1905); MS 596 L12.

9. 8.12.

10. 8.129 (1902). For other texts supporting the same thesis but which were written from 1890 on see Chapter II above.

11. See footnote 8 above.

12. 8.16 (1871).

13. 5.311 (1868). See also 5.408 (1877).

14. 5.431 (1905).

15. 6.95 (1903).

16. 6.327 (1905). See also 7.337–40 (1873).

17. These results remove major difficulties (alluded to in Chapter II) surrounding the soundness of Peirce's second type of argument in defense of the thesis that there is an external world. See pp. 154ff above.

18. M. G. Murphey, "Kant's Children: The Cambridge Pragmatists," *Transactions of the Charles S. Peirce Society*, IV, No. 1 (Winter 1968).

19. 6.24 (1891). See also 4.551 (1905); 6.264ff (1891).

20. 6.102–8.

21. 6.163.

22. 6.238–71 (1891). See also 6.287–317 (1891).

23. 6.265 (1891).

24. B. Gresham Riley in his interesting article, "Existence, Reality and Objects of Knowledge," *Transactions of the Charles S. Peirce Society*, IV, No. 1 (Winter 1968), pp. 34ff argues that Peirce was never an epistemological idealist and that the sense in which Peirce was an idealist was simply the sense in which he insisted that real objects must be knowable and hence dependent upon mind for their status as objects of knowledge. While I believe that a good case could be made for the claim that Peirce was never an epistemological idealist, it seems to me patently false to urge that the only sense in which Peirce is an idealist is the sense in which he insists that real objects are knowable. Indeed, such an interpretation clearly obfuscates and overlooks the true nature and substance of Peirce's later commitment to objective idealism as put forth above. Moreover, it seems that if one were to argue that Peirce was *never* an epistemological idealist one would be obliged to show that Murphey's interpretation of Peirce's earlier thought is false and this is not accomplished very well by pointing to the fact that there are early texts (Riley gives two) supporting the view that the sense in which the real is dependent upon the mind of the community is not the sense in which the existence and properties of physical objects are logically and causally dependent upon mind. Indeed, if one were to question Murphey's interpretation of Peirce's earlier idealism, one would be obliged to show, among other things, that Peirce's denial of first impressions of sense and the consequent location of the real at the end of inquiry does not entail epistemological idealism. Whether or not this can be shown is another matter. In general, I think Murphey's interpretation of Peirce's later thought sound and illuminating although, as I have shown, I have extensive doubts as to whether or not the early Peirce was an epistemological idealist. I have not pursued the issue very far since my primary concern is with the nature of Peirce's later thought and whether or not the nature of his later idealism is consistent with his later commitment to epistemological realism.

25. See 5.539; 7.335; 8.106.

Chapter V

Peirce's Pragmatism and Scotistic Realism

I. INTRODUCTION

Without some extended discussion of Peirce's intellectual debt to the medieval philosopher Duns Scotus, it is unlikely that a thorough understanding of Peirce's philosophy is possible. Peirce claimed that the doctrines of the medieval realists, and especially the doctrines of Duns Scotus, had a monumental influence on the development and nature of his own thought. Indeed, he even went so far as to claim that pragmaticism is merely an outgrowth of Scotistic realism and that pragmatism could never have entered the mind of anyone who was not already convinced of the truth of Scotistic realism. A good deal has already been written on this topic and while it is clear that Scotus greatly influenced Peirce, I do not think that that influence has yet been properly characterized. As we shall see, one can make a very good case for the claim that Peirce was not at all a Scotistic realist. In a sense, this latter claim is true but uninteresting and misleading. Uninteresting because the claim sheds no light on the reasons why Peirce thought he was a Scotistic realist; and misleading because, after it is understood why Peirce thought himself a Scotistic realist and how he qualified his commitment, there is a perfectly legitimate sense in which his claim is true and important for understanding his philosophy. As James Ross has pointed out, we need to know precisely what adjustments Peirce made in the conceptual scheme he derived from Scotus and why he considered those adjustments necessary.[1] Unfortunately, in seeking to satisfy this need we shall be obliged to repeat some fairly familiar facts about the doctrines of Peirce and Scotus. Hopefully, however, it will be seen that our conclusion is anything but a re-hash and that a certain amount of re-hash is not so terribly perverse if it leads to a clear comprehensive thesis not yet provided.

Before beginning our discussion, however, it should be noted that when Peirce claimed to be a Scotistic realist his concern was with *logical* and not *epistemological* realism. The term 'realism' admits of two distinct definitions. On the one hand, it can be taken to designate that epistemological doctrine which insists that there is a world of knowable physical objects whose existence and properties are logically and causally independent of the noetic or perceptual act of any number of finite minds. On the other hand, the term 'realism' may also be taken to designate the logical doctrine that *universals* are in some sense real and function as the referent for general terms. This latter doctrine is the doctrine of logical realism which is usually contrasted with various species of nominalism the fundamental tenet of which is that only individuals exist while the universal is some sort of mental or linguistic fiction. The term 'realism' then, can be taken to designate two distinct philosophical theses which arise out of two distinct philosophical problems; the first of which is the problem of whether or not our belief in the existence of a knowable external world is justified, while the second of which is the problem of whether or not the elements of our experience exist (independently of knowing or otherwise) as individuals or universals or both. Epistemological realism does not imply logical realism and logical realism does not imply epistemological realism.

When Peirce claimed to be a Scotistic realist he was referring not to the epistemological doctrine but rather to the logical doctrine and the claim itself would seem to suggest that Peirce endorsed Scotus' solution to the problem of universals. We shall begin by looking briefly to Scotus' solution to the problem of universals. Thereafter we shall state Peirce's solution, show by comparison the fundamental differences between Peirce and Scotus, and finally point to the sense in which it is legitimate, important and illuminating to say that Peirce was a Scotistic realist.

II. *SCOTUS ON UNIVERSALS*[2]

With respect to the problem of universals, Scotus distinguished two acts of the intellect which correspond to the distinction between intuitive and abstractive knowledge. The first act of the intellect is the immediate and simple apprehension of an individual in so far as it is present and existing, and, as such, the first act of the intellect is opposed to the second or abstractive act of the intellect which reaches the object in its essence. Unlike the intuitive or the first act of the intellect, the act of abstraction is indifferent to the existence or nonexistence, to the presence or absence of the object apprehended. This second act of the intellect gives us knowledge of the essence of an object considered in abstraction from existence, whereas the former act gives us knowledge of an object as existent and actually present. The passage from sensible and intuitive knowledge of individuals to speculative or intellectual knowledge of the universal is effected by the act of abstraction which Scotus characterized in much the same way as Aristotle and his medieval followers.

But Scotus' solution to the problem of universals is actually more detailed and subtle than the Aristotelian solution. As a matter of fact, Scotus distinguished three senses of the term 'universal'. First, there is what Scotus called the *metaphysical* universal, or the remote subject of the first intention, which remote subject is a common nature existing in many individuals of the same species, not as it actually exists in concrete things but rather as it exists independently of being concretized in a state of positive indetermination. Secondly, there is the *physical* universal, or the near subject of the first intention, which is the common nature as it exists in individuals such that it is a specific nature. The *physical* universal results from the contraction of the common nature in its original undetermined state (the *metaphysical* universal) to the mode of individuality via the addition of an individuating principle, *haecceitas*, to the common nature. The *metaphysical* universal, or the common nature as it exists in itself prior to determination, is real but neither individual nor universal (*equinitas est equinitas tantum*). As remote subject of the first intention, the common nature or the *metaphysical* universal is the universal in the broad sense; whereas the common nature as near subject, or as contracted to the mode of individuality, is the universal in the strict sense. Neither of these however is the *logical* universal. Thirdly, there is the *logical* universal which is the metaphysical universal conceived reflexively in its predicability and analyzed into its constitutive notes.[3] The *logical* universal is neither the near nor the remote subject of the first intention but rather is a second intention. The *logical* universal is an *ens rationis*. The intellect confers logical universality but not real metaphysical commonness. The common nature then, as it is in itself, is real but neither individual nor universal, but in potency with respect to individual and universal determination. It is contracted to the mode of individuality by the addition of *haecceity* (from which it is *formally* distinct[4]) and rendered logically universal by the agent intellect abstracting it from its mode of individuality and rendering it predicable of many on the basis of real metaphysical commonness.[5] Thus Socrates and

Plato have the same nature but that nature is not numerically one for both of them. For this reason the common nature prior to determination is said to have a unity less than numerical:

> I say ... that the unity of the sense object is not some universal unity in act, but nevertheless something one, by some prior unity a real unity, by which the understanding is moved, so that there should result something common abstracted from this or that singular of the same species, rather than of diverse species, as otherwise the universal would be a fiction only. The understanding being taken away, that white would rather agree with another white than with something of another genus. Wherefore I say that the real unity preceding the act of understanding is one *in* many, not however, one *of* many but is made one of many through the understanding and then is actually universal, not before.[6]

Gilson has maintained that Scotus Platonized the common nature by giving it an extra-mental reality.[7] Such a view is obviously false if taken to imply that the metaphysical universal has numerical unity. The common nature does not lose its commonness by being contracted to the mode of individuality since it is still formally distinct from its principle of individuation, although it must be admitted that only individuals exist. Scotus avoided extreme Platonic realism by insisting that the metaphysical universal, which is the foundation of logical universality, is not numerically one; while at the same time he apparently avoided nominalism by insisting that there is something really (though not numerically) common to many individuals of the same species. It is precisely the formal distinction between the common nature and the principal of individuation which allowed Scotus to insist that only individuals exist but also that each individuals possesses a real commonness which is the foundation for the logical universal and the objective referent for universal terms.

The universal as the common nature possessing less than numerical unity, as reduced to the mode of individuality (but still maintaining its distinctive commonness) may be understood, as Charles McKeon has pointed out, as the universal *ante rem* and *in re* respectively. It is neither actually universal nor individual but a habit, tendency, or disposition to be individually or universally actualized, universally actualizable as the immediate ground of predicability of many. The common nature as contracted to the mode of individuality is the immediate, though of itself the incomplete ground of the logical universal.[8] Let us now examine Peirce's solution to the problem of universals.

III. *PEIRCE AND THE PROBLEM OF UNIVERSALS*

With regard to the problem of universals, Peirce claimed, like Scotus, that the most important point to be insisted upon is that universals are in some sense real. Peirce once expressed the problem of universals by maintaining that fundamentally the question was whether or not "man," "horse," and any other names of natural classes correspond with anything which all men, or all horses, really have in common, independent of our thought, or whether these classes are constituted simply by a likeness in the way in which our minds are affected by individual objects which have in themselves no resemblance or relationship whatsoever. Peirce maintained that the nominalist does not admit that two men really have anything in common, for to say that they are both men is only say that one mental term or thought-sign "*man*" stands indifferently for either of the sensible objects (8.12).[9] Peirce's Scholastic or Scotistic realism consisted in positing the reality of generals or universals but it should be noted that what Peirce meant by the universal and what Scotus meant by the universal are quite different.

In the 1870's, according to M. G. Murphey, Peirce had come to the conclusion that if relations were as abstract and as fundamental as qualities, the meaning of a concept or the essence of an object might very well consist in its relations to other objects.[10] Hence the relations of a thing or its operations would be the source of its embodied quality rather than the embodied quality being the source of the operations or relations of a thing. This in effect would simply imply that there is no reason why a law governing the operation of a thing should not be as essential as any abstract property which it may embody. Murphey goes on to say that the analogy between a general law and a habit was pointed out by Peirce in 1868 and it only remained for him to extend the concept of essence to include laws for the essence of an object to be identified with the habits it involves. Peirce took this step in 1871 in his review of Fraser's edition of the works of Berkeley. In this review Peirce asserted that the meaning of any concept consists in its translation into a set of conditional statements whose antecedents prescribe certain operations to be performed and whose consequents list sensible experience which would occur (as the result of performing the operations specified in the antecedent) if the concept were true. 'Intellectual concepts', then, find their meaning expressed in an appropriate set of conditionals relating certain operations on an object to expected sensible consequences. These hypotheticals, which express the meaning of any intellectual concept, are nothing other than statements of law or habit specifying the object of that conception.[11] The point to be emphasized here is that the law which is expressed in the meaning of a concept or proposition and which accounts for the meaning of our propositions is Thirdness which Peirce claims is the element of habit, mediation, continuity, and rationality immediately perceived in our experience.[12] Moreover, it is the indeterminacy of Thirdness which accounts for the generality and vagueness of all predicates which in turn accounts for Peirce's claim that the meaning of any proposition consists in a *theoretically infinitely* long list of conditionals which in turn accounts for Peirce's claim that the *meaning* of any proposition can only be partially specified and the *truth value assigned* to any proposition is corrigible.[13] The phenomenological analysis of Thirdness in its material aspect provided Peirce with a metaphysical foundation and justification for the pragmatic theory of meaning and truth.

Hence, by 1872 Peirce, had developed a theory of meaning and truth the substance of which committed him to specifying the meaning of *any* concept or proposition in terms of law, habit, continuity or Thirdness. It may be, as Murphey maintains, that Peirce's earlier writings committed him to a scholastic theory of essence in so far as his earlier writings were committed to the subject-copula-predicate theory of the proposition. In any event, with the introduction of the logic of relations and the pragmatic theory of meaning, Peirce's view on the nature of the universal was hardly scholastic. For Peirce, the essence of anything is the sum of habits it involves. Instead of seeking a qualitative essence from which the behavior of a thing follows, Peirce identified the essence of a thing with its behavior. Our objective in the investigation of a thing is to discover the laws governing its behavior and not a form which serves as the basis of natural classification.[14] The discovery of the logic of relations and the pragmatic theory of meaning, then, led Peirce to rephrase the problem of universals from 'Are universals real?' to 'Are laws or general types real or are they merely figments of the mind?' In order to refute nominalism Peirce then set out to prove that there is real law or continuity in the universe.

And in 1903, when Peirce delivered the Lowell Lectures at Harvard, he proposed to show conclusively, by way of experiment, that indeed laws are real and not mere figments of the mind.

Although somewhat lengthy, this argument is sufficiently important to warrant quoting it before offering an assessment of it. He said:

> I proceed to argue that *Thirdness* is operative in Nature. Suppose we attack the question experimentally. Here is a stone. Now I place that stone where there will be no obstacle between it and the floor, and I will predict with confidence that as soon as I let go my hold upon the stone it will fall to the floor. I will prove that I can make a correct prediction by actual trial if you like. But I see your faces that you all think it will be a very silly experiment. Why so? Because you all know very well that I can predict what will happen, and that the fact will verify my prediction.
>
> But *how can* I know what is going to happen? You certainly do not think that it is by clairvoyance, as if the future event by its existential reactiveness could affect me directly, as in an *experience* of it, as an event scarcely past might affect me. You know very well that there is nothing of the sort in this case. Still, it remains true that I *do know* that that stone will drop, as a *fact*, as soon as I let go my hold. If I *truly know* anything, that which I know must be *real*. It would be quite absurd to say that I could be enabled to know how events are going to be determined over which I can exercise no more control than I shall be able to exercise over this stone after it shall have left my hand, that I can so peer in the future merely on the strength of any acquaintance with any pure fiction.
>
> I know that this stone will fall if it is let go, because experience has convinced me that objects of this kind always do fall; and if anyone present has any doubt on the subject, I should be happy to try the experiment, and I will bet him a hundred to one on the result.
>
> But the general proposition that all solid bodies fall in the absence of any upward forces or pressure, this formula I say, is of the nature of a representation. Our nominalistic friends would be the last to dispute that. They will go so far as to say that it is a *mere* representation—the word *mere* meaning that to be represented and really to be are two different things; and that this formula has no being except a being represented. It certainly is of the nature of a representation. That is undeniable, I grant. And it is equally undeniable that that which is of the nature of a representation is not *ipso facto* real. In that respect there is a great contrast between an object of reaction and an object of representation. Whatever reacts is *ipso facto* real. But an object of representation is not *ipso facto* real. If I were to predict that on my letting go of the stone it would fly up in the air, that would be mere fiction; and the proof that it was so would be obtained by simply trying the experiment. That is clear. On the other hand, and by the same token, the fact that I *know* that this stone will fall to the floor when I let it go, as you all must confess, if you are not blinded by theory, that I *do* know—and you none of you care to take up my bet, I notice—is the proof that the formula, or uniformity, as furnishing a safe basis for prediction, is, or if you like it better, *corresponds to,* a reality.
>
> Possibly at this point somebody may raise an objection and say: You admit, that (it) is one thing really to be and another to be represented;

and you further admit that it is of the nature of the law of nature to be represented. Then it follows that it has not the mode of being a reality. My answer to this would be that it rests upon an ambiguity. When I say that the general proposition as to what will happen, whenever a certain condition may be fulfilled, is of the nature of a representation, I mean that it refers to experiences *in futuro,* which I do not know are all of them experienced and never can know have been all experienced. But when I say that really to to be is different from being represented, I mean that what really is, ultimately consists in what shall be forced upon us in experience, that there is an element of brute compulsion in fact and fact is not a mere question of reasonableness. Thus, if I say, "I shall wind up my watch every day as long as I live," I never can have a positive experience which *certainly* covers all that is here promised, because I never shall know for certain that my last day has come. But what the real fact will be does not depend upon what I represent, but upon what the experiential reactions shall be. My assertion that I shall wind up my watch every day of my life may turn out to accord with facts, even though I be the most irregular of persons, by my dying before nightfall.

If we call that being true by chance, here is a case of a general proposition being entirely true in all its generality by chance.

Every general proposition is limited to a finite number of occasions in which it might conceivably be falsified, supposing that it is an assertion confined to what human beings may experience; and consequently it is conceivable that, although it should be true without exception, it should still only be by chance that it turns out true.

But if I see a man who is very regular in his habits and am led to offer to wager that that man will not miss winding his watch for the next month, you have your choice between two alternative hypotheses only:

1. You may suppose that some *principle* or *cause* is *really* operative to make him wind his watch daily, which *active principle* may have more or less strength; or

2. You may suppose that it is mere chance that his actions have hitherto been regular; and in that case, that regularity in the past affords you not the slightest reason for expecting its continuance in the future, any more than, if he had thrown sixes three times running, *that* event would render it either more or less likely that his next throw would show sixes.

It is the same with the operations of nature. With overwhelming uniformity, in our past experience, direct and indirect, stones left free to fall have fallen. Thereupon two hypotheses only are open to us. Either—

1. the uniformity with which those stones have fallen has been due to mere chance and affords no ground whatever, not the slightest, for any expectation that the next stone that shall be let go will fall; or

2. the uniformity with which stones have fallen has been due to some *active general principle*, in which case it would be a strange coincidence that it should cease to act at the moment my prediction was based upon it.

That position, gentlemen, will sustain criticism. It is irrefragable.

Of course, every sane man will adopt the latter hypothesis. If he could doubt it in the case of the stone—which he can't—and I may as well drop the stone once and for all—I told you so!—if anybody doubts this still, a thousand other such inductive predictions are getting verified every day, and he will have to suppose every one of them to be merely fortuitous in order reasonably to escape the conclusion that *general principles are really operative in nature*. That is the doctrine of scholastic realism. (5.64–67)[15]

Notice that in arguing for the reality of laws, Peirce asserted that he was defending the doctrine of scholastic realism, or the view that general principles are really operative in nature. Notice, too, that, in the end, his reason for saying that there are laws is that the behaviour of certain objects (the falling stone) is predictable because regular. The fact that we *know* the stone will fall when once released shows that the behaviour of the stone is rule governed or lawlike—otherwise we could not know that this stone, when released, will fall toward the earth. Stones released never 'fall' up. Furthermore, that the law governing the behaviour of the stone is real, and not a mere figment of the mind (as the nominalist asserts) is a function of the fact that we have no control over the fall of the stone when once released. The difference between a fiction and an external fact (real fact) is that the former, and not the latter, is subject to control by our will. Hence it is the compulsiveness, or the Secondness of the stone's behaviour, when released, which shows that the observable lawlike behaviour is not mental in origin but rather real and external. Recall that in Chapter II it was argued that Peirce's criterion for externality is Secondness, compulsiveness, or the inability of the mind to control the object of perception. And here the same criterion is brought into play to demonstrate the reality, or externality, of laws or real Thirdness in the world. We also saw in Chapter II (pp. 168ff) that Peirce's criterion for externality derives its force from his general argument to the effect that we know that there is an external world because we find our opinions constrained by a force of experience outside ourselves. So, by way of assessing the above proof for the (external) existence of universals (laws), it would appear that Peirce's proof is no stronger and no weaker than his general argument to effect that we know an external world exists because some of our opinions are constrained by a force outside ourselves and over which our wills have no control. We have already assessed the strength of this argument (pp. 114ff) and in the light of that assessment I think we can conclude once again that, at the very least, Peirce has succeeded in casting the burden of proof back upon the sceptic who, in this case, is the nominalist.[16]

It should now be clear that the scope of Peirce's epistemological realism extends beyond the view that there is a knowable external world and further asserts that what is so knowable are universals or laws, individuals (as traditionally conceived) being figments in this synechistic universe. Hence we cannot grasp the full scope of Peirce's epistemological realism without viewing it in conjunction with his defense of logical realism. This is why we cannot understand Peirce's epistemological realism without a close examination of his commitment and defense of logical realism. Accordingly, Peirce's debt to medieval philosophy is by no means incidental to a full understanding of his metaphysics.

Finally, we argued at the beginning of this chapter that epistemological realism as traditionally conceived, does not imply, and is not implied by, logical realism. But we also saw that when Peirce came to Harvard to defend his view that laws or universals are not fictions of the mind but are real (external) and operative in nature, he appealed fundamentally to the very same basic argument which he offered in defending his belief in the existence of an external world, namely, that some of our opinions are constrained by a force of experience over which we have no control. In virtue of this alone, we have seen that if Peirce's defense of epistemological realism fails, then so too does his logical realism. But more importantly, it also suggests that, if we can argue along with Peirce that there are no individuals, and if the sceptic cannot shoulder the burden of proof which Peirce's defense of epistemological realism places upon him, then epistemological realism, properly argued, entails logical realism. And this would have the effect of casting a long dark shadow over the view that epistemological realism does not imply logical realism just as much as it would over the view that logical realism, properly defended, does not imply epistemological realism.

But none of this should be taken to imply that, in so defending what he called 'the scholastic doctrine' on the reality of universals, Peirce was thereby defending Scotus' solution to the problem of universals. Nor, as we shall see, was he offering a straightforward defense of the existence of what the scholastics meant by universals. Indeed, I shall now show how radically Peirce's solution to the problem of universals differs from that of the scholastics and Scotus. Thereafter the nature and significance of Scotus' influence of Peirce will be taken up. So, let us proceed.

Peirce understood Scotus' position on Universals as follows: Such natures or sorts of things as a man or a horse which are real, and are not necessarily of themselves *this* man or *this* horse, are in the *species intelligibilis* always represented positively indeterminate, it being the nature of the mind to so represent things. Peirce then maintained:

> Accordingly, any such nature is to be regarded as something which is of itself neither universal nor singular, but is universal in the mind, singular in things outside the mind. ... It is the very same nature which in the mind is universal and *in re* is singular; for if it were not, in knowing anything of a uiniversal we should be knowing nothing of things, but only of our thoughts, and our opinion would not be converted from true to false by a change in things. (8.18ff)[17]

Peirce understood Scotus to maintain that the universal as it actually existed in things was contracted to the mode of singularity. For Peirce, however, the universal *in re* is not a singular having something in common with all the other singulars of its species; rather, the universal *in re* is law, continuity, mediation, generality actually existing and not contracted to any mode of singularity. The universal *in re* is a quasi Platonic entity of a truly general or continuous nature which is essentially real Thirdness immediately perceived in the phaneron or percept.[18] Hence the terms "*man*" or "*horse*," existing in the mind, correspond to something which is common to all horses or men and as such is a general law which determines their natural classification. General law thus determines the general character and natural class of the singular and is that which is represented in a general proposition or term.

The nominalistic contention, according to Peirce, is that wherever generality is found, it is a function of the sign and does not reflect a generality independent of the mind. It should now be clear that Peirce's pragmatism involves not only a belief that generals or universals are real but also a very special conception of the nature of generality or universality. It was precisely this new conception of the nature of generality which turned Peirce into such a critic of the schoolmen who attempted to explain real universality in terms of form alone. The schoolmen, as Peirce saw them, realized the importance of habits or dispositions but unfortunately treated them as forms. The Scholastics were unable to do justice to the relational structure of real generals. The result was a static doctrine of forms which could not account for the important elements of continuity and process. For Peirce, scholastic realism was a step beyond nominalism because it could account for the generality of monadic predicates, but even the best of scholastic realists (Scotus) was too nominalistic. Boler has alluded to this point rather clearly:

> Peirce's objection to the scholastic substantial form as the universal *in re*, apart from his criticism of Scotus and aside from the question of how scientific one is in determining distinguishing characteristics (6.361) is that it fails to reveal the relational structure which is ultimately involved. Every general predicate is relational, hence, what it denotes must of itself be equally relational, or mediative. For Peirce the scholastics were correct as far as they went but their limited logic did not allow them to see that the nature, essence, power or disposition represented in mondadic predicates is only a truncated image of a relational law.[19]

For this reason Gallie calls Peirce's realism a "relational realism" in contrast to a "substantival realism" of the scholastics.[20]

The extremity of Peirce's logical realism, however, can only be assessed in terms of his doctrine on the nature of individuality. Up until the 1890's Peirce had explicitly denied the existence of individuals on the grounds that the vagueness and generality of all our predicates makes it impossible that anything ever be rendered completely determinate. Peirce defined an individual as that which is absolutely determinate with respect to having or not having every known property. If this definition is taken literally no absolute individual (except the universe itself) can exist (3.393 n. 1, 1870). For whatever exists must exist for some period of time however short, and however short the period of time may be, the object will experience some changes in its relations to other objects; hence it will not be absolutely determinate in having or not having certain relations to other objects. From this it follows that no absolutely determinate object can exist.[21] But for the purpose of discourse we may neglect some aspect of an object and treat it as though it were an individual completely determinate, except with reference, for example, to temporal relations. An object so treated Peirce called a *singular* and a singular is one in number from a particular point of view (3.93). Peirce's example is the term "The second Phillip of Macedon" which may be divided into "Phillip drunk" and "Phillip sober" but strictly neither one is an individual. We may call it a singular, if we keep in mind that we are neglecting differences of time and differences which accompany time (3.93).[22] This is also why, I think, Peirce maintained that it is the nominalist and not the realist who is putting forth metaphysical figments (5.312).[23] Had Peirce never said anything more about the nature of individuality after 1870 there would be little doubt about the extremity of his logical realism. However, around 1890 he characterized the category of Secondness as the category of individuality and equated it with the Scotistic notion of *haecceitas*:

> *Hic et nunc* is the phrase perpetually in the mouth of Duns Scotus, who first elucidated individual existence. (1.458, 1896)

> ... the individual is determinate in regard to every possibility, or quality, either as possessing it or as not possessing it. This ... does not hold for anything general, because the general is partially indeterminate ... (1.434)

> Combine quality with quality after quality and what is the mode of being which such determinations approach indefinitely but altogether fail ever to attain? It is ... the *existence* of the individual. (1.456)

But in what sense can *haecceities* or individuals be truly said to exist if in fact all that is is general or continuous? If Peirce was correct in stating that only generals exist, then it follows that what we call individual things (Socrates) are not strictly speaking individuals but rather fragments of systems and never fully determinate singulars. And, indeed, Peirce sometimes speaks as though individuality is a pure figment:

> When we come to study the great principle of continuity ... it will appear that individualism and falsity are one and the same. (5.402 n. 2, 1893)

Moreover, according to Charles McKeon, the indeterminacy of Thirdness and continuity is so pervasive in Peirce's later thought as to raise a serious doubt whether for Peirce anything absolutely individual can be known or can exist, since what exists undergoes some change in its relations during whatever interval of time it exists; and consequently is capable of logical division.[24] Either Peirce was completely contradictory in his later thoughts about the existence of *haecceities* or individuals, since the existence of individuals would be incompatible with his synechism, or he was speaking of *haecceities* or individuals in some sense compatible with his contention that all that is is general or continuous. We have already shown that in Peirce's earlier thought there is no room for individuals but only singulars which are objects fully determinate from a specific point of view in abstraction from all their relations. If the singular is taken as the individual, it must be taken as a fictive entity since arbitrarily determined.

McKeon is of the opinion that when Peirce equated Secondness with individuality and *haecceitas*, the language he was using could only be metaphorical since there is no room for individuals in Peirce's synechistic universe:

> The possibility of an individual changing its relation in however short an interval of time it exists, contains the conception of individual existence as a limit to be approached but never reached. Approaching individuality through Firstness entails a similar conception, the indefinite addition and combination of qualities failing to attain the mode of being of the existence of the individual. (1.456; 1.464; 1890)[25]

McKeon insists that Secondness as a mode of being consists merely in opposition and that Peirce in effect denied the substantial *per se* character of individuals in favor of relational, operational accidental individuating principle.[26] And, as we shall see shortly, Peirce's stated reasons for rejecting Scotus' solution to the problem of universals confirms McKeon's suspicions.

M. G. Murphey agrees in substance with McKeon that there are in fact no individuals for Peirce, but rather than say that Peirce is speaking in a purely metaphorical way when he speaks of individuality and *haecceitas*, Murphey insists that Peirce's doctrine of haecceites is quite compatible with his synechism given a correct understanding of Peirce's thought on the nature of haecceities. Murphey begins by quoting the following section from Peirce:

> According to this definition that which alone immediately presents itself as an individual is a reaction against the will, but everything whose identity consists in a continuity of reactions will be a single logical individual. Thus any portion of space, as far as it can be regarded as reacting, is for logic a single individual; since existence (not reality) and individuality are essentially the same thing; and whatever fulfills the present definition equally fulfills ... the principles of contradiction and excluded middle ... (3.613)

On the basis of this text Murphey maintains that what we actually experience as individual is the reaction and not the entity. ... Its existence is dependent solely upon its dynamic functions—not upon its inherring qualities. Murphey favors this interpretation of Peirce's view the doctrine of haecceities, which Peirce introduced late in life along with the phenomenology, not only because it does not reduce Secondness to Thirdness (the reactions themselves remain irreducibly Seconds) but also because haecceities still remain subject to the laws of excluded middle and non-contradiction at any one instant. The value of Murphey's interpretation is that it would not force us to maintain that Peirce was either metaphorical or contradictory in introducing the category of

Secondness as the criterion of haecceiatic individuality. Still, I think an excellent case can (and shortly will) be made for the claim that Murphey's view is consistent with McKeon's and that, in fact, when Peirce uses the term 'individual' it stands metaphysically for 'singular' as Peirce understood it. Moreover, if a universal must have real instances, I see no reason why it cannot be instanced in 'singulars' (as Peirce conceived them) rather than individuals. The behavior of *this* stone when released is an instance of "all stones when released, fall to the earth". Even *this* stone (and its behavior when released) is not an individual (as determined by Peirce) rather than a singular.[27] What all this does imply, at any rate, is that Peirce's use of the term '*haecceitas*' and his notion of haecceiatic individuality differs quite radically from the substantival individuality espoused by Scotus who used the same word.[28]

IV. *COMPARISON OF PEIRCE AND SCOTUS*

Is Peirce a Scotostic realist, then, in the sense that he held the same position as Scotus with regard to the problem of universals? Many Peirce scholars have insisted that Scotus' solution to the problem of universals is unambiguously present in Peirce's doctrine on the categories.[29]

E. C. Moore, R. Goodwin, and T. Goudge find the Scotistic solution to the problem of universals in Peirce's doctrine on the categories. They claim that Scotus' *Common Nature, Haecceitas,* and *Logical Universal* correspond in nature and function with Peirce's Firstness, Secondness and Thirdness. But on the basis of our analysis of Scotus and Peirce, we will now see that Firstness does not correspond with the *Common Nature,* Secondness does not correspond with *Haecceitas,* and Thirdness does not correspond with the *Logical Universal.*[30]

For Peirce, Firstness is primarily described as the sensuous quality of our perceptual experience. It is simply a phenomenal suchness. It is what the world was to Adam on the day he opened his eyes to it, before he had drawn any distinctions or had become conscious of his own existence. Whatever the *Common Nature* is for Scotus, it definitely is not a phenomenal suchness. Moreover even though Peirce describes Firstness as pure possibility or negative generality, which corresponds with the indeterminateness of the *Common Nature;* nevertheless Firstness cannot be conceptualized (and hence can not exist in the mind as the logical universal) nor is it the common element among many individuals of the same species.

Moreover *Haecceitas*, as Scotus conceived it, does not correspond with the category of Secondness which Peirce often equated with the Scotistic principle of individuation. No doubt, Peirce used Secondness as a principle of individuation just as Scotus used *Haecceitas as a principle of individuation. We have urged above that, for Peirce, what Secondness individuates is 'singulars' and not 'individuals'; whereas, for Scotus, what Haecceitas* individuates is 'individuals' and not 'singulars' as Peirce defined them. And shortly I shall attempt to show that, in the end, Peirce set himself off from Scotus for the stated reason that there are in fact no individuals. For these reasons it is decidedly dangerous to suggest that *Haecceitas* corresponds to Secondness since there is good reason for thinking that while they are both principles of individuation, they individuate quite different kinds of entities. For Scotus the addition of *Haecceitas* to the *Common Nature* reduces the *Common Nature* to the mode of individuality and makes of what was originally general, a *de se haec*, a metaphysical individual possessing a *Common Nature*. For Peirce, however, there is every good reason to suppose that the universal does not exist under the mode of individuality and is not contracted to the mode of individuality rather than singularity. If the nature of a principle of individuation is to be specified in terms of its function as contracting the universal (as is the case in Scotus), then the principle of individuation could not be the same in Scotus and Peirce. More can be said on the nature of individuals in Peirce and how the existence of such entities is compatible with the thesis of synechism, but even then (for reasons which we shall see shortly) I think it clear that the identity between the Scotistic notion of *Haecceitas* and the category of Secondness is not all reasonable.

Is it the case, then, that Peirce's category of Thirdness corresponds with the *Logical Universal* of Scotus? Here again the answer is no. The *Logical Universal* for Scotus exists formally in the mind as a concept predicable of many on the basis that many individuals actually possess what is denoted by the concept, namely, the *Common Nature*. The *Logical Universal* is a second intention. It is an *ens mentis* which is not arbitrarily mental since it has a foundation in fact. For Peirce, however, Thirdness is not simply an *ens mentis* with a foundation in fact; it is real operative law, mediation or habit in the universe. Thirdness is the universal *in re*; whereas for Scotus the *Logical Universal* does not exist *in re*—it is an abstraction of the universal *in re* which is the common nature individuated. Hence the *Logical Universal* of Scotus does not correspond with the category of Thirdness because the *Logical Universal* is not the universal *in re*, whereas Thirdness *is* the universal *in re*.

Not only do the scotistic notions of *Common Nature, Haecceitas* and *Logical Universal* not correspond in nature and function with Firstness, Secondness, and Thirdness, but also there is nothing in Scotus' thought that can stand as a counterpart for Firstness or Thirdness. The most that can be said is that what Peirce *meant* by Thirdness corresponds with what Scotus meant by the *Common Nature* as contracted. Here again, however, the universal *in re* is characterized quite differently by both men.

All this, of course, only tells us the sense in which it is illegitimate to claim that Peirce is a Scotistic realist. The more important task is to determine precisely to what extent Peirce was *legitimately* influenced by Scotus, and whether or not the sense in which he was legitimately influenced by Scotus is important for an adequate understanding of Peirce's pragmatism. I submit that this matter has not yet been carefully or clearly discussed.

V. PEIRCE'S SCOTISTIC REALISM

In spite of the foregoing considerations, it would be rash, I think, to maintain that Scotus had no significant influence on Peirce. After all, Peirce considered Scotus a philosophical genius and honored him as one of the two greatest metaphysicians of all time.[31] Moreover, Peirce explicitly claimed (both early and late) not only to have been greatly influenced by Scotus, but also that he was himself a Scotistic Realist.[32]

But whenever he endorsed Scotistic Realism he usually also rejected it for being too nominalistic, that is, too committed to the existence of individuals. That Peirce thought Scotus was too nominalistic is reflected in his concise analysis of Scotus' solution to the problem of universals. Consider the only two texts in the *Collected Papers* in which Peirce states the Scotistic doctrines:

(a) He [Scotus] holds, therefore, that such natures (i.e. sorts of things) as a *man* and a *horse*, which are real, and are not of themselves necessarily *this* man or *this* horse, though they cannot exist *in re* without being some particular man or horse, are in the *species intelligibilis* always represented positively indeterminate, it being the nature of the mind so to represent things. Accordingly any such nature is to be regarded as something which is of itself neither universal nor singular, but is universal in the mind, singular in things outside the mind. If there were nothing in the different men or horses which was not itself singular, there would be no real unity except the numerical unity of the singulars; which would involve such absurd consequences as that the only real difference would be numerical difference, and that there would be no real likenesses among things. *If therefore it is asked whether the universal is in things, the answer is that the nature which in the mind is universal, and is not in itself singular, exists in things* (italics added). It is the very same nature which in the mind is universal and *in re* is singular; for if it were not, in knowing anything of a universal we should be knowing nothing of things, but only of our own thoughts, and our opinion would not be converted from true to false by a change in things. This nature is actually indeterminate only so far as it is in the mind. But to say that an object is in the mind is only a metaphorical way of saying that it stands to the intellect in the relation of known to knower. The truth is, therefore, that the real nature which exists *in re* apart from all action of the intellect, though in itself, apart from its relations, it be singular, yet is actually universal as it exists in relation to the mind. But this universal only differs from the singular in the manner of its being conceived (*formaliter*), but not in the manner of its existence (*realiter*).

And:

(b) The great argument for nominalism is that there is no man unless there is some particular man. That, however, does not affect the realism of Scotus; for although there is no man of whom all further determination can be denied, yet there is a man, abstraction being made of all further determination. There is a real difference between man irrespective of what the other determination may be, and man with this or that particular series of determinations, although undoubtedly this difference is only relative to the mind and not *in re*. Such is the position of Scotus.[33] Occam's great objection is, there can be no real distinction which is not *in re*, in the thing-in-itself; but this begs the question for it is itself based only on the notion that reality is something independent of representative relation. (5.312)

Hence Peirce understood Scotus to be asserting that the actually indeterminate universal exists only in the mind, whereas the same nature existing *in re* is contracted to the mode of individuality in such a way as to imply that only determinate individuals exist. When it is recalled how strenuously Peirce argued not only for the non-existence of individuals (actually determinate states of affairs) but also for the existence of real generality (Thirdness, continuity, law, mediation, habit) it becomes quite apparent why he rejected Scotus' solution as too nominalistic and called it a halting realism (6.175). He himself claimed to be a more extreme scholastic realist which he considered essential for pragmatism:

> Even Duns Scotus is too nominalistic when he says that universals are contracted to the mode of individuality in singulars, meaning, as he does, by singulars, ordinary existing things. The pragmatist cannot admit that. I myself went too far in the direction of nominalism when I said that it was a mere question of the convenience of speech whether we say that a diamond is hard when it is not pressed upon, or whether we say it is soft until it is pressed upon. I *now* say that experiment will prove that the diamond is hard, as a positive fact. That is, that it is a real fact that it *would* resist pressure, which amounts to extreme scholastic realism. (8.208, 1905)

And:

> But it follows that since no cognition of ours is absolutely determinate, generals must have a real existence. Now this scholastic realism is usually set down as a belief in metaphysical fictions. But, in fact, a realist is simply one who knows no more recondite reality than that which is represented in a true representation. Since, therefore, the word "man" is true of something, that which "man" means is real. The nominalist must admit that man is truly applicable to something; but he believes that there is beneath this thing in itself, an uncognizable reality. His is the metaphysical figment. ... (5.312)

But it is also clear that Peirce accepted Scotus' solution to the extent that he found in Scotus an affirmation of the reality of the universal which Peirce endorsed in his attack on nominalism:

> The great argument for nominalism is that there is no man unless there is some particular man. That, however, does not affect the realism of Scotus; for although there is no man of whom all further determination can be denied, yet there is a man, abstraction being made of all further determination. There is a real difference between man irrespective of what the other determinations may be, and man with this or that particular series of determinations, although undoubtedly this difference is only relative to the mind and not *in re*. (5.312)

And, moreover, when Peirce claimed that he was a scholastic realist it is evident that he was asserting not only the Scotistic doctrine on the reality of the universal, but also his own particular conception of the universal as the real operative law governing the objects of which general terms are predicated:

> It must not be imagined that any notable realist of the thirteenth or fourteenth century took the ground that any "universal" was what we in English should call a "thing," as it seems that, in an earlier age, some

realists and some nominalists, too, had done; though perhaps it is not quite certain that they did so, their writings being lost. Their very definition of a "universal" admits that it is of the same generic nature as a word, namely, it is: "Quod natum optum est *praedicari* de pluribus." Neither was it their doctrine that any "universal" *itself* is real. They might, indeed, some of them, think so; but their realism did not consist in *that* opinion, but in holding that what the word *signifies*, in contradiction to what it can be truly said of, is real. Anybody may happen to opine that "the" is a real English word; but that will not constitute him a realist. But if he thinks that, whether the word "hard" itself be real or not, the property, the character, the predicate, *hardness*, is not invented by men, as the word is, but is really and truly in the hard things and is one in them are, as a description of habit, disposition or behavior, *then*, he *is* a realist. (1.27 n. 1, 1901)

Peirce claimed that Pragmatism was the new Scholastic Realism and insisted that Pragmatism presupposed Scholastic Realism because he found in Scotus and the Scholastics the doctrine that what the general term signifies is real and is truly in things and this, in part, he sought to prove in his famous 'Harvard Experiment'. But Peirce extended that doctrine by identifying the universal *in re* not with a somewhat static essence determined to a particular mode of existence but rather with real operative law (Thirdness, habit, mediation, continuity) governing the behavior of objects. It is precisely this law which determines the nature or activities of objects in the universe and is truly represented in the meaning of our propositions.

Scotus' solution to the problem of universals presented Peirce with a halting realism which he described as only a hair's breath away from nominalism, but yet the same doctrine also presented Peirce with arguments in favor of the reality of universals. Peirce rejected Scotus' nominalism and turned Pragmatism into extreme scholastic realism by simply denying the existence of individuals and identifying the undetermined common nature with real operative law governing the behavior of objects. This law, or Thirdness, determines the meaning of our empirical propositions which are statements or descriptions of it. Needless to say, although Peirce's emendation of the Scotistic solution was technically minor, the effect was of such a magnitude that Peirce felt he had supplied the only justifiable metaphysics capable of being harmonized with the physical sciences. Such a metaphysics accounts for the generality and vagueness of all predicates which, in turn, accounts for the essential corrigibility of all our physical knowledge.

While it must be denied that Peirce and Scotus put forth the same solution to the problem of universals; nevertheless, it cannot be denied that Scotus' solution to the problem of universals had an inspirational effect on Peirce to the extent that it provided Peirce with a partial justification of his own realistic thesis which, in denying the existence of individuals and identifying the universal *in re* with law or Thirdness, went considerably beyond the thesis of Scotus.

NOTES

1. See James Ross' review of John Boler's *Charles Peirce and Scholastic Realism: A Study of Peirce's Relationship to John Duns Scotus* (Seattle: University of Washington Press, 1963) in *The Journal of Philosophy*, February 1965, pp. 80–3.

2. For those who are already familiar with Scotus' solution to the problem of universals, it would be better that they proceed immediately to Section III below.

3. "... primo distinguendum est de universale. Sumitur enim, vel sumi potest tripliciter; quoniam pro intentione secunda quae scilicet est quaedam relatio rationis in praedicabili, ad illud de quo est praedicabile, et hunc respectum significat hoc nomen universale in concreto, sicut et universalitas in abstracto. Alio modo accipitur universale pro illo, quod denominatur ab illa intentione, quod est aliqua res primae intentionis, nam secundae intentiones applicantur primis et sic accipi potest dupliciter. Uno modo, pro illo quod quasi ut subjectum remotum denominatur ista intentione; alio modo pro subjecto propinquo. Primo modo dicitur natura absolute sumpto universale quia non est de se haec, et ita non repugnat sibi ex se dici de multis. Secundo modo non est universale, nisi sit actu indeterminatum ita quod unum intelligible numero sit dicible de omni supposito, et illud est complete universale." *Quaest Subt.* Bk. 7, 18, 3, n. 6. See also *Meta.* 8, 18.

4. The formal distinction is a distinction mid-way between a real distinction and a purely logical distinction. A real distinction exists between two or more physical entities (inter rem et rem) separable at least by divine power, whereas a logical distinction is a distinction created totally by the mind. The formal distinction is a distinction of reason with a foundation in fact. See Wolter, *The Transcindentals and their Function in the Metaphysics of Duns Scotus* (Washington, D.C.: Catholic University Press, 1946), pp. 21–2.

5. *Quaest. Subt.* Lib. vii, q. 18, Sch. V, p. 459.

6. *Quaest. Subt.* Lib. I, q. 6, n. 5. See also *Oxon.* II, d. 3.

7. Etienne Gilson, Jean Duns Scot (libraire philosophique), Paris: J. Vrin, 1952, p. 451. "L'universalite dans l'intellect presuppose au moins la communaute reele de "quod quid est." And in note 2: "... mais il n'est pas impossible de soutenir que notre docteur platonise en attribuant a la nature commune, etiam in rerum natura, verum esse extra animam reale."

8. II *Oxon.* 3, 1, n. 7–9. Also *Quaest. Subt.* 18, Sch. IV, VI, p. 460. See also Charles McKeon's fine article, "Peirce's Scotistic Realism" in *Studies in the Philosophy of Charles Sanders Peirce*, eds. P. Wiener and Frederick H. Young, Cambridge, Mass.: Harvard University Press, 1952, pp. 238–50.

9. See also MS 440; MS 623 (p. 48): MS 624.

10. On the logic relatives see MS 532 and MS 533.

11. Recall, too, that in Chapter I above (pp. 14ff) it has to be argued that what

Peirce means by 'Intellectual concept' is a descriptive statement (sentence) which admits of verification under the method of science.

12. See Buchler's interpretation of Peirce's theory of meaning in *Peirce's Empiricism* as cited by Murphey in *The Development of Peirce's Philosophy* (Cambridge: Harvard University Press, 1962), pp. 115ff.

13. See Chapter I above (pp. 23ff).

14. See Murphey, *Development*, p. 256, and John Boler's *Charles Peirce and Scholastic Realism*, pp. 414–44. It is important to note, as Boler has pointed out (p. 102), that there is a sense in which one might argue that Peirce's conception of the universal in terms of law is not a repudiation rather than a restatement of the scholastic theory of essence. Indeed, the scholastic maxim *operari sequitur esse* would seem to suggest that the essence of an object is to be specified in terms of its activities or operations. If what the scholastics meant by essence, form, or nature was simply the activities of an object, rather than an embodied quality which accounts for an object's ability to act in a certain way, then Peirce's conception of generality in terms of law or habits would not be so remote from the scholastic theory of essence. But it seems rather clear that what the scholastics ordinarily meant by *operi sequitur esse* was that we come to know what the embodied quality is in virtue of the activities of the object and that the embodied quality, which is referred to by the general term, is the cause of the object's ability to act in a particular way. In short, it seems that the scholastics distinguished between the essence of an object and its activities through which we acquire a knowledge of the object. The distinction of course Peirce rejected.

15. See also MS 309 (p. 3); MS 309 (p. 18); MS 1 (DM 49).

16. Boler has offered a negative assessment of Peirce's famous 'Harvard Experiment' (pp. 21 and 67ff); but, for the reasons just mentioned, it should be clear why I disagree with that assessment

17. Notice the use of the word 'singular' rather than 'individual'.

18. See MS 949 (pp. 2ff).

19. Boler, op. cit., p. 103.

20. W. B. Gallie, *Peirce and Pragmatism* (Middlesex, England: Penguin Books, 1952), pp. 153, 156–7.

21. See pp. 16ff above.

22. See also 1.457.

23. See also 280 (p. 36); MS 280 (p. 49); MS 434 (Logic IV, p. 29); MS 434; MS 530 (p. 17).

24. See 3.93 n. 1; 1.456; 1.464.

25. McKeon, op. cit., p. 247. In general I am indebted to this fine article, not only for its precise exposition of Scotus' theory on universals but also for some of its illuminating insights with respect to the differences between Peirce and Scotus on the problem of universals.

26. Ibid. p. 251.

27. On this point see Boler (op. cit., pp. 138–49).

28. Actually, Peirce's extreme realism was further enforced by his work on the nature of the continuum. See Murphey, *Development*, p. 440.

29. See Ralph Bastian, "The Scholastic Realism of C. S. Peirce," *Philosophy and Phenomenological Research*, 14 (1953), pp. 246–9; Robert Goodwin, "Charles Sanders Peirce: A Modern Scotist?", *New Scholasticism*, 35 (1961), pp. 478–509; Edward C. Moore, "The Scholastic Realism of C. S. Peirce," *Philosophy and Phenomenological Research*, 12 (1952), pp. 406–17, and "The Influence of Duns Scotus on C. S. Peirce" in *Studies in the Philosophy of Charles Sanders Peirce, Second Series* (Amherst: University of Massachusetts Press, 1964); Thomas Goudge, *The Thought of C. S. Peirce* (Toronto: University of Toronto Press, 1950), pp. 100ff.

30. In much of the following analysis I am indebted to the insights of W. P. Haas

as expressed in his book, *The Conception of Law and the Unity of Peirce's Philosophy* (Indiana: University of Notre Dame Press, 1964).

31. 2.166 (1902); 8.18 (1871); 5.40 (1893); 1.6 (1897); 4.28 (1893); 1.29 (1869); 6.175 (1905); 8.208 and 577 n. 1.

32. 1.560 (1907); 4.50 (1893); 1.6; 6.605; 1.6; 6.605; 1.560; MS 309 (pp. 2 and 3) and 514 (p. 5).

33. Peirce here quotes the authentic text. *Quaest. Subt.* Lib. 7, Q. 8: "Eadem natura est quae in existentia per gradum singularitatis est ut cognitum ad cognoscens, est indeterminata." Peirce was also commenting on the same text in the preceding quotation.

Conclusion

In seeking an answer to the question posed back in the introduction to this essay, we have seen that Peirce was committed to *both* an epistemological realism that extends itself to embracing logical realism *and* also to what he called objective idealism. And, although Peirce felt the combination quite consistent, one cannot consistently endorse both epistemological realism and objective idealism as each is traditionally defined. This is because epistemological realism makes no sense if it does not suppose a real distinction between minds and physical objects; and *that* distinction is effectively undermined with the objective idealist's claim that everything is mind, material objects being merely a form or aspect of mind. Presumably, after all, the terms 'epistemological realism' and 'objective idealism' are meant to designate mutually exclusive doctrines inasmuch as one asserts, and the other denies, the existence of physical objects understood by definition to be things not reducible to a property of consciousness. So, if objective idealism is true, then epistemological realism must be false; and if epistemological realism is true, the objective idealism must be false. One cannot be both a monist and a dualist; but that is precisely what one must be, if one is to be both an epistemological realist and an objective idealist. Thus, it is hard to see how we can effectively defend the claim that Peirce successfully synthesized epistemological realism and objective idealism.[1] At present, it seems difficult to imagine how such a synthesis can be achieved by anyone without the changing of what we traditionally mean by 'realism' and 'idealism'.

Moreover, owing to his commitment to objective idealism, it would appear that Peirce was very much interested in asserting that everything in the universe is some form of psychic energy, physical objects and minds being merely two accidentally different aspects of the same stuff, i.e. Evolving Mind, the Absolute. And if we were to take this view as the central thrust of Peirce's metaphysics, then, in the interest of offering a consistent reading, his commitment to epistemological realism would need to be considered as something subsumed into an idealism which, in the absence of individuals, would not be at all unlike the idealism of

Hegel even though Peirce criticized Hegel for neglecting individuals. "Even an idealist need not deny the existence of an external world" (5.539) if by 'external world' we mean merely a certain aspect of Mind, namely, that aspect over which the other aspect has no control. On this construal, of course, the combination of epistemological realism and objective idealism turns out to be consistent only because we change the traditional meaning of 'epistemological realism'. Also, on this reading Peirce's definition of Truth as the destined product of the scientific community would need to be viewed not as asserting a relationship between what we ordinarily mean by thought and extra-linguistic fact, but rather as between two different aspects of Mind wherein one aspect comes to reflect or mirror the other without ever obliterating the distinction in Mind between the two.

But even if this, or something very much like it, is the way consistently to read Peirce, there is the tragic flaw that comes with the strongest evidence he offered for believing that objective idealism is true, namely, that the property of consciousness is irreducible to a property of matter. Indeed, he gave no commanding evidence for the truth of this latter claim; and even if it were true, it is difficult to see how one can move from here to the claim that therefore *everything* is of the nature of Mind. If some things are conscious and irreducible to a property of matter, does it not follow that some things are not? At any rate, it seems incontestable that, in defending his idealism Peirce was given over to the questionable assumption that matter cannot be conscious or think.[2] This is not to say that the assumption is false, but only that Peirce did not prove it. But for this unfortunately central assumption, it is unlikely that Peirce would have embraced objective idealism.

Shorn of its love affair with objective idealism, however, Peirce's system presents a realistic proposal which appears quite attractive and capable of persuasive defense. Although Peirce failed to provide an adequate defense of the view so essential to his realism, namely that science *will* come to a final answer on any answerable question and, moreover, that that answer is True because it will tell us how things really are independently of any relationship they have to minds; still, as we have seen, the thesis can be argued forcefully. Apart from a well-developed theory of inquiry and meaning, what seems both novel and exciting in Peirce's realism is the thesis that although truth is always a matter of what is warrantedly assertible by the scientific community under its current conceptual framework, we are warranted in asserting that, owing to the nature of scientific progress, what is warrantedly assertible under the final conceptual framework will tell us how the external world really is. Naturally, this assumes that there is scientific progress (construed in terms of theories building on each other) and that we can determine when one theory is better than another. So understood, Peirce's theory of truth seeks not only to synthesize coherence and correspondence theories of truth (and so, in an attenuated sense, both idealism and realism in a system ultimately realistic) but also conceptual relativism and epistemological realism. Given what we have seen at the end of Chapter One, we can hope that this aspect of Peirce's thought will be studied more carefully in the future, if only because it holds out the promise of synthesizing idealism and realism in a system which is ultimately realistic.

NOTES

1. The view that Peirce's endorsement of both epistemological realism and objective idealism can be quite consistent has been frequently offered by various Peirce scholars and most recently defended by S. Rosenthal in "On the Epistemological Significance of What Peirce is Not," *The Transactions of the Charles S. Peirce Society: A Quarterly Journal in American Philosophy* (Winter 1979).

2. On this item see Richard Taylor's "How to Bury the Mind-Body Problem," *The American Philosophical Quarterly*, Vol. 6, no. 2 (April 1969), pp. 136–43.

Selective Bibliography

This bibliography contains only those works to which reference has been made in the foregoing pages. For the most complete and current bibliography of both primary and secondary materials on Peirce, see the bibliography recently published with the microfiche edition of Peirce's published works entitled *Charles Sanders Peirce: Complete Published Works, including selected secondary materials.* This bibliography is included with the microfiche edition and may be obtained together with this edition or separately from Johnson Associates Inc., Greenwich, Connecticut.

For Peirce's writings, see *The Collected Papers of Charles Sanders Peirce* edited by Charles Hartshorne and Paul Weiss (vls. 1–6) and Arthur W. Burks (vls. 7–8) (Cambridge, Mass.: Harvard University Press, 1931–35, 1958). The unpublished papers are available on a microfilm edition and can be obtained from the Widener Library at Harvard University, Cambridge, Massachusetts.

There are other useful and more readily available bibliographies of both primary and secondary sources. For primary sources, see Arthur W. Burks' bibliography in *The Collected Papers of Charles Sanders Peirce*, vol. 8, pp. 251–330 and Appendix I; "A First Supplement to Arthur W. Burks' Bibliography of the Works of Charles Sanders Peirce," compiled by Max H. Fisch, in *Studies in the Philosophy of Charles Sanders Peirce, Second Series* edited by Edward C. Moore and Richard S. Robin (Amherst: University of Massachusetts Press, 1964) pp. 477–85. The same volume contains a bibliography of secondary sources in Appendix II, "A Draft of a Bibliography of Writings about C. S. Peirce," compiled by Max F. Fisch with the assistance of Barbara E. Kretsmann and Victor F. Lenzen, pp. 486–514.

CHAPTER I

Books

Aristotle, *Posterior Analytics.* In *The Oxford Translation of Aristotle.* 12 vols. Ed. J. A. Smith and W. D. Ross, Oxford: Clarendon Press, 1908–31.

Armstrong, David M. *Belief, Truth and Knowledge.* Cambridge: Cambridge University Press, 1973.

Ayer, A. J. *The Origins of Pragmatism.* San Francisco, Calif.: Freeman, Cooper & Co., 1968.

Chisholm, Roderick M. *Perceiving: A Philosophical Study.* Ithaca, New York: Cornell University Press, 1957.

Corman, James W. and Keith Lehrer. *Philosophical Problems and Arguments, An Introduction.* New York: Macmillan Co., 1968.

Feyerabend, Paul. *Against Method* (N.J.: Humanities Press, 1975).

Fitzgerald, John. *Peirce's Theory of Signs as Foundation for Pragmatism.* The Hague: Mouton, 1966.

Goudge, Thomas. *The Thought of Charles Sanders Peirce.* Toronto: University of Toronto Press, 1950.

Greenlee, Douglas. *Peirce's Concept of Sign.* The Hague: Mouton, 1973.

Korner, Stephen (ed.). *Observation and Interpretation* (New York: Academic Press, 1957).

Laudan, Larry. *Progress and its Problems (Berkeley: University of California Press, 1978).*

Lewis, Clarence Irving. *Mind and the World Order.* New York: Dover Publications, 1956.

———. *An Analysis of Knowledge and Valuation.* LaSalle, Ill.: Open Court Publishing Co., 1946.

Murphey, Murray G. *The Development of Peirce's Philosophy.* Cambridge, Mass.: Harvard University Press, 1961.

Naess, Arne. *Scepticism.* New York: Humanities Press, 1968.

Popper, Karl R. *The Logic of Scientific Discovery.* New York: Harper and Row, 1959.

Price, H. H. *Truth and Corrigibility.* Oxford: Clarendon Press, 1936.

Quine, Willard Van Orman. *From a Logical Point of View.* New York: Harper and Row, 1961.

———. *Word and Object.* Cambridge, Mass.: M.I.T. Press, 1960.

Rescher, Nicholas. *The Coherence Theory of Truth. Oxford: Oxford University Press, 1973.*

———. *Peirce's Philosophy of Science* (Notre Dame: Notre Dame Press, 1978).

———. *Scientific Progress* (Basil Blackwell, 1978).

Russell, Bertrand. *The Problems of Philosophy.* London: Home University Library, 1912.

Scheffler, Israel. *The Conditions of Knowledge: An Introduction to Epistemology and Education.* Glenview, Ill.: Scott, Foresman and Company, 1965.

Sellars, Wilfrid. *Science, Perception and Reality.* London: Routledge and Kegan Paul, 1963.

Smith, John. *Purpose and Thought: The Meaning of Pragmatism* (New Haven: Yale University Press, 1978).

Thayer, H. S. *Meaning and Action.* New York: Bobbs-Merrill Co., 1968.

Articles

Almeder, Robert. "Science and Idealism," *Philosophy of Science,* Vol. 40, No. 2 (June 1973), pp. 242–54.

———. "Fallibilism and the Ultimate Irreversible Opinion," *American Philosophical Quarterly, Monograph Series: Studies in Epistemology,* Monograph No. 9, 1975, pp. 33–54.

———. "Peirce on Meaning," *Synthese* (July 1979).

Aronson, Jerrold L. "Connections: A Defense of Peirce's Category of Thirdness,"

The Transactions of the Charles S. Peirce Society: A Quarterly Journal in American Philosophy (Summer 1969).

Aune, Bruce. "Two Theories of Scientific Knowledge," *Critica,* Vol. 5, No. 13 (1971), pp. 3–20.

Austin, J. L. "Other Minds" in *Philosophical Papers,* 2nd ed., ed. J. O. Urmson and G. J. Warnock, Oxford: Oxford University Press, 1970, pp. 76–116.

Boorse, Christopher l. "The Origins of the Indeterminacy Thesis," *The Journal of Philosophy,* Vol. LXII, No. 13 (July 17, 1975), pp. 369–87.

Burks, Arthur W. "Peirce's Two Theories of Probability" in *Studies in the Philosophy of Charles Sanders Peirce, Second Series.* Ed. Edward C. Moore and Richard S. Robin, Amherst, Mass.: University of Massachusetts Press, 1964, pp. 141–50.

Delaney, C. F. "Peirce's Critique of Foundationalism," *The Monist* 57 (1973), pp. 240–51, and "Basic Propositions, Empiricism and Science" in *The Philosophy of Wilfrid Sellars: Queries and Extensions,* ed. by J. C. Pitt. Dordrecht: D. Reidel, 1978.

Foelsdall, Dagfinn. "Indeterminacy of Translation and the Underdetermination of the Theory of Nature," *Dialectica,* Vol. 27, No. 3–4 (1973), pp. 289–301.

Gentry , George. "Habit and the Logical Interpretant" in *Studies in the Philosophy of Charles Sanders Peirce,* eds. Philip P. Wiener and Frederic H. Young, Cambridge, Mass.: Harvard University Press, 1952, pp. 75–90

Goodman, Nelson. "Words, Works, Worlds," *Erkenntnis,* Vol. 9 (May 1975).

Grunbaum, Adolf. "Can a Theory Answer More Questions Than One of it Rivals," *British Journal for the Philosophy of Science (*Vol. 27, 1976), pp. 1–22.

Hintikka, Jaakko. "Quine vs. Peirce," *Dialectica,* Vol. 30, No. 1 (1976).

Hooker, M. "Peirce's Conception of Truth" in J. C. Pitt (ed.) *The Philosophy of Wilfred Sellars: Queries and Extensions,* Dordrecht: Reidal, 1978.

Kitcher, Phillip. "The Plight of the Platonist," *Nous* (May 1978).

Kohl, Marvin. "Bertrand Russell of Vagueness," *Australasian Journal of Philosophy,* Vol. 47, No. 1 (May 1969), pp. 31–41.

Kneale, William. "Scientific Revolutions Forever?", *The British Journal for the Philosophy of Science,* Vol. 19, No. 1 (May 1968), pp. 27–42.

Kuhn, Thomas. "Reflections on my Critics" in *Criticism and the Growth of Knowledge,* eds. Lakatos and Musgrave (Cambridge: Cambridge University Press, 1970).

Lakatos, I. "The Methodology of Scientific Research Programs" in *Criticisms and the Growth of Knowledge,* eds. Lakatos and Musgrave (Cambridge: Cambridge University Press, 1970, pp. 91–195).

Laudan, Larry. "Two Dogmas of Methodology," Philosophy of Science (Vol. 43, No. 4, Dec. 1976), pp. 585–97.

——. "Peirce and the Trivialization of the Self-correcting Thesis" in R. N. Giere and R. S. Westfall (eds.) *Foundations of Scientific Method: The Nineteenth Century,* Bloomington: Indiana University Press, 1973, pp. 275–306.

Levi, Isaac. "Truth, Fallibility and the Growth of Knowledge" in *Local Induction* ed. by Radu J. Bogdan, Dordrecht: Reidel, 1976 (pp. 1–71), and "Induction as Self-Correcting According to Peirce" in *Science, Belief and Behaviour: Essays in Honor of R. B. Braithwaite.*

Madden, Edward H. "Peirce on Probability" in *Studies in the Philosophy of Charles Sanders Peirce, Second Series.* Ed. Edward C. Moore and Richard S. Robin, Amherst, Mass.: University of Massachusetts Press, 1964, pp. 122–40.

Moore, Edward C. "On the World as General," *The Transactions of the Charles S. Peirce Society: A Quarterly Journal in American Philosophy* (Spring 1968).

Niiniluoto, I. "Notes on Popper as Follower of Whewell and Peirce," *Ajatus,* 37 (1978), pp. 272–327.

Popper, Karl. "Truth, Rationality and the Growth of Scientific Knowledge" in *Conjectures and Refutations* (New York: Basil Books, 1962).

Putnam, Hilary. "Realism and Reason," 1976 APA Presidential Address, in *The Proceedings of the American Philosophical Association*, Vol. 50 (August 1977).

Quine, Willard Van Orman. "Whither Physical Objects" in Cohen, Feyerabend, and Wartofsky (eds.), *Essays in Memory of Imre Lakatos*. Dordrecht: D. Reidel, 1976, pp. 303–10.

——. "On Empirically Equivalent Systems of the World," *Erkenntnis*, Vol. 9 (May 1975).

——. "The Pragmatist's Place in Empiricism," in *Pragmatism: Its Sources and Prospects*, South Carolina Univ. of South Carolina Press, 1981 (Forthcoming).

Rescher, Nicholas. "Peirce on the Economy of Research," *Philosophy of Science*, Vol. 43 (1976), pp. 71–98.

Russell, Bertrand. "Dewey's New Logic" in *The Philosophy of John Dewey*, ed. Paul Arthur Schilpp, New York: Tudor Publishing Company, 1939.

Schuldenfrei, Richard. "Quine in Perspective," *The Journal of Philosophy*, Vol. LXIX, No. 1 (Jan. 13, 1972), pp. 5–16.

Swinburne, R. G. "Vagueness, Inexactness and Imprecision," *The British Journal for the Philosophy of Science*, Vol. 19, No. 4 (Feb. 1969), pp. 281–99.

CHAPTER II

Books

Haas, William P. *The Concept of Law and the Unity of Peirce's Philosophy*, Notre Dame, Indiana: University of Notre Dame Press, 1964.

Hirst, R. J. (ed.). *Perception and the External World*, New York: Macmillan Co., 1965.

Scheffler, Israel. *Science and Subjectivity*, New York: Bobbs-Merrill Co., 1967.

Slote, Michael A. *Reason and Scepticism*, New York: Humanities Press, 1970.

Articles

Almeder, Robert. "The Epistemological and Metaphysical Realism of Charles S. Peirce," Ph.D. Dissertation, University of Pennsylvania, 1968.

——. "Charles Peirce and the Existence of the External World," *The Transactions of the Charles S. Peirce Society: A Quarterly Journal in American Philosophy* (Spring 1968).

——. "Peirce's Epistemological Realism," *The Transactions of the Charles S. Peirce Society: A Quarterly Journal in American Philosophy* (Winter 1975).

Bernstein, Richard. "Peirce's Theory of Perception" in *Studies in the Philosophy of Charles Sanders Peirce, Second Series*, eds. Edward C. Moore and Richard S. Robin, Amherst, Mass.: University of Massachusetts Press, 1964, pp. 165–89.

Hall, Richard. "Kuhn and the Copernican Revolution," *The British Journal for the Philosophy of Science*, Vol. 21, No. 2 (May 1970), pp. 196–7.

Lehrer, Keith. "Why Not Scepticism?", *Philosophical Forum*, Vol. II, No. 3 (Spring 1971), pp. 283–98.

Montague, William Pepperell. "The Story of American Realism," *Philosophy*, Vol. 12, No. 46 (1937), pp. 140–161.

Stearns, Isabel. "Firstness, Secondness, Thirdness" in *Studies in the Philosophy of Charles Sanders Peirce*, eds. Philip P. Wiener and Frederic H. Young, Cambridge, Mass.: Harvard University Press, 1952, pp. 195–208.

CHAPTER III

Books

Ayer, A. J. *The Problem of Knowledge,* Oxford: Penguin Books, 1966.
Ryle, Gilbert. *The Concept of Mind,* London: Hutchinson & Co. Ltd., 1949.

Articles

Almeder, Robert. "Peirce's Theory of Perception," *The Transactions of the Charles S. Peirce Society: A Quarterly Journal in American Philosophy* (Vol. VI, No. 2, 1970).

Hirst, R. J. "The Difference Between Sensing and Observing" in *The Philosophy of Perception,* ed. G. J. Warnock, London: Oxford University Press, 1967, pp. 25–43.

Price, H. H. "Appearing and Appearances," *American Philosophical Quarterly,* Vol. I, No. 1 (1964).

Rosenthal, Sandra B. "Peirce's Theory of Perceptual Judgment: An Ambiguity," *Journal of the History of Philosophy,* Vol. VII, No. 3 (July 1969), pp. 303–17.

CHAPTER IV

Books

Ayer, A. J. *The Origins of Pragmatism* (San Francisco: Freeman, Cooper, and Co., 1968).

Articles

Almeder, Robert. "The Idealism of Charles S. Peirce," *The Journal of the History of Philosophy* (Jan. 1971).

Murphey, Murray G. "Kant's Children: The Cambridge Pragmatists," *The Transactions of the Charles S. Peirce Society: A Quarterly Journal in American Philosophy,* Vol. IV, No. 1 (Winter 1968).

Rosenthal, Sandra. "On the Epistemological Significance of What Peirce is Not," *The Transactions of the Charles S. Peirce Society: A Quarterly Journal in American Philosophy* (Winter 1979).

Riley, Greshham B. "Existence, Reality and Objects of Knowledge," *The Transactions of the Charles S. Peirce Society: A Quarterly Journal in American Philosophy,* Vol. IV, No. 1 (Winter 1968).

Smith, John E. "Community and Reality" in *Perspectives on Peirce,* ed. R. J. Bernstein, New Haven: Yale University Press, 1965, pp. 92–119.

CHAPTER V

Books

Boler, John. *Charles Peirce and Scholastic Realism: A Study of Peirce's Relationship to John Duns Scotus,* Seattle: University of Washington Press, 1963.

Buchler, Justus. *Charles Peirce's Empiricism*, New York: Harcourt, Brace & Co., 1939.

Gaillie, W. B. *Peirce and Pragmatism*, Middlesex, England: Penguin Books, 1952.

Gilson, Etienne Henry. *Jean Duns Scot*, Libraire Philosophique, J. Vrin, Paris, 1952.

Scotus, John Duns. Opus Oxoniense. In *Joannis Duns Scoti Opera Omnia*, 26 vols., ed. L. Vives, Paris 1891–5, Vols. VIII–XXI.

——. *Quaestiones Subtilissimae in Metaphysicam Aristotelis* in *Joannis Duns Scoti Opera Omnia*, 26 vols., ed. L. Vives, Paris, 1891–5, Vol. VII.

——. *Quaestiones subtilissimae super libros Metaphisicorum Aristotelis*, Venetiis, Ioannes Hamann, 1499.

Wolter, Allan B. *The Transcendentals and their Function in the Metaphysics of Duns Scotus*, Washington D.C.: Catholic University Press, 1964.

Articles

Almeder, Robert. "Peirce's Pragmatism and Scotistic Realism," *The Transactions of the Charles S. Peirce Society: A Quarterly Journal in American Philosophy* (Winter 1975).

Bastian, Ralph J. "The 'Scholastic' Realism of C. S. Peirce," *Philosophy and Phenomenological Research*, Vol. XIV, No. 2 (December 1953), pp. 246–9.

Goodwin, Robert P. "Charles Sanders Peirce: A Modern Scotist?", *New Scholasticism*, 35(1961) pp. 478–509.

McKeon Charles. "Peirce's Scotistic Realism" in *Studies in the Philosophy of Charles Sanders Peirce*, ed. Philip P. Wiener and Frederic H. Young, Cambridge, Mass.: Harvard University Press, 1952, pp. 238–50.

Moore, Edward C. "The Scholastic Realism of C. S. Peirce," *Philosophy and Phenomenological Research*, Vol. XII, No. 3 (March 1952) pp. 406–77.

——. "The Influence of Duns Scotus on Peirce" in *Studies in the Philosophy of Charles Sanders Peirce, Second Series*, eds. Edward C. Moore and Richard S. Robin, Cambridge, Mass.: University of Massachusetts Press, 1964, pp. 401–13.

Ross, James. Rev. of *Charles Peirce and Scholastic Realism: A Study of Peirce's Relationship to Duns Scotus* by John F. Boler (Seattle: University of Washington Press, 1963) in *The Journal of Philosophy*, Vol. LXII, No. 3 (Feb. 4, 1965) pp. 80–3.

Conclusion

Taylor, Richard. "How to Bury the Mind-Body Problem," *The American Philosophical Quarterly*, Vol. 6, No. 2 (April 1969), pp. 136–43.

NAME INDEX

Adam, 174
Aristotle, 80, 81, 162
Armstrong, D. M., 91, 94, 95
Augustine, Saint, 85, 89
Aune, B., 91, 95, 96
Austin, J. L., 133

Bentham, J., 34, 35
Berkeley, G., 126, 164
Bohm, 68, 69
Boler, J., 171
Boorse, C., 42, 44
Buchler, J., 47

Chisolm, R., 133
Columbus, C., 66
Comte, A., 22

Descartes, R., 5–7, 56, 81, 88, 89, 120,
    154
Duhem, 34, 35, 38, 43

Feyeraband, P., 116, 121
Foelsdall, D., 38, 43
Fraser, 164

Gallie, W. B., 171
Gilson, 163
Goodman, N., 98
Goodwin, R., 174
Goudge, T., 174

Hamilton, 126
Hegel, G. W. F., 184
Hintikka, J., 43, 44
Hume, D., 20, 33–35, 41, 44

James, 77

Kant, I., 70, 71, 140
Kitcher, P., 72
Kneale, W., 68, 69
Kuhn, T., 116, 121

Laudan, L., 74
Lewis, C. I., 49
Locke, D., 133

Macbeth, 129
McKeon, C., 163, 172–174
Moore, E. C., 174
Moore, G. E., 133
Murphey, M. G., 153, 156, 164, 165,
    173

Napoleon, 66
Newton, I., 12, 13

Ockham, W., 54, 83, 177

Peirce, C. S., 3–5, 7, 8, 10, 13–16, 47,
    48, 52, 54, 60, 62, 75, 76, 83–85, 89,
    109, 111–114, 117, 123–125, 127,
    128, 138, 149–155, 166–168, 170,
    172, 173, 176–179
Phaneron, 169
Phillip of Macedon, 171
Planck, M., 69
Plato, 72, 163, 170
Popper, K., 81, 82
Price, H. H., 81
Putnam, H., 98

Quine, W., 4, 9, 19, 33–39, 41–44,
    63–65, 96, 98, 118

Reid, T., 126, 133
Rescher, N., 69–71
Ross, J., 160
Royce, J., 151, 152
Russell, B., 10, 63, 65, 66, 118

Scheffler, I., 62–65, 96, 118
Schelling, F., 154
Schiller, F., 36
Schuldenfrei, R., 42
Scotus, J. Duns, 160–164, 169–176,
    178, 180
Sellars, W., 81, 82, 91, 133
Shakespeare, W., 124
Socrates, 162, 172

Tooke, J. H., 34, 35

Vigier, 68, 69

Welby, L., 28
Wundt, W., 89

SUBJECT INDEX